Remaking the Postwar World Economy

Also by Peter Burnham

A MAJOR CRISIS: THE POLITICS OF ECONOMIC POLICY IN BRITAIN IN THE 1990s
(*with Werner Bonefeld and Alice Brown*)

THE POLITICAL ECONOMY OF POSTWAR RECONSTRUCTION

SURVIVING THE RESEARCH PROCESS IN POLITICS (*editor*)

Remaking the Postwar World Economy

Robot and British Policy in the 1950s

Peter Burnham
Reader in Politics and International Studies
University of Warwick

First published 2003 by
PALGRAVE MACMILLAN
Houndmills, Basingstoke, Hampshire RG21 6XS and 175 Fifth Avenue, New York, N. Y. 10010
Companies and representatives throughout the world

PALGRAVE MACMILLAN is the global academic imprint of the Palgrave Macmillan division of St. Martin's Press, LLC and of Palgrave Macmillan Ltd. Macmillan® is a registered trademark in the United States, United Kingdom and other countries. Palgrave is a registered trademark in the European Union and other countries.

ISBN 0–333–55725–5

This book is printed on paper suitable for recycling and made from fully managed and sustained forest sources.

A catalogue record for this book is available from the British Library.

Library of Congress Cataloging-in-Publication Data
Burnham, Peter, 1959–
    Remaking the postwar world economy : Robot and British policy in the 1950s / Peter Burnham.
      p. cm.
    Includes bibliographical references and index.
    ISBN 0–333–55725–5
    1. International finance – History – 20th century. 2. Great Britain – Foreign economic relations – United States. 3. United States – Foreign economic relations – Great Britain. 4. Monetary policy – Great Britain – History – 20th century. I. Title.
HG3881.B853 2003
330.941'0855 – dc21

                                                    2003048294

10   9   8   7   6   5   4   3   2   1
12   11   10   09   08   07   06   05   04   03

Printed and bound in Great Britain by
Antony Rowe Ltd, Chippenham and Eastbourne

Contents

Acknowledgements

I would like to thank the following individuals who helped support this project over a number of years: my colleagues in the Department of Politics and International Studies at the University of Warwick (in particular the late Jim Bulpitt, Wyn Grant, David Carlton, Shirin Rai and Hazel Smith), Rosemary Aris, Werner Bonefeld, Alice Brown, Simon Clarke, David Coates, Mick Cox, Nick Crafts, Tony Elger, Andrew Gamble, Colin Hay, Phil Mizen, Robert Skidelsky, Helen Thompson and Geoffrey Underhill.

A number of people assisted with various aspects of the research, including Henry Gillett, Sarah Millard, the late John Fforde, Fred Atkinson, Sir Donald MacDougall, Christine Woodland and Richard Temple.

Lastly, the following individuals and institutions kindly granted me permission to use and quote from documents of which they hold the copyright: the Bank of England; Charles Clarke; Churchill College, Cambridge; the Modern Records Centre, University of Warwick; the National Archives, Washington, DC; Nuffield College, Oxford; Stephen Procter; the Keeper of the Public Record Office, London; Special Collections Department (Avon Papers), University of Birmingham; Trinity College, Cambridge; the Trustees of Harold Macmillan's papers; and the Earl of Woolton.

List of Abbreviations

APU	Atlantic Payments Union
BE	Bank of England
BIS	Bank for International Settlements
CBI	Confederation of British Industry
ECA	Economic Co-operation Administration
ECSC	European Coal and Steel Community
EDC	European Defence Community
EEC	European Economic Community
EFTA	European Free Trade Area
EMA	European Monetary Agreement
EPU	European Payments Union
ERP	European Recovery Programme
FOA	Foreign Operations Administration
GATT	General Agreement on Tariffs and Trade
GDP	Gross Domestic Product
GNP	Gross National Product
HC	House of Commons
IMF	International Monetary Fund
IPE	International Political Economy
ITO	International Trade Organization
MRC	Modern Records Centre
MSA	Mutual Security Agency
NAC	National Advisory Council on International Monetary and Financial Problems
NATO	North Atlantic Treaty Organization
NSC	National Security Council
OEEC	Organization for European Economic Co-operation
OF	Overseas Finance Division of the Treasury
PEC	Cabinet Committee on Preparations for the Commonwealth Economic Conference
PRO	Public Record Office
RG	Record Group
TUC	Trades Union Congress
UN	United Nations

1
Britain, Bretton Woods and the Crisis of the World Economy, 1945–1951

I Introduction

For most scholars working in the field of international political economy (IPE), the 1950s is a forgotten decade. Sandwiched between the well-trawled period of postwar reconstruction (1945–51) and the so-called 'golden age' of the 1960s, the decade is seen almost exclusively through the lens of the Suez crisis, the Treaty of Rome and the consolidation of bipolar Cold War politics. There has been relatively little academic interest in charting the development of international economic relations in the 1950s, and this is particularly true with respect to international monetary policy. As a result, most IPE studies tend to assume that during this period the world economy was governed by the rules and institutions established in accordance with the Bretton Woods Agreement of 1944. Although it is often pointed out that the practice of the 'system' diverged from the theory of its founders, it is nevertheless a cardinal assumption of the discipline (and of political science and international relations more generally) that Bretton Woods operated quietly and effectively in the 1950s to usher in a period of unrivalled growth and prosperity in the world economy.[1] This study shows, however, that there is little evidence to support this assumption.

The inauguration of the IMF and the International Bank at Savannah, Georgia in March 1946, was followed not by the smooth unfolding of 'embedded liberalism',[2] but by waves of economic crisis which forced the 'system' to shut down in August 1947. The multilateral ideals of Keynes and White were sidelined as European economies were kick-started by dollar aid in a world context dominated by discriminatory blocs and bilateral trade and payments agreements. By 1951, as the consequences of Korean rearmament began to bite, the world economy faced its most severe postwar test. The Bretton Woods institutions were dormant and currencies inconvertible. The future of the world economy would be decided not by the Fund and the GATT, but by governments in London, Paris and Washington struggling to correct the critical weaknesses in the world economic structure.

This study presents a detailed, archive-based account of the key aspects of international monetary relations in the 1950s – and in particular in the period of the dormancy of Bretton Woods, 1951–58. The restoration of general currency convertibility, on 29 December 1958, represents for many the rebirth of the Bretton Woods 'system' and the dawn of the modern global economy. However, whilst there are numerous studies of the decline of Bretton Woods in the early 1970s, the move to convertibility which led to the resuscitation of the 'system' is almost totally unresearched within the field of IPE.[3] To make good this deficiency, and to begin to lay bare the dynamics of the international economic system in the 1960s, this study focuses specifically on the conditions surrounding the move to sterling convertibility in the context of wider Anglo-American economic relations. With over 50 per cent of world trade still conducted in sterling in the early 1950s, struggles over British policy assumed particular significance in the international arena and drove broader policy shifts towards the convertibility of other key European currencies. Towards the end of the decade, however, the limits of British leadership in international monetary affairs, as in international politics more broadly, were becoming all too obvious and the final push to convertibility came not from the British but from the French and German governments.

At the heart of this book is the claim that in the midst of economic crisis in February 1952, the British government had a unique opportunity to take a bold, almost revolutionary, step in the external field which would have transformed the international political economy (through the abolition of the fixed rate system, the International Monetary Fund, and the European Payments Union) and restructured Britain's domestic economy to tackle the long-standing productivity, export and labour market problems. The move was discussed under the codename Operation Robot. Seen by many economic historians simply as a Bank plan to achieve sterling convertibility, its real significance lay in its political impact on international economic relations and on Britain's domestic political economy. Arising in the Bank of England and the Overseas Finance Division of the Treasury, and supported to the last by the Chancellor Rab Butler, Robot was, above all else, a unilateral British plan of action. On Budget day, 11 March 1952, Butler would announce that sterling was to be made convertible (for non-residents of the Sterling Area) on a floating rate of exchange and that sterling balances (net sterling liabilities of the UK) would, to all intents and purposes, be frozen and funded into long-term Treasury bonds. The pound would fall, import prices would rise and unemployment, it was judged, would in all probability shoot over the one million mark (from an existing figure of around 400,000). This would 'free-up' the labour market, encourage economic adjustment in line with market forces, and the exchange rate would 'take the strain' as payments came back into balance. Soft markets would disappear and British exports would be forced to compete with dollar goods. Internationally, it was envisaged that a number of European countries (including France but excluding Germany) would wish to become part of a wider Sterling Area 'Payments Club', floating with sterling against the dollar. This would put paid to Franco-German moves towards closer European integration and finally end what was left of the faltering Bretton Woods 'system'. Britain would now be at the head of new international monetary system, recovering a general freedom of action in the international arena, and policy makers in Washington would simply have to adapt to the new order. The political moment had finally arrived for a solution to Britain's external monetary problems – one which would also begin to address the fundamental weakness of the domestic political economy.

Borrowing from Keynes' famous discussion of the opportunities open to Britain in 1945,[4] John Fforde, the Bank of England's official historian of the period, likened Britain's position in the postwar world economy to the proverbial squirrel trapped in the cage.[5] At one end of the cage was an apparently attractive exit marked 'Grand Multilateral Solution'. Through this exit Britain negotiated with the Sterling Area and Western Europe, and went on to reach a comprehensive agreement with the United States for the provision of substantial financial underpinning for convertibility and exchange control. But when examined closely, this exit sooner or later turned out to be blocked since sympathetic US trade policies and large-scale financial aid were generally not forthcoming after 1950. At the other end of the cage was an exit marked 'Unilateral Trapdoor: for emergency use only'. Through it one immobilized the sterling balances and took a unilateral decision to introduce convertibility on a floating rate. It involved great risks, hence its 'emergency use' designation, but it would provide a solution to Britain's external economic policy dilemmas whilst simultaneously disciplining the domestic economy. Finally, in the middle of the cage, one found an easily opened and hauntingly familiar exit marked 'Temptation'. Through it Britain was led to the restoration of fixed rate convertibility without adequate underpinning or adequate restraints on the sterling balances. It was a long-term option involving delicate negotiation and compromise and the likelihood of recurrent sterling crises with no solution to the problems of the domestic economy.

In essence, this book explores the tensions between these three solutions and in so doing charts Britain's approach to the international political economy through an analysis of the move to sterling convertibility in the 1950s. The issues raised by the convertibility debates are fundamental to understanding not only state–economy relations in Britain but also to correcting the myopia which currently exists in, what may be called, historical studies in IPE, in particular in relation to Bretton Woods.

The structure and argument of the book

To understand why policy makers in Britain opened the trapdoor and took a long look down the emergency exit, it is necessary, firstly, to highlight the nature of the world economic crisis in the period 1945–50 and, secondly, to pinpoint the precise causes of the British balance of payments crisis in 1951 which provided the context and justification for the articulation of radical solutions. This is the task of the rest of this chapter which concludes with some brief comments on the key individuals involved in the floating rate convertibility disputes. Chapter 2 traces the currents which converged over the winter of 1951 to produce the Robot plan. Many of the arguments later deployed in favour of floating rates were developed early by Marcus Fleming (then Deputy Director of the Economic Section) and then by Lucius Thompson-McCausland (a flamboyant Advisor to the Governors in the Bank of England). But the real impetus for change came from the deadlock in Anglo-American relations which signalled the dwindling of dollar aid to Britain, and from the problem posed by so-called 'cheap sterling' operations undermining confidence in the official sterling–dollar exchange rate. By January 1952, Otto Clarke, Leslie Rowan and George Bolton,[6] were hammering out the details of a new course for Britain and the international political economy. Chapter 3 discusses in detail the Robot plan. Particular attention is paid to its impact on the postwar world economy charting its likely effect on the Sterling Area, Europe and the United States. The boldness of the Robot plan, and the manner of its presentation to Cabinet Ministers, ensured that it would generate doubters and opponents. Chapter 4 looks at the counter arguments presented principally by Robert Hall and Lord Cherwell. On 28 February 1952, the Cabinet met at 10.00 p.m. for the first of three meetings to discuss Robot and the economic situation. Macmillan described the next 24 hours as the most extraordinary he had ever spent. The events leading up to the Cabinet's shelving of Robot are analysed in full in this chapter using private diaries and primary documents. Throughout the spring and early summer of 1952, Clarke, Rowan, Bolton and Cobbold worked on a 'new look' Robot to make the plan, at least in principle, acceptable to the Foreign Office and the Board of Trade. Chapter 5 details the modifications made to Robot (particularly as regards the sterling balances and impact of the plan on Europe and the EPU) in the context of alternative policies presented by the Economic Section of the Cabinet Office. Robot was rejected again on 30 June by a select group of Ministers before it reached the full Cabinet. Unilateral British action was now ruled out. But, from the debris and recriminations emerged a new route to floating rate convertibility, christened the Collective Approach to Freer Trade and Currencies. Chapter 6 discusses both Cherwell's plan for an Atlantic Payments Union and the steps which led to the adoption by the government and the Commonwealth of the Collective Approach. The success of this approach rested on a positive endorsement (including financial assistance) from the new United States Administration. Chapter 7 focuses on the Washington talks of March 1953 which effectively killed off the grand designs of the Collective Approach. The US Treasury had concluded that a bilateral stabilization fund of several billion dollars to support convertibility would, to all intents and purposes, be a repetition of the disastrous Anglo-American Loan Agreement of 1946. It was now left to the Bank to devise a more low-key 'depoliticized' approach to convertibility which bore fruit in March 1954 with moves to unify transferable sterling alongside the reopening of the London gold market. In February 1955 the Cabinet agreed to support the transferable rate at a one per cent discount on the official rate, a move widely seen as introducing de facto convertibility. Eddie Bernstein, at the IMF, announced that the UK action was the greatest single move in the history of the Fund. Chapter 8 indicates that between the summer of 1955 and the start of Operation Unicorn in October 1958, the Treasury steadfastly refused to move to de jure convertibility by bringing together the transferable and official rates for sterling. However, by the summer of 1958 the reserves had been strengthened, mainly by drawings and stand-by credits from the IMF and the Export–Import Bank, the balance of payments was back in surplus and it appeared that the dollar shortage was finally over. Unicorn, the unification of the transferable and official rates, could be launched. However, the balance of power had begun to shift to Continental Europe and Britain would be forced to dovetail operations with France and West Germany. Monday 29 December 1958 saw the introduction of convertibility across Europe and the replacement of the European Payments Union by the European Monetary Agreement. Despite much rhetoric this did not herald a bright new dawn for Britain or the world economy. The Conclusion sketches the tensions present in the world economy in the late 1950s which ultimately led to the demise of fixed rates in the early 1970s. Finally, it is suggested that in the light of continued economic and political decline, the British government missed a golden opportunity in February 1952. Robot was a gamble, but the alternative was 'creeping paralysis' which by the late 1970s forced violent reform without altering the structure of the external environment. Robot, in short, should not be misinterpreted simply as a 'bankers' ramp'. Rather, it was an attempt to breakout of postwar constraints and remake the world economy in an effort to check the relative economic and political decline of Britain.

II Bretton Woods and the falsification of the IMF assumptions

International trade and financial relationships between 1944 and 1950 were dominated by discussions surrounding the Bretton Woods Agreement, the Anglo-American Loan Agreement, the Marshall Plan and the European Payments Union. There is a large literature on each, and so this introduction will highlight salient points rather than presenting an exhaustive history.[7]

Bretton Woods enshrined the following multilateral objectives: currencies freely convertible at fixed exchange rates, with controlled capital movements; no discrimination in trade (except by the formation of full Customs

Unions); and the abolition of quotas (except to meet temporary balance of payments difficulties), the reduction of tariffs and the progressive elimination of preferences (although there was no obligation to reduce preferences except in return for tariff concessions of equivalent value).[8] The aim of the Articles of Agreement of the International Monetary Fund, the International Bank for Reconstruction and Development and the Havana Charter for an International Trade Organisation, was to translate these objectives into international rules of behaviour in the economic field and establish institutions to administer the rules and promote further action towards the objectives.[9] The ITO was, of course, stillborn, but the commercial policy provisions of the draft Charter for the ITO were incorporated into the General Agreement on Tariffs and Trade.[10] It was envisaged that after a relatively short 'transitional period' (which allowed members to maintain restrictions for a five-year period in order to adapt to changing circumstances), a smoothly working international system would be established.[11] It was anticipated that balance of payments difficulties would arise but it was thought that such problems would, over time, be the exception rather than the rule. The Articles of Agreement indicated that in such cases, there should be no pressure on countries to deflate (for this would jeopardize full employment). Rather, difficulties could be rectified by import restrictions and short-term borrowing from the IMF. Universal discrimination against a persistent creditor was permissible, in theory, under the provisions of the Scarce Currency clause, if the IMF's resources of that country's currency were approaching exhaustion. In short, the architects of Bretton Woods assumed that, provided import and exchange restrictions were removed – and their reimposition in time of emergency strictly controlled – and provided that there were no discriminatory blocs, a smoothly working multilateral system would come about automatically.[12]

At the close of the Bretton Woods conference on 22 July 1944, as a band played the 'Star-Spangled Banner', Keynes and Morgenthau spoke of the creation of a new 'brotherhood of man' and of the Bretton Woods signpost 'pointing down a highway broad enough for all men to walk in step and side by side'.[13] However, this was not the view of the American banking community who pushed for the rejection of the IMF on the basis that 'it embodies lending methods that are unproven and impractical . . . it might tempt borrowing countries to continue on the easy political way, instead of making the maximum effort to put their economic affairs in order'.[14] According to a clutch of influential New York bankers, including John Williams (professor of economics at Harvard and vice-president of the Federal Reserve Bank), Leon Fraser (president of the First National Bank of New York), and Winthrop Aldrich (Chase National Bank), Bretton Woods failed, in particular, to recognise the importance of key currencies in international trade.[15] Extensions of credit, they argued, should be negotiated on a bilateral basis, not centrally through an international organization. In short, to secure the interests of American capital, the best way to kick-start the world economy would be to offer a substantial credit to Britain (Fraser suggested $5 billion; Williams and Aldrich $3 billion) to underwrite the use of sterling and act as a financial lever on Britain forcing an early commitment to convertibility and non-discrimination.[16] Although the US Senate passed the Bretton Woods agreements bill on 19 July 1945, by 61 votes to 16, the issue of US aid to Britain remained unresolved until the war against Japan was concluded. VJ Day (2 September 1945) saw the abrupt termination of Lend-Lease and a shift in the American position towards the key currency approach. Truman and Vinson (replacing Roosevelt and Morgenthau) now took the opportunity to recast Bretton Woods offering a $3.75 billion dollar loan to Britain in exchange for sterling convertibility, non-discrimination in trade, the dissolution of the Sterling Area dollar pool (and by implication, the Sterling Area) and the freeing of the blocked sterling balances (accumulated British war debts). The obligations would become effective one year from the formal ratification of the Agreement. Despite opposition, particularly from the Bank of England and Otto Clarke in the Overseas Finance division of the Treasury, the Anglo-American Financial Agreement was signed on 6 December 1945, and Britain's ratification of Bretton Woods received Royal Assent 14 days later, on 20 December.[17] Congress now approved the line of credit, in the context of furthering the purposes of the Bretton Woods Agreement, on 15 July 1946.[18] Britain would now be forced to ignore any 'transitional period' rights and undertake the full rigours of convertibility and non-discrimination, in the name of global multilateralism, on 15 July 1947.[19] From the perspective of the US State Department, the Agreement was fundamental to the realization of American political and economic objectives. Domestic economic growth depended on maintaining large export surpluses which were only achievable in the long term if currencies were fully convertible and discrimination reduced.[20] As Assistant Secretary of State for Economic Affairs, Will Clayton privately noted, 'if we succeed in doing away with the Empire preference and opening up the Empire to United States commerce, it may well be that we can afford to pay a couple of billion dollars for the privilege'.[21]

It soon became apparent, however, that the assumptions of Bretton Woods, particularly in its Loan Agreement guise, were to be falsified by events. Not only had the scale of the wartime disruption been gravely underestimated, but the extent of the change in the basic underlying factors had not been perceived. In a review of the postwar situation, British Treasury and Bank officials concluded that the architects of the 'new system' had failed to appreciate six key factors.[22] Firstly, the scale of the disruption in Europe and Asia and the double advantage which North America had gained by both escaping physical damage during the war and having developed its production of essentials under the forced drought of wartime necessity. Secondly, the revolution in the international economy resulting from the impoverishment of the UK and the transformation of Britain from the world's biggest creditor to the world's biggest debtor – including the weakening of sterling and competitive power. Thirdly, the move towards industrialization and development in the 'underdeveloped' countries of the world, and the effect which this would have on world trade. Fourthly, the abnormality of the great surpluses of primary products in the 1930s and the major change in the terms of trade between primary products and manufactures. Fifthly, the great demand for investment in the disrupted world, and the resulting rapid world inflation. Finally, the inadequacy of the gold reserves outside the United States in view of the rise in prices and the size of the balance of payments deficits. The worldwide demand for food, consumer goods, fuel and capital goods – which could be supplied in sufficient quantities only from North America – created the 'world dollar shortage' with the United States amassing balance of payments surpluses of $7 billion and $10 billion in 1946 and 1947 respectively. As US aid was rapidly exhausted, the world's gold reserves flowed back to Fort Knox; European economies were plunged into crisis; trade began to seize up around the world and bilateral trade and payments systems were reactivated.

In the UK, the effect of convertibility was to increase significantly the pressure on external resources and to create expectations that an acute crisis, demanding drastic action, was fast approaching.[23] Two weeks into the convertibility experiment, the Governor of the Bank summed up the official position noting, 'I have always personally believed that the whole pack of cards of Bretton Woods, Washington Loan, ITO etc., was unsoundly or at any rate prematurely built and that it would collapse under "transitional period" stresses. I agree therefore that convertibility as contemplated in the Loan Agreement (by which our hands are tied and which precludes us from using our trade, etc., negotiating weapons) must be modified'.[24] By mid-August, with the drain in Britain's dollar reserves running at $180 million a week, the government concluded that convertibility must be suspended.[25] At a special Cabinet meeting on Sunday 17 August the government agreed to implement 'Operation Gearcrash', involving intensified discrimination against dollar goods and emergency monetary action limiting the transferability of sterling (sterling would no longer be freely convertible outside of North America). To soften the impact of this unilateral legal breach of the Agreement, Treasury and Bank officials flew to Washington and agreed an exchange of face-saving letters that took place on 20 August, the day of the suspension itself.[26]

Bretton Woods was now in tatters. Europe returned to an international system dominated by bilateral trade and payments agreements whilst officials in Washington concluded that, 'the entire foreign economic policy of the United States was in jeopardy'.[27] As George Bolton perceptively commented in the wake of the convertibility crisis, 'We are back to the discussion which took place from 1941 onwards as to what policy we should adopt, but with the added difficulty of having made a false start'.[28] Currency convertibility and non-discrimination in trade remained the principal objectives of US foreign economic policy but they were now pursued in the context, not of Bretton Woods, but of Marshall Aid. In brief, this second postwar phase was based on the creation of a discriminatory bloc in Europe in accordance with a limited notion of increased European co-operation and toleration of the discriminatory Sterling Area system. It now seemed self-evident to the US Treasury that Britain and the Sterling Area constituted a 'far greater danger to US objectives than continental bilateralism' and thus 'it is not in the Sterling Area but only on the continent that we have any hope of seeing any ally emerge to prove the prowess of convertibility when the struggle for hard dollars gets underway'.[29] In economic terms, the period 1948–50 was marked by two characteristics.[30] The first was the weakening of competition and price as the determining factors of international trade, and the absence of a single world market price for most important commodities. Secondly, inflation continuously stimulated internal demand for goods without creating effective external purchasing power.[31] This increased the 'gaps' in international payments which could only be met by special financial provision. Trade therefore depended fundamentally on the credits doled out by the United States, which in theory should have been restricted to the phase of immediate postwar reconstruction. The net result was that while employment and production remained high, trade was distorted and no stable pattern of exchanges emerged. Consequently, the US Treasury was willing to accept the formation of the European Payments Union, retroactively established on 1 July 1950, provided there could be a satisfactory solution to the conflict between 'the deliberate creation of a sheltered trading area within Europe (including the colonies and the Sterling Area) and the firm US objective of the highest possible degree of commercial and financial unity in the free world'.[32] Accordingly the State Department's advocacy of European integration – as a means of deterring Soviet aggression and utilizing German resources whilst preventing the resurgence of an independent, aggressive and highly nationalistic Germany – was accepted by the Treasury in the hope that it would strengthen Europe as a competitive unit securing a multilateral future for the global economy.[33] It soon became apparent, however, that the EPU could not resolve the serious imbalances in the international economy and by 1951 it had encountered severe monetary problems trying to reconcile the positions of large creditor and debtor countries.

By the end of 1951 it was clear to both the United States Administration and the British government that the international political economy was in a state of chaos. The Bretton Woods 'system' had lasted less than six weeks in the summer of 1947 before falling victim to the world dollar shortage. The future of the IMF and the GATT looked in doubt as international trade and payments were characterized by discrimination against US exports and inconvertibility of currencies. Marshall Aid had boosted industrial production but the end of the European Recovery Programme raised the spectre of the re-emergence of the dollar gap, particularly in the context of the commodity boom associated with Korean rearmament. The Marshall Aid phase had also sanctioned the creation of a large discriminatory bloc in Western Europe and further weakened the position of the IMF by virtue of the so-called ERP decision of 5 April 1948, under which the Fund agreed not to finance countries participating in the Marshall Plan.[34] In a review of US foreign financial policy, the US Treasury now admitted that 'it was common knowledge that the objectives of the basic policy have generally not been realised'.[35] In London, Bank and Treasury officials drew three main conclusions regarding the state of world economy in 1951.[36] Firstly, there had been a clear failure to establish a stable pattern of trade and payments. Neither the IMF nor the GATT were designed to deal with the tremendous structural weaknesses created by the wartime and postwar changes. Bretton Woods had, in effect, been largely irrelevant and its institutions 'have neither been a major help nor a major hindrance'.[37] Secondly, the most obvious and worrying feature of the world economy was the continuance of structural imbalance. The non-dollar countries had not yet adapted themselves sufficiently to the difficult conditions: their investment programmes had been insufficiently concentrated into fields contributing to righting their balances of payments; with certain important exceptions, their economies overloaded displaying a tendency to inflation and dollar squandering. Thirdly, the weakness of the non-dollar world in relation to the United States had magnified the significance of fluctuations in the US economy. A relatively small adjustment of United States production and commodity stocks in 1949 had been a major factor in the devaluation of sterling. Fluctuations since the outbreak of the Korean War had wrought catastrophic consequences on the economies of many countries – both on the upswing and the down. In short, the gold reserves of the non-dollar countries had proved entirely inadequate to bear the strain placed upon them and the fluctuations had exposed critical weaknesses in the world economic structure. These weaknesses, as Raymond Mikesell clarified, could not be rectified by the IMF and GATT, whose role could, at best, be 'auxiliary'.[38] The forces determining whether the world would move towards or away from a system of multilateral trade and payments and currency convertibility lay outside the Fund and GATT. Power in this field resided largely in three cities:

(1) in London where decisions were taken with respect to the sterling area; (2) in Paris where decisions were made regarding the European Payments Union or any possible successor organisation; (3) in Washington where financial and political support would have to be obtained for any major effort in the direction of freeing the world's trade and payments from its shackles.[39]

To the governments in all three cities it was now evident that the 'critical weaknesses' in the world economy had been cloaked by American aid, which had enabled Western Europe to maintain commitments, both internal and external, far beyond its resources. Governments thus faced a period in which economic potentialities were as explosive as the political – the problem of how non-dollar countries could earn a living would have to find a solution.[40]

III The British problem and the 1951 balance of payments crisis

Although the British problem was, of course, an aspect of the world dollar problem, the Treasury recognized that a solution of the world problem would not necessarily carry with it a solution of the special problem of the United Kingdom – in fact, under certain circumstances it might have the reverse effect.[41] To understand the precise difficulties facing the British government in 1951 it is necessary to trace in detail the economic situation as it developed in the run-up to the General Election of 26 October 1951.

1950 saw Britain record a healthy balance of payments surplus and, for the first time since 1945, gain an increase in reserves (by $1,612 million).[42] But, by the second quarter of 1951, it was clear that the British economy was, once again, heading towards crisis. Gaitskell's bold assertion that 'by the end of 1950 the immediate tasks of postwar recovery would be complete',[43] looked overly optimistic as the terms of trade began to move against Britain in October 1950 and suffered a rapid deterioration in the first half of 1951 (increasing almost twenty points in the 12-month period from June 1950).[44] Consequently, at the close of 1951, the UK's earnings from visible and invisible exports had fallen short of its expenditure on imports and invisible account by some £521 million.[45]

The immediate cause of the imbalance was an astronomical rise in the *price* of imports combined with an increase in the *volume* of imports into Britain and the rest of the Sterling Area. Increased economic activity in the United States and the recovery of the West German economy, in the context of world rearmament, put severe pressure on raw material supply, and shortages of textiles, metallic ores and sulphur developed rapidly.[46] The situation was exacerbated by the US Government's policy of stockpiling strategic materials and by speculative demand for commodities in all countries, engendered by expectations of price rises and further shortages. The price of raw materials increased from an index which stood at 100 in December 1949, to 215 points by June 1951.[47] This increased UK import prices overall by 60 per cent over the same period. The total import bill for 1951, therefore, showed an annual increase of £1,100 million. Two-thirds of the rise was due to higher import prices resulting from the scramble for raw materials, but there was also an increase of 16 per cent in the volume of imports to counteract the reckless run-down of strategic stock in 1950.[48] The biggest volume increases were in fuel and materials, notably crude oil, timber, paper, rubber, textile yarns and manufactures for processing. Significantly, the proportion of goods arriving from the Sterling Area fell, whilst those from the Dollar Area and the OEEC increased.[49] The value of imports from the Dollar Area was 62 per cent higher, and the volume almost a third higher, than in 1950. Larger quantities of foodstuffs and tobacco together with imports of refined petroleum accounted for over half the increase in the volume from the United States.[50]

On the export side, although earnings totalled £2,708 million in 1951 (compared with £2,225 million in 1950), the bulk of the increase was due to higher export *prices*. The *volume* of exports increased by only 3 per cent in 1951, compared with an increase of 16 per cent in 1950.[51] In terms of geographical distribution, the proportion of exports sent to the Sterling Area increased from 46.3 per cent in 1950 to 49 per cent in 1951, whilst those sent to the United States and Canada fell by 0.4 per cent.[52] The most general cause of the export crisis was, as Bridges outlined to Butler, 'sluggishness of total industrial production'.[53] The large increases in export volume in earlier years were accompanied by a rapid rise in level of industrial production. In 1951, production increased at less than half the rate of previous years. This was largely due to difficulties in securing imports of scarce materials (particularly steel), manpower problems in key industries (such as coal) and the impact of rearmament on the metal goods sector (in particular, aircraft, vehicles, shipbuilding and electronics producers).[54] Even without an up-rated rearmament programme in Britain, the rise in import prices elsewhere would have created difficulties for export industries. The government's three-stage increase in defence expenditure merely added to the problems facing Britain's major producers. From an expenditure ceiling for defence over the period 1951–53 which stood at £2,340 million in December 1949, an increase to £3,400 million was announced in August 1950, revised to £3,600 million in September of that year, with a final increment to a level, excluding strategic stockpiling, of £4,655 million unveiled on 19 January 1951.[55] Consequently, defence production in the second quarter of 1951 was some 30 per cent greater than the average for 1950, and rose steeply throughout the year exacerbating labour shortages and difficulties for exports of metal goods.

Further pressure was placed on the precarious balance of payments by a fall in the UK's net invisible earnings. Although in the first half of 1951, invisibles amounted to £243 million, by December they had reduced to £25 million.[56] As a consequence invisible earnings dropped by £123 million between 1950 and 1951. This was as a result of four main factors. First, purchases of dollar oil to replace the Persian seizure of the oil refineries at Abadan cost approximately £100 million. Second, interest on the US and Canadian loans, which began on 31 December 1951, cost £39 million (excluding the £23 million capital repayment). Third, the government increased its military expenditure in Europe, Malaya, the Middle East and, of course, Korea. Finally, the steady annual rise in net earnings on shipping account was checked in 1951.[57]

Overall, in terms of balance of payments, the government's 'Economic Survey for 1952' summarized,

> The chief reason for the change was a large increase in expenditure on imports and a decline in invisible earnings coming at a time when exports were handicapped by shortages of steel and other raw materials, by the competing claims of defence and investment upon the engineering industries and by a fall in world demand for textiles . . . the result was that we could not sell enough of the things we could supply and we could not supply enough of the things we could sell.[58]

This, however, was only part of the problem. Britain could not, of course, continue indefinitely increasing its external indebtedness in order to consume more than it produced. However, as part of the Sterling Area system, Britain could, within limits, run an external deficit without disastrous consequences as long as the Sterling Area as a whole was spending in the rest of the world no more than it received. This, in fact, was the situation from mid-1950 until the end of the first quarter of 1951. Higher prices and a higher volume of imports was manageable (even favourable) whilst UK manufactured goods found a home in North America, and, more importantly, the overseas Sterling Area (in particular Australia, Ceylon, Malaya and many of the Colonial territories in Africa) made substantial dollar earnings selling wool, tin and rubber. In this way the overseas Sterling Area helped to produce surpluses in the European Payments Union resulting in considerable gold receipts.[59] However between June and December 1951, the dollar earnings of the overseas Sterling Area fell by nearly 50 per cent, as the United States cut purchases of wool, rubber and tin and the prices of Sterling Area raw materials fell. In addition, spurred on by earnings in the first half of 1951, the overseas Sterling Area substantially increased its spending on dollar imports between June and December, to a level twice the 1950 rate.[60] Since the prices of the specific raw materials imported by the UK from outside the Sterling Area did not fall appreciably, and the UK struggled to expand the volume of its exports, severe economic crisis was inevitable. In this context, the Treasury noted correctly, that 'the UK and the overseas Sterling Area each accounted in roughly equal measure for the swing which took place during 1951 in the balance of payments of the Sterling Area as a whole with the outside world'.[61]

Inevitably, the gold and dollar reserves which peaked on 31 June 1951 at £1,381 million, fell at a greater rate than at any time since the war.[62] By 31 December 1951 they had plummeted by £548 million and the drain continued until October 1952, when the reserves flattened out at a total figure of £602 million.[63] Predictably, this was accompanied by a sizeable UK deficit with the European Payments Union, with the consequence that by November 1951 the UK's gold-free credit in the Union had run dry.[64] Not without good reason did Churchill describe the situation as a 'financial super-crisis',[65] which threatened to destroy the value of sterling.

The problems of Britain's external economic policy

Britain's freedom of choice in external economic policy was limited by three factors which emerge from a consideration of the crises of 1947, 1949 and 1951.[66] Firstly, any policy would have to attend to the problem of the reserves. Even achieving a level of nearly £1,400 million in June 1951 could not, Treasury officials noted, stop a loss of confidence in sterling three months later. At a figure of just over £600 million the reserves could hardly accommodate the inevitable swings in the worldwide trading and financial transactions which were ultimately settled from them. According to Treasury calculations, on average the quarterly change in gold reserves (up or down) was approximately £100 million. Only four times in the period 1947–51, had it been as small as £50 million.[67] The first problem therefore was to adjust to this situation, either by acquiring substantial resources to strengthen the gold reserves or by altering the external financial situation in a way which reduced the strain on the gold reserves (or, of course, both).

Secondly, the balance of payments problem could only be solved in the long term by expanding exports and invisible earnings, and by obtaining an increased share of world trade. There were four dimensions to this problem. First, to cover capital commitments (debt repayment and overseas investment), it was calculated that an annual current surplus of at least £300 million was required.[68] Even this, whilst reducing liabilities, would allow nothing for rebuilding the gold reserves. Second, as regards import reduction, while there was scope over a period for increased production of essentials currently imported (food, steel, chemicals), this would not, over the long term, yield a decisive reduction in the size of the import bill. Demand for imports was bound to grow as the economy expanded; import-saving production might moderate this expansion of demand but was unlikely to reverse it.[69] Similarly, the Board of Trade's experience of import restriction was that the limits of useful action were reached fairly early. Over the medium term, import cuts either did grave damage to the competitiveness of the economy (as did paying discriminatory premium prices for raw materials) or resulted in retaliation and therefore loss of exports.[70] Third, righting the current account required an expansion of exports by at least 20 per cent over the 1951 volume with much more than proportionate increases in certain products (manufactured exports) and in certain markets. This task would be eased if there was an expansion in the total world trade in manufactured goods, but if trade stayed at the 1951 level, Britain's share would have to be increased to 23 per cent (compared with 19 per cent in 1951).[71] Finally, a large expansion on invisible account was required, particularly in respect of oil income.

The third – and what the Treasury perceived to be the hard core – problem of Britain's external economic policy was to provide an effective basis for eliminating the UK's £500 million deficit with the dollar area, either by direct action or by multilateral earning of gold or dollars. This required consideration of policies to reduce UK imports from the dollar area (already pressed intensively in the period 1947–1950); possibilities of earning gold from non-dollar, non-sterling countries (deemed by the Treasury to extremely limited); and earning gold from the rest of the Sterling Area – Britain's traditional strategy now thrown into doubt because a number of Sterling Area dollar-earning commodities (wool, rubber, tin, cocoa, jute) seemed vulnerable to substitution and fluctuation in US demand.[72] This left the obvious, though seemingly most difficult route, UK export expansion in the dollar area. This, however, was the point where United States competition was the keenest and, in respect of exports in general, highlighted the importance of adopting a policy which increased competitive earning power in the widest sense.

1951 saw a serious weakening of the UK's competitive power in relation to the United States.[73] Both wages and prices rose faster in this year than at any time since 1946, increasing by over 11 per cent, whilst the United States experienced a rise of only 5 per cent.[74] This was accompanied in Britain by a slight fall in output per man over the period 1951–52, increasing unit labour costs by 9 per cent.[75] As Cairncross has calculated, although average weekly wage rates between 1945 and 1951 increased by only 33 per cent (rather less than consumer prices), the rise in wages exceeded increases in productivity and added to labour costs in each of the immediate postwar years.[76] In Britain, export prices rose by 20 per cent in 1951, compared with a rise of only 4 per cent in the United States. Moreover consumption in the US fell from 70 per cent of gross national product to 62.5 per cent in 1951, whilst in Britain the share of consumption increased. Productivity and competitiveness were also affected in Britain by the existence of relatively full employment which considerably enhanced the bargaining power and general strength of the labour movement. July 1951 saw the registered number of unemployed drop to 0.8 per cent of the total civilian workforce. By mid-1951, the number of unfilled vacancies had risen to 504,000 – the highest total since 1947 – with the unemployed total standing at 188,000.[77] Severe labour shortages were experienced in the railway, coal and metal-using industries.[78] In such labour market conditions, it was almost inevitable that government exhortations to increase competitiveness would simply fall on deaf ears. Christopher Dow, a member of the Economic Section in 1950, later calculated that had the government pursued policies resulting in higher levels of unemployment – 2 to 2.5 per cent rather than the postwar average of 1–1.5 per cent – this would probably have made a major difference to the rate of rise in prices and, consequently, competitiveness.[79] As it was, without moves to create a more 'progressive and adaptable' economy, it seemed that the goal of making exports more plentiful and competitive would remain unattainable.[80] This was also the diagnosis of the US State Department, who conducted a number of surveys into 'the British problem' in 1951.[81] Inflation and over-full employment had 'deranged' the balance of payments by creating excess demand for imports and diverting resources from exports to domestic markets. Business had become inefficient because of the atmosphere of a seller's market and the tight labour market had encouraged restrictive practices and impeded the transfer of labour to essential industries. According to State Department economists, studies of British productivity showed that in the 14-year period, 1935–1948, for 22 key industries, productivity in eight had declined (including coal, coke, cotton spinning and paper), productivity in seven had increased less than 10 per cent and in only seven had it increased by more than 10 per cent. In general it was found that real product per man-hour was rising very slowly and by the end of 1951 was only 5 per cent higher than in 1938.[82] The State Department concluded,

> Restrictive practices of industry and labour are primarily to blame for the inflexibility of the British economy. These practises impede production and cause prices to be kept at artificial levels, either through price agreements or inflated costs. Psychology of labour is dominated by fear of new techniques which might jeopardise jobs or wages.[83]

Britain's competitive power in export markets was in decline principally because newer industrial rivals had a higher rate of growth of labour productivity and lower wage levels. According to the US State Department, action needed to be taken in the sphere of 'domestic British politics' to reduce the scale of the welfare programme (which had adversely affected incentives), reduce the level of direct controls and introduce greater flexibility.[84]

In short, a solution to the problems of Britain's long-term external economic policy would have to be consistent with increasing industrial potential and competitive power, and relieving pressure on the reserves to enable confidence in sterling to rise. Alternatives to a 'one-world' multilateral trade and payments system, such as bilateralism, permanent discriminatory groups and extended preference arrangements, would, in the long term, be inconsistent with these objectives. Hence the Bank and Treasury's commitment, by the first quarter of 1952, to the creation of a multilateral system in which sterling was freely convertible (except for residents of the Sterling Area), discriminatory or quantitative restriction of imports were kept to a minimum and market forces, through a floating exchange rate, were allowed to effect a structural adjustment of the domestic economy and a restructuring of the global economy, in order to enhance overall competitiveness. By contrast, a 'gradualist' approach was advocated by the Economic Section and the Paymaster General's Office favouring retention of the fixed rate, intensified import restrictions and the development of more dollar-earning and dollar-saving production with full co-operation from the United States and Europe. As clarified by a group of officials drawn from both camps, the issue was essentially between those thought it too dangerous to make sterling convertible too soon and who believed that as a result of vigorous action by Britain, the Commonwealth, the United States and Europe, the world dollar shortage could be reduced to a point at which fixed rate convertibility could be introduced without serious risk; and those who considered the risks of waiting greater than the risks of an early decisive step towards convertibility on a floating rate, that the attempt to wait would probably be frustrated by the course of events and that the move would in itself set up constructive pressures that would help to lead the economy in the right direction.[85]

The debate over Robot therefore was not a dry discussion of the merits of exchange rate regimes or the technicalities of convertibility – although, of course, it encompassed both. At heart, Robot was about the future direction of British, and by implication, global capitalism. In one fell swoop Robot would demolish what remained of Bretton Woods and re-establish Britain as a leading power alongside the United States. At home, market forces would destroy the 'rigidities' set up under Attlee and help cure the economy of the 'creeping paralysis' induced by over-full employment and the lure of 'soft' markets for uncompetitive goods. The following chapters detail the remarkable struggles which took place over Robot and the direction of British policy in the early 1950s. However, before considering the emergence of the plan in detail, it is important to acknowledge the pivotal role played by high-ranking Treasury and Bank officials in the currency management debates of the 1950s. To help reveal the struggles which took place and the alliances which were formed among Ministers and higher civil servants, this introduction concludes with some biographical details of the key Treasury and Bank officials involved in policy formation at the highest level.

IV Dramatis personae[86]

Bolton, George (1900–82)
Executive Director of the Bank of England 1948–57, with primary responsibility for questions of external financial policy. Principal supporter of Robot in the Bank. Recognized, in 1954, that the Collective Approach had run its course and began to push, with some success, for a new low-key, market-based approach to convertibility. Said to have had an 'engagingly pugilistic personality', he was thought 'a reckless adventurer' by Frank Lee. Critical of overly cautious politicians, he resigned in February 1957 to take the Chairmanship of the Bank of London and South America.

Clarke, R.W.B. 'Otto' (1910–75)
Perhaps the most influential figure in the Robot episode and certainly the prime mover behind floating rate convertibility from late January 1952 until Robert Hall engineered his departure from Overseas Finance (OF) in October 1953. Passionate about chess, bridge and betting, Otto was a chain smoker and is reputed to have read at least five books a week. An Under-Secretary in the Overseas Finance Division of the Treasury from 1947, he exerted an influence far greater than his official position. Termed by Lord Cherwell, 'brilliant but volatile', he was distrusted by Robert Hall, who likened him to an 'evil genius'. Later, Permanent Secretary at the Ministry of Aviation (1966) and Ministry of Technology (1966–70).

Cobbold, Cameron (1904–87)
Deputy Governor (1945–49) and then Governor of the Bank of England (1949–61). A qualified supporter of Robot, he laid stress on the need for stability alongside more flexibility in exchange rate policy. Following the shelving of Robot, he fought a constant battle to persuade the Chancellor and the Treasury to move quickly to convertibility. A commanding personality, who ruled the Bank in almost military fashion, he 'never ceased to argue fearlessly for what he believed was right'.

Hall, Robert (1901–88)
Director of the Economic Section, Cabinet Office, 1947–53. From 1953 to 1961 Economic Advisor to HM Government (Treasury). A formidable opponent of Robot and of other floating rate 'crash course' schemes. Increasingly influential after the defeat of Robot II, he convinced Bridges and Butler in 1953 to move Otto Clarke and Herbert Brittain from OF. Renowned for his 'subtle and hard-won common sense', he also had great success every year at the Treasury Horticultural Society where sweetcorn, grown on his Oxford allotment, often won first prize in the Any Other Vegetable category.

MacDougall, Donald (b. 1912)
An economist tutored by Maurice Allen at Oxford, he was Chief Advisor to the Prime Minister's Statistical Section headed by Lord Cherwell ('the Prof') 1951–53. A staunch opponent of Robot, he worked tirelessly with the Prof to defeat the plan in the run-up to the crucial February Robot Cabinet meetings. An architect of the Atlantic Payments Union proposals he later became head of the Government Economic Service and Chief Economic Advisor to the Treasury 1969–73.

Plowden, Edwin (1907–2001)
Chief Planning Officer and Chairman of the Economic Planning Board, 1947–53. Allied himself with Hall against Robot. A 'businessman in Whitehall', he had a reputation for courage and tenacity when in debate,

and self-doubt when there was no struggle on which to focus. Became Chairman of the Atomic Energy Authority in 1954.

Rowan, Leslie (1908–72)
Second Secretary, HM Treasury 1947–49 and Second Secretary, Head of the Overseas Finance Division 1951–58. Famously captained England at hockey. The most senior advocate of Robot in Overseas Finance, he was contemptuously termed 'really nothing more than Otto Clarke's creature' by Robert Hall in 1952. Maintained close contact with Bolton and Cobbold in the Bank until 1955 when OF and the Bank differed over the timing of moves towards convertibility. He was passed over for the post of Permanent Secretary when Bridges retired in June 1956. On his resignation from the Treasury in 1958 (to join Vickers Ltd), Hall commented that he was a 'considerable international figure' and that the Treasury was 'certainly much weaker with him gone'.

Thompson-McCausland, L. P. 'Lucius' (1904–84)
Advisor to the Governors 1949–65. A self-taught economist, he took a double first in classics at King's College, Cambridge. A strong supporter of floating rate convertibility in the Bank. Known as 'Lucifer' in Treasury circles, he had accompanied Keynes to the United States in 1943 to discuss plans for the new monetary order. An Ulsterman and a violet anti-Papist, he was called by Bolton, the 'most tenacious controversialist I have ever encountered'. Served as Consultant to the Treasury on international monetary problems in the late 1960s before becoming Director of Tricentrol Ltd.

2
Emergency Action and the Route to Floating Rate Convertibility

By the end of August 1951, with a General Election imminent, it seemed likely to many government officials that the Conservative Party would form the next government.[1] Edwin Plowden, the Chief Planning Officer, announced his decision to resign on 3 August, fearing that a Conservative government would 'organise his job out of existence and him out of the Civil Service'.[2] Leslie Rowan succeeded Henry Wilson Smith as head of Overseas Finance, and it was expected that Edward Bridges would soon retire as Permanent Secretary, to be replaced by Norman Brook, the Cabinet Secretary.[3] In the event both Plowden and Bridges were persuaded to stay on and it seems that Bridges in particular saw the advent of a Conservative government as a long-awaited opportunity to put a stop to the policy drift since 1945 and convince Ministers of the need to 'take painful decisions'.[4] In the run-up to the election, Bridges chaired a number of high-level meetings (involving Gilbert, Rowan, Brook, Hall and Clarke) to clarify the main issues facing the new government and the major objectives of government policy.[5] It was agreed that the main objectives of government policy were, firstly, to restore the external financial position, secondly, to carry through the defence programme, and thirdly, to avoid open wage inflation. A special report, 'Economic Prospects for 1952', was prepared for the incoming Chancellor and Bridges insisted that it 'emphasize the need for speedy action'.[6]

On entering office, Churchill set up a somewhat over-elaborate and confusing Ministerial structure for dealing with economic policy. Butler, a former Cambridge history don, became Chancellor over 'the obvious candidate'[7] Oliver Lyttelton, who took the office of Colonial Secretary. As a junior Minister at the Foreign Office in the late 1930s Butler had been associated with the policy of Appeasement and it was widely believed that Churchill thought he would need detailed guidance on important policy matters.[8] Consequently, Arthur Salter, then 70 years old, became Minister of Economic Affairs and Lord Cherwell was given Ministerial rank as Paymaster General with a roving commission to advise Churchill on economic issues, assisted by Donald MacDougall in the Prime Minister's Statistical Section. Despite Churchill's attempt to cage the Chancellor – Hall reported 'alarms about wanting to reduce the Chancellor to a tax collector'[9] – Treasury officials tended to ignore Salter and thought Cherwell both eccentric and an irritant.[10] However, as subsequent chapters will show, the retention of Plowden as Chief Planning Officer and the appointment of Cherwell as economic advisor proved crucial in the later Robot debates. Bridges would later confide to Butler that although he thought Churchill had supported the Chancellor in the actions which had enabled the short-term position to be dealt with, the Prime Minister had failed to support him in his efforts to tackle the long-term problems.[11] It is plausible to suggest an entirely different outcome to the debates had Lyttelton become Chancellor, Butler been appointed Foreign Secretary and had Norman Brook been in post as Chief Planning Officer.

Butler began his Treasury life by responding to an invitation to meet Bridges and William Armstrong at the Athenaeum Club.[12] Here Bridges outlined the essentials of the report he had prepared on 'Economic Prospects for 1952'. The report indicated that five features of the current situation gave cause for serious concern.[13] The external financial position was seriously unbalanced; the domestic price and wage level was moving steadily upwards; different parts of the productive system were grossly unbalanced; the intense demand for labour was hampering the government's redeployment programme; and, as a result, the expansion of defence production at the speed required was endangered. Butler recalled, 'their story was of blood draining from the system and a collapse greater than had been foretold in 1931'.[14] At the first Cabinet meeting on 31 October 1951, Churchill, in typically belligerent fashion, suggested that 'a copy of the note by the Permanent Secretary to the Treasury should be sent to the Leader of the Opposition; he should at once be made aware of the factual position as it had been made known to the government when they first took office'.[15] Later that evening Butler met with Cameron Cobbold, Governor of the Bank, who stressed that the safety of the currency required that a comprehensive programme be announced and all possible measures taken without delay. Heavy cuts in expenditure and investment programmes were required and as regards monetary policy, Cobbold noted, it 'will not really bite directly on inflation unless it goes much further. It would begin really to bite and bite hard with Bank Rate at 4 per cent and upwards with the shake-outs and upsets which this would cause. This may well prove necessary before confidence in the currency can be fully restored'.[16] Now fully appraised of the severity of the situation, Butler circulated a memorandum to the Cabinet outlining the 'UK's insupportable position, one in which even apart from speculative pressure, we stand to lose virtually the whole of our remaining reserves in 1952'.[17] Accepting the advice of Bridges and Cobbold, Butler declared that the restoration of confidence in sterling 'should be the first and most important object of our policy'.[18] Accordingly he recommended four measures to be effective from his first statement to the House on 7 November. First, imports would be cut by £350 million (£150 million by direct cuts of imports of food, wine and spirits; £100 million saved by the suspension of the strategic stockpiling programme; £50 million cut in the import of rationed foods; and miscellaneous measures including reducing the tourist ration from £100 to £50 and limiting timber imports). Second, after twelve years of 'No change' in the Bank Rate, the Chancellor proposed a move of 0.5 per cent raising the Rate to 2.5 per cent. Cobbold had finally advised against a move to 3 per cent on the grounds that the government would probably achieve its objective with a small increase signalling the resumption of the use of short-term interest rate policy in support of other measures.[19] Third, Butler called for an urgent review of all government expenditure. Finally, he proposed measures to reduce the level of home investment in plant, machinery and vehicles to make more metal goods available for export.[20]

It seems clear that although Butler thought these measures necessary, he knew they were not sufficient. Despite the optimism of Robert Hall that 'a combination of Tory Government and Bank Rate' would lessen the capital outflow,[21] the economic crisis deepened through November and December. In the final quarter of 1951, the dollar deficit stood at $940 million (£337 million) and a deficit of $700 million was forecast for the first quarter of 1952.[22] On this estimate, gold reserves would fall to the Treasury's absolute minimum figure of £500 million by June 1952. Without emergency action further deterioration looked inevitable. In the context of an overloaded economy with wages and prices increasing and productivity sluggish, the rate of export was low and demand for costly imported raw materials high. As Butler explained to the Cabinet in January,

> On the import side, prices have risen against us (cotton and non-ferrous metals) and there have been increases in volume (steel, coarse grains) too. On the export side, the general conditions (for example, textiles) are at present unfavourable, and – much more serious – our competitive position in certain industries appears to be deteriorating. Except in the markets of the sterling Commonwealth we are tending to lose ground in many lines of business.[23]

The deficit of the other Sterling Area countries which amounted to £156 million in the second half of 1951, was forecast to continue to the tune of £120 million in 1952. Therefore with a predicted UK balance of payments deficit of £533 million for 1952, the Sterling Area as a whole looked to be amassing a combined deficit of £650 million for the coming year with total reserves of £835 million.[24]

In these circumstances Bridges and a number of Second Secretaries managed to convince Butler that unless further drastic action was taken, the government would find it impossible to hold the pound at $2.80. The Permanent Secretary emphasized that the 'mixture as before' was no longer good enough and that the Conservatives would need to 'do things from which their predecessors shrank'.[25] However, Bridges' suggestion, that Butler cut deep into food subsidies and take measures to restructure social services, was resisted. Items under consideration included suspending general dental and ophthalmic services, abolishing exemptions from prescription charges, increasing the use of hospital pay beds, increasing charges for school meals and raising the school starting age from five to six.[26] Bridges was aware that cutting food subsidies would increase the retail price index and this might well fuel demands for wage increases. However, in his view, these measures were necessary to indicate the 'startling gravity of the situation' and show that sacrifices were required all round.[27] In discussion, Robert Hall countered by arguing that the measures would undoubtedly lead to wage increases and industrial unrest given the confidence and militancy of the labour movement.[28] Although on this occasion Hall's advice was heeded by Butler, it was clear that the Chancellor was now receptive to radical suggestions on how to deal with both the short- and long-term problems facing the British economy. Solutions involving exchange rate management and convertibility were brought to the fore by Treasury and Bank explorations of the benefits of a floating rate.

I Fleming and Thompson-McCausland on the advantages of a floating rate

Many orthodox accounts of international monetary policy often imply that governments in the postwar period were wholeheartedly committed to the fixed rate system agreed at Bretton Woods. However, it's important to be aware that official thought in Britain regarding exchange rate policy fluctuated broadly in line with perceptions of the severity of the balance of payments deficit. As early as 1944, James Meade and Marcus Fleming of the Economic Section advocated the use of exchange rate variations and clashed with Keynes on the relative merits of import quotas and depreciation to correct a persistent external deficit.[29] The convertibility crisis of 1947, and the recurrent difficulty of inducing exporters to expand sales in dollar markets, prompted the government once again in 1948 to open serious debate on exchange rate management, including the merits of floating. In an early influential paper, Ernest Rowe-Dutton, Third Secretary in Overseas Finance, expressed general Treasury concern that failure to secure equilibrium in the balance of payments would, sooner or later, 'make a floating rate inevitable'.[30] However, it was thought that this would be inconsistent with the Labour government's emphasis on planning and might possibly lead to the break-up of the Sterling Area. For these reasons, Rowe-Dutton, and at this stage Otto Clarke, concluded that 'a floating rate should not be regarded as an alternative to devaluation to a fixed rate'.[31] This was a view shared at the time by George Bolton in the Bank. In what he described as a 'very hastily drafted memo', Bolton noted that although there was no scientific basis for a correct rate of exchange, variable rates 'could not be regarded as a policy but simply the inevitable result of an economic catastrophe'.[32] It was important, Bolton noted, to retain the protection offered by the comprehensive character of the Sterling Area controls which 'rest upon a fixed pattern of rates dependent in the first instance on a fixed sterling/dollar rate and a fixed sterling price of gold'.[33] A floating inconvertible pound would be incompatible with comprehensive exchange control, and low reserves would not permit intervention tactics to offer any effective protection to the British economy. This argument would be reiterated by Bolton in the course of the revaluation debate in early 1951 and supported by Bridges, Plowden and, to a lesser extent, Clarke. Against this orthodoxy stood the Economic Section. A variable rate, it was argued in the Section, would provide a useful method of insulating the UK economy from economic fluctuations abroad; if the rate selected should prove inappropriate it could easily be adjusted; and it could go down sufficiently far to make people expect the rate to rise again, thereby removing the tendency for capital to leak away.[34]

The devaluation of sterling on 19 September 1949 from $4.03 to $2.80 did not dampen the enthusiasm of those who had begun the push for a floating rate.[35] Informal discussions between Edward Playfair and Marcus Fleming (Deputy Director of the Economic Section) led Fleming to prepare a paper on 'the practicability and relative merits and demerits' of a floating system.[36] On 3 March, Fleming produced a devastating critique of the Rowe-Dutton/Bolton fixed rate orthodoxy.[37] It is particularly significant that the memo was copied to Otto Clarke, with a covering note from Playfair indicating that on this important issue, Overseas Finance must 'have a line'.[38]

Fleming's memorandum is a remarkable document inasmuch as it prefigures many of the arguments later deployed by Rowan, Bolton and Clarke in the floating convertibility Robot debates. Although he does not consider the problem of the sterling balances, Fleming directly links floating to convertibility and provides many of the raw materials for Clarke's seminal paper of 25 January 1952 which formally marks the opening shot in the Robot controversy. Fleming's central argument was that as a medium-term stabilizer of the balance of payments, the floating rate system was the only feasible alternative to the use of import restrictions, bilateral agreements and restrictions on convertibility. He carefully developed five main points. Firstly, it was inevitable that exchange rates would have to be altered at intervals to correct not only fundamental disequilibria but disequilibria lasting only a few years. In a world where the economies of some countries were relatively stable whilst those of other important nations were subject to involuntary fluctuation, the case for floating was strong. Secondly, contrary to Rowe-

Dutton's memo, Fleming argued that the floating rate system would not weaken the Sterling Area system. A floating pound would perhaps increase the number of adherents to the Area since it would provide a 'respectable way' of devaluing vis à vis the dollar at times of US recession and low dollar prices. Thirdly, floating would, of course, create difficulties with bilateral trade and payments arrangements. The point of adopting a floating system, however, would be to help abolish bilateralism and import restrictions. As regards uncertainty for traders, the provision of forward exchange facilities would cover the short term, whilst in the medium term floating would encourage exports and discourage imports at times when the former would otherwise have been tending to fall and the latter to rise, thus reducing hazards for industries providing exports or competing with imports. Fourthly, in respect of exchange control and capital movements, Fleming noted that floating rates operated largely by harnessing capital movements. In a passage echoed two years later by Clarke, he argued, 'we usually think of "hot money" as a destructive force but the examples we have in mind are usually those where a country has tried to maintain a patently overvalued currency. Thus it seems to me at least arguable that, if we adopted a floating rate, we might *want* to remove exchange control altogether'.[39] Sweeping aside Bolton's casual remarks on the problems of exchange rate management in the 1930s, Fleming continued,

we survived in 1937–38 a decline in US business conditions by comparison with which the recession of 1949 was the merest fleabite without denting our exchange rate by more than a few points and we did it with reserves we had picked up since the initiation of the floating rate system. I do not know any financial or commercial regime which has a better record than our floating exchange rate system in the 1930s.[40]

Finally, the memorandum acknowledged that floating was incompatible with Bretton Woods and the IMF. This, however, was not necessarily a bad thing since, in Fleming's eyes, IMF conceptions of the world economy were contradictory and in present form, unworkable: 'The maxim for the Fund must be: "Adapt or perish!" Certainly I believe a flexible exchange rate system is the only one which will permit the Fund's other desiderata, of convertibility, freedom from exchange control etc to be realised'.[41]

As the Sterling Area gold and dollar reserves continued to improve in the early months of 1950 – rising from $1,417 million in August 1949 to $2,125 million in April 1950[42] – it was inevitable that Fleming's radical approach to exchange rate management would be sidelined. Robert Hall, an advocate of floating in 1949, now deferred to Bolton's memo and decided that floating was 'totally impracticable'.[43] Likewise, Playfair, who had earlier admitted to being 'knocked out by Fleming', now declared that the real drawback of floating was that it was incompatible with Labour's 'kind of social policy', based on planning, controlled prices and 'fair shares' philosophy.[44] On these points, and the reservations expressed by Martin Flett concerning the 'potentially disruptive impact' of floating on the Sterling Area, Herbert Brittain was in full agreement.[45] Only Otto Clarke, in Overseas Finance, felt confident enough to explore the radical implications of Fleming's paper. In a brief comment, Clarke noted that 'theoretically' Fleming was correct.[46] It was absolutely necessary to have some 'equilibrating factor – for instance changes in reserves or changes in exchange rates or changes in import restrictions or changes in internal purchasing power'.[47] From this list, Clarke agreed with Fleming that only changes in exchange rates made any long-term sense. Furthermore, he rejected the common assumption that traders prefer a fixed rate: 'give them a choice between stability of import restrictions and stability of exchange rates and they'll choose the first every time'.[48] However, with reserves rising, Clarke sided with the rest of his colleagues in Overseas Finance. Fleming, he concluded, was

> entirely right if we are talking about the 'British pound', the factors affecting which are predominantly those of the UK economy in relation to the whole world. But we are talking about 'sterling', the factors affecting which are at least as much rest of the Sterling Area, as UK (on the dollar side probably more so). I think I favour an undervalued fixed rate for sterling.[49]

Clarke would maintain this position until January 1952 when his preference would be for radical change and in this respect it seems plausible that Fleming's paper had a lasting, though generally unacknowledged, influence.

The recovery of the British economy in the final quarter of 1950 led Gaitskell and Cobbold to reopen discussion on the merits of floating, this time in the context of the revaluation of sterling – meaning an appreciation in the dollar value of the pound.[50] The debate in the Bank, and specifically the interventions of Lucius Thompson-McCausland, proved to be of particular significance for the emergence of floating rate convertibility schemes in early 1952.

The revaluation debate

Revaluation, as a defence against inflationary pressures arising from the worldwide increase in commodity prices, had been suggested by the Economic Committee of the TUC and transmitted to the government's Economic Planning Board by the TUC's economic guru, Lincoln Evans.[51] Gaitskell's view, that potentially there were advantages in an appreciation of the dollar value of the pound, was soon tempered by more cautious advice from Overseas Finance.[52] Henry Wilson Smith, Head of Overseas Finance, set the tone in January 1951 by asking Herbert Brittain and Otto Clarke to prepare a 'contra revaluation note'.[53] This note was the first of many outlining the case against revaluation.[54] In principle, revaluation would cheapen, in terms of sterling, the 20 per cent of UK imports coming from the dollar area (which would mean cheaper bread, sugar and cotton). However, against this 'limited advantage' to the cost of living, Brittain and Clarke set two 'formidable objections'.[55] First, it was important to acknowledge that changes in exchange rates should be reserved for occasions when it was necessary to correct fundamental disequilibria. If it was thought that the government would alter the rate at will, this would give 'a most unfortunate encouragement to speculators and to disturbing pressure on the exchanges between the UK and other countries'.[56] The exchange value of sterling, it was argued, should be kept as stable as possible to maintain overseas confidence. Second, although the dollar balance of payments on current account had improved since September 1949, it was forecast that rising import prices, exacerbated by rearmament, might change the dollar surplus of the Sterling Area into a deficit by the second half of 1951. It would thus be a rash move to increase the dollar value of sterling. Brittain and Clarke concluded that nothing should be done to impede UK exports to the dollar area and 'nothing whatever should be done to aggravate the probable adverse effect of rearmament on those exports'.[57]

Similar conclusions were reached by Nita Watts of the Economic Section and by Clarke in later memos who ridiculed the belief that 'we can wangle ourselves an improvement in the terms of trade by revaluation – it is essentially a selfish case for competitive appreciation, which would no doubt be so regarded by other countries, who might follow suit'.[58] This advice was heeded by Gaitskell who decided on 1 June that in light of the levelling off of reserves, he would not pursue the idea of appreciating sterling, although he suggested that the question be kept under review and revisited in the autumn.[59]

The case for revaluation melted away as the reserves fell. However, the real significance of the debate was that it refocused attention on the issue of the floating rate. Nita Watts had ended her assessment of the pros and cons of revaluation by suggesting, 'it seems that some consideration might well be given to the possible advantage of making any future change in the exchange rate by allowing it to "float" for a while before adopting a new fixed parity'.[60] This was now taken up in the Bank and pursued independently by Clarke in Overseas Finance.

On 14 March, John Fisher, Advisor to the Governors, indicated that, in his view, the Bank could not support proposals for non-resident inconvertibility and a floating rate.[61] A floating rate had certain attractions – it could be used as a weapon to mitigate the effects of capital movements on the domestic financial situation and also the effects on the balance of payments of price movements. However, in Fisher's eyes, floating was more appropriate for the management of a currency not in international use. In the case of sterling, he doubted whether a floating rate would maintain the confidence of holders of sterling overseas and this was vital 'so long as confidence cannot be assured by convertibility'.[62] In addition, it would mean the renegotiation of existing monetary agreements, the reopening of the London gold market, and withdrawal from the European Payments Union. It might well prompt similar action by other trading nations as a measure of defence, and carried the prospect of 'a greater turning to the US dollar as the only major currency anchored to gold'.[63]

George Bolton shared Fisher's concerns. On 22 March, Bolton circulated a document which drew on Fisher and his own pre-devaluation paper on variable rates.[64] The Bolton memo was judged to be significant enough to figure as the Bank's only contribution to the Treasury debate on revaluation.[65] After rehearsing Fisher's argument concerning confidence in sterling, Bolton focused (as he had in 1949) on the problem of managing exchange control with a floating rate. The current system, he noted, rested on a relatively stable pattern of rates dependent on a fixed sterling–dollar parity and a fixed sterling price of gold. The administration of sterling was technically operated through the provisions of monetary and payments agreements, by the European Payments Union and the Sterling Area, and by official intervention in the New York market by the Exchange Equalisation Account.[66] There was, he noted, 'no system of administration whereby fluctuating rates could be transmitted to all the Area Controls so as to enable all traders and producers in the Area to have comparable and similar facilities to all others'.[67] The only feasible method of organizing a fluctuating sterling rate of exchange, he concluded suggestively, was 'to have a free exchange and gold market with no Exchange controls, all pressures making themselves felt through the rate of exchange and the price of gold'.[68] However, with limited UK gold reserves and large sterling balances in the hands of non-residents, Bolton considered it quite impossible to adopt a floating rate. Cobbold saw Gaitskell on the same day as the circulation of Bolton's memo, and the Governor and Chancellor agreed that 'in the present circumstances there could be no question of letting the pound go free and having a freely fluctuating rate'.[69]

This decision did not prevent Lucius Thompson-McCausland, the flamboyant Advisor to the Governors who had accompanied Keynes to the United States in 1943, from continuing to probe the idea of floating. On 9 April 1951, he produced the first Bank memorandum since Fleming, arguing explicitly for the adoption of floating rate convertibility.[70] Echoing Fleming (and Clarke's comments on Fleming), Thompson-McCausland began by noting that while economic and monetary policy in the UK was an important factor in the wider non-dollar world, there could be no question of counterbalancing fluctuations in the US balance of payments solely by adjustments in the UK itself: 'the only adjuster available to us which affects the non-dollar world as a whole is the sterling–dollar rate'.[71] This was the inevitable consequence of having two international currencies, one of which was based on a much smaller home economy than the other. A rigidly fixed sterling–dollar rate was deemed, by Thompson-McCausland, to be increasingly inappropriate: 'we must envisage a future in which the rate will fluctuate'.[72] The essential problem of convertibility was not to define the conditions in which Britain could sell gold or foreign exchange but to find a means of maintaining convertibility once it had been established. Once again, a fluctuating exchange rate seemed the only viable adjuster that could keep sterling convertible.

Thompson-McCausland followed up this brief memo with a much longer and considered document setting out a five-point case for floating on 4 May 1951.[73] Firstly, direct controls, other than on outward capital movements, had, he noted, been almost entirely ineffective in practice. In consequence, the defence of the exchange rate had fallen almost completely on the reserves, so that the defence of the rate meant in practice the defence of the reserves. Secondly, when the defence of the reserves ultimately meant that the defence of the rate (at $4.03) be abandoned, the reserves recovered and increased rapidly following the movement of the rate. Thirdly, at root, he claimed, the pound's difficulties were merely an aspect of the new 'Problem of the Colossus' posed by the growth of the US economy. It was now simply impossible to maintain a fixed sterling–dollar rate by adjusting the UK economy to that rate. In prophetic terms Thompson-McCausland warned, 'we shall fatally compromise our economic position by continuing to pursue a fixed rate . . . as a principle which must be defended until overwhelming forces compel its abandonment'.[74] Fourthly, Thompson-McCausland pointed to the great advantage of floating: 'the burden of adjustment will no longer be concentrated on the reserves and new vistas open on the adequacy of reserves for other purposes – in particular for convertibility'.[75] The disadvantage of a reserve currency fluctuating in terms of other currencies would be reduced if a sufficient number of them moved in line with sterling. In this way, the 'great prize of convertibility' would at long last 'come in sight with a moving rate'.[76] Finally, Thompson-McCausland refused to be bound by the mentality of Bretton Woods: 'since support of the rate to the last makes us dependent on our reserves, it thereby makes us dependent on America, which is the only source of help when our reserves run out'.[77] However, US authorities were an unreliable source as they had reneged on Bretton Woods by limiting access to IMF funds and preventing use of the Scarce Currency clause. As a result, Britain, he argued, was no longer bound by the agreement since 'the remaining principles of the Fund amount in practice to a capitulation by the non-dollar world to the Americans at any time when America is in heavy or continuous surplus'.[78] Exchange flexibility and convertibility supported by the use of indirect controls (such as Bank Rate) would, Thompson-McCausland maintained, provide the only secure foundation for sterling.[79] If American co-operation was not forthcoming, Britain could move independently with support from the non-dollar world.

Thompson-McCausland's proposals were radical and somewhat cavalier. They were not well received in the Bank. Both John Fisher and William Allen (Assistant Adviser to the Governors) recommended that they be rejected outright. Fisher, predictably, drew attention to the problem posed by the sterling balances; the danger of the break-up of the Sterling Area; and the blow that would result to confidence in sterling.[80] He concluded, 'to my mind the fixed rate policy seems the better with freedom to use such controls as seem necessary in its defence – unless we prefer to abandon the international character of sterling'.[81] Allen similarly emphasized the unpredictable effect of floating on the Sterling Area and doubted whether Thompson-McCausland's assumption, that devaluation had been responsible for the improvement in UK reserves, was in fact correct.[82] Floating, in his view, would deter the use of sterling as a reserve currency and expose Britain to counter action. Allen's most interested comments, however, centred on the politics of the floating rate. Anticipating Cherwell's later objections, he noted

> the prospects for convertibility are little helped if depreciation fails through domestic resistance to lower real incomes, or if, for fear of such resistance, the rate was not allowed to fall to the point where a temporary external balance was reached. Capital movements might be as severe as with a fixed rate, for it would not be clear that a floor to the depreciation had been reached.[83]

At this stage, of course, Bolton needed little convincing. The case against floating rate convertibility prevailed and Thompson-McCausland's memos were, for the time being, quietly sidelined. But, as John Fforde notes, Thompson-McCausland had provided a persuasive insight.[84] As a reserve and trading currency, sterling was in a unique position. Yet it was supported by inadequate reserves and an economy whose competitiveness was in decline. In the teeth of a crisis, floating rate convertibility might be a suitable option if the Bank were to become convinced that the fixed rate could not be held and 'that a virtue had to be made of necessity'.[85] This was precisely the conclusion reached independently by Otto Clarke who, whilst in agreement with Bolton, nevertheless noted that if the impact of US inflation on the economy and the rest of the Sterling Area became intolerable, 'we could then consider changing the fixed rate'.[86] This would mean the adoption of a floating rate since 'frequent changes in a fixed rate is the worst system of all'.[87] Although both Plowden and Bridges agreed in principle that the floating rate had advantages they also accepted the orthodoxy that the time was not yet ripe for the abandonment of the fixed rate parity (and, by implication, for a move towards convertibility).[88]

However, as the economic tide began to turn, attention would be refocused on the merits of floating rate convertibility. Three developments in particular helped push the Fleming/Thompson-McCausland solution back on to the agenda at the end of 1951: first, the re-emergence of the problem of 'cheap sterling'; second, apparent deadlock in Anglo-American economic relations, in particular over the question of continued financial assistance; and third, the preparations for the Conference of Commonwealth Finance Ministers which was due to open in London on 8 January 1952.[89]

II Inconvertibility and the problem of cheap sterling

The term 'cheap sterling' was shorthand for a variety of financial manipulations designed to evade UK exchange control regulations. Despite government efforts to maintain the inconvertibility of transferable sterling (that is, all sterling held outside of the Sterling Area and the Dollar Account Area) a world market had arisen in transferable sterling with dealings taking place in a variety of centres across the globe.[90] The most active markets were to be found in New York and Zurich, but dealing also occurred in centres such as Bangkok, Macao, Beirut and Tangier. The difficulty of tracking such trade was illustrated by the Bank of England's example of the dealing carried out by the Zilkha organisation.[91] Iraqi Jews by origin, the Zilkhas were active bankers in the Middle East before the war with headquarters in Syria and branches in Egypt. According to Bank sources, they were amongst the most active operators in transferable sterling and conducted their transactions through the American Nile Corporation in New York, and in particular through one of the latter's Venezuelan subsidiaries which traded in exchange throughout Europe and the East from a small office in Paris.[92]

Cheap sterling operations took a number of forms including: the trans-shipment of Sterling Area goods to the United States or other dollar markets; the use of cheap sterling by American purchasers for meeting invisibles payments in the Sterling Area; the use of cheap sterling to finance trade between non-Sterling Area soft currency countries; purchase of sterling by Americans to meet sterling obligations to non-Sterling Area countries; and the use of cheap sterling for purposes of capital flight.[93] The most widespread of these operations was the trans-shipment of Sterling Area goods, commonly termed 'commodity shunting'.[94] This did not involve the direct sale of discounted transferable sterling against dollars, but rather took the form of a complicated series of transactions involving trade in a variety of commodity markets. Typically a two-stage process, the seller of transferable sterling might, for example, be a Belgian exporter of steel to Australia who would be paid in sterling but would prefer dollars; while the buyer might be a Dutch merchant 'shunting' sterling tin to the United States and converting the dollars obtained for the tin back into sterling to cover his initial expenditure on the tin.[95] In more complicated instances, as Fforde clarifies, commodity shunting might take the form of, for example, a Dutch merchant beginning the first leg by importing a raw material from the Sterling Area (such as rubber which was readily saleable in the United States), paid for in sterling from a Dutch account.[96] This would then be exported to the United States where it would be sold at a discount undercutting US traders. The dollars received would be used to buy scarce dollar goods which would then be shipped back to Holland. Having completed the first leg of the operation, the Dutch trader would now begin stage two by re-exporting the dollar goods to, for example, Egypt. The goods, likely to be in short supply, would be sold for transferable sterling substantially above their American dollar price at the official rate of exchange. Thus the sterling profit on the second leg would exceed the loss on the first and to all intents and purposes 'inconvertible' sterling had been exchanged for dollars evading the complex structure of administrative transferability. Typical 'first leg' commodities were identified by the Bank as rubber, furs, wool, tea, hides and skins, whilst examples of 'second leg' commodities included US refrigerators, Swiss watches and Brazilian coffee.[97] Harry Siepmann, the Bank official responsible for monitoring exchange control, could only watch as commodity shunting became an increasingly specialized branch of industry from 1950 onwards. He reported to Cobbold that radical measures to tackle the trade in transferable did not exist within the present structure of exchange control and nothing better than harassing tactics were available to the government. Pessimistically, Siepmann concluded,

> We see a selection of unrepresentative samples which happen to come our way, and they often astonish us because there is no general type of pattern. Wool, tin, rubber, spices or any other raw material of Sterling Area origin can form the basis. Shipment may be to any one of a number of intermediate destinations. The ultimate outcome may be almost any sort of luxury export to a country which is short of dollars. The technique will vary according to the facilities offered in a wide choice of markets – Tangier and Beirut, Zurich and Amsterdam, with Paris as co-ordinator. The degree to which laws and regulations have to be evaded or broken may vary from one extreme to another. The boldness with which they are flouted is certainly increasing.[98]

Second in importance to commodity shunting was the direct sale of transferable sterling usually to an American resident for dollars at a discount on the official rate.[99] Arranged quite openly and legally by a number of banks and brokerage houses in Zurich or New York, the seller would use the dollar proceeds to buy dollar goods for sale at a profit elsewhere, whilst the buyer would use the sterling proceeds to shunt Sterling Area commodities to the United States or pay for 'invisible' services from the UK or the Sterling Area.[100] As Fforde again clarifies, 'this was a straight avoidance, off-shore, of the UK control, but one of which the British authorities could not usually be aware and could not effectively stop without at the same time stopping almost all use of sterling in the countries concerned'.[101]

Although the problem of 'cheap sterling' had occupied official thought since the reintroduction of inconvertibility in 1947, exchange control officials were reporting in late 1951, that cheap sterling transactions were probably on a greater scale than at any time since the summer of 1949. In the early days, reported the Bank, cheap sterling operations were conducted by a 'floating population of experienced tricksters' who actually gained by the growing complexities of regulated trade.[102] Gradually, however, the possibilities of the cheap sterling business 'began to attract the attention of more substantial people', and by the middle of 1951, more sophisticated organisation resulted in a huge expansion of the market in volume.[103] Although the Bank admitted that no absolute figures could be given, estimates for January 1952 put trade in cheap sterling at £2.5 million a week in the New York market alone.[104] Not only was such trade weakening confidence in official sterling, it was also undermining the dollar trade of legitimate Sterling Area firms and contributing to the UK's general dollar crisis.

Senior Bank officials now began to ask whether the UK's exchange control system had been overtaken by events. The exchange control system inherited from the war when trade was physically controlled by the Allied Navies and finance was supervised by comprehensive postal censorship and economic warfare organizations increasingly relied on the assumption that 'the foreigner will observe the wishes of the UK Government'.[105] As Thompson-McCausland outlined, in the early postwar years, with a great part of business still in government hands, inconvertibility had been effective (though never absolute).[106] But with trade returning to private hands overseas and foreign markets for sterling reopening beyond British jurisdiction, it was clear that 'sterling in non-resident hands cannot now be kept inconvertible'.[107] No exchange policy based on inconvertible sterling, whether at a fixed parity or otherwise, could offer an escape from the problems of cheap sterling. Thompson-McCausland posed a stark choice between reducing sterling to a domestic currency with little or no international use, and retaining sterling as key international currency (and Britain as a centre of international trade and commodity markets) which meant accepting the need for an early move to convertibility for non-resident sterling. Each time, he argued, the United States went into surplus and the dollar became scarce, the pressure on inconvertible European currencies mounts and the threat of devaluation resurfaces. Despite the risk of making the move with low reserves, Thompson-McCausland was adamant by November 1951 that 'the dangers of convertibility are less than the dangers of a pretended inconvertibility'.[108] His conclusion was that Butler should approach the US Administration and offer convertibility in exchange for a relaxation of IMF drawing rights and stabilization measures. If this failed, he advised once again that Britain should opt for unilateral action. The question to be decided, he stressed to Cobbold, was not that between convertibility and inconvertibility, 'for inconvertibility and the devices to which it leads are an illusion damaging to international balance and above all to ourselves'; the fundamental question was 'whether America can be brought to co-operate and, if so, will it be on terms that we can accept'.[109] Although Thompson-McCausland did not say so specifically,[110] Fforde is surely right to note that his arguments added up to a case for floating rate convertibility:

> Bretton Woods considerations apart, periodic prompt downward adjust-ments of a fixed parity would obviously have been impossible to handle in the case of an international currency with very inadequate reserves. A floating rate would have had its own dangers but could have been a supe-rior operating technique in such conditions.[111]

The ineffectiveness of exchange control had also begun to convince George Bolton that there was now no alternative to a policy based on the intro-duction of convertibility which must entail 'substituting measures which act with price incentives, for controls which attempt to act against them'.[112] Convertibility for non-resident sterling would not be 'easy or painless' but was the 'only alternative to reducing sterling to a local domestic currency with the collapse of the Sterling Area'.[113] Alongside the reintroduction of convertibility, Bolton pressed for the reopening of commodity markets in the UK and the reopening of the London gold market. But, instead of seeking financial assistance from the US government, Bolton proposed raising a banking credit from US and Canadian commercial banks supported by access to increased IMF funds. Unlike Thompson-McCausland, Bolton remained silent on the issue of unilateral action and he emphasized clearly that his preference, at this point in time, was for fixed rate convertibility.[114]

In general terms, the Governor of the Bank was initially reluctant to endorse the radical plans put forward by Thompson-McCausland and Bolton.[115] He had encouraged the pair to 'think aloud' about exchange policy, in the view that 'everything ought to be turned out by the roots and looked at, if it were only to conclude that we could not do much about it at present'.[116] He would, however, become a staunch advocate of an early move to convertibility as it became clear that the United States would offer very little financial aid to Britain in 1952, and that, as the crisis deepened, even the soundest domestic policies agreed at the Commonwealth Finance Minister's Conference would be no guarantee against the recurrent threat of devaluation unless accompanied by radical action on the external front.

III Anglo-American economic relations and dollar aid

Relations between Britain and the United States in the field of external eco-nomic policy had hit a difficult phase by late 1951. Since the signing of the Bretton Woods Agreements in 1944 and more specifically following the conclusion of the Washington Loan Agreement (ratified by the US on 15 July 1946), US foreign economic policy regarding Britain had been based on the twin themes of currency convertibility and non-discrimination in trade.[117] As Frank Southard of the IMF outlined in a review of US foreign financial policy in 1952, 'currency convertibility and freedom from restrictions are considered to contribute to the best allocation of economic resources. Currency inconvertibility ordinarily has to be regarded as *prima facie* evidence of disequilibrium in the balance of payments and instability in the economy as a whole'.[118] Despite granting $6.7 billion to Britain between 1946 and 1951, Southard concluded it was 'common knowledge that the objectives of the basic policy have generally not been realised. Currency inconvertibility is widespread and the continued inconvertibility of sterling is especially important'.[119]

Judd Polk of the US Treasury clarified that the significant improvement in Britain's gold and dollar reserves in the first quarter of 1951, made the question of dollar grants to Britain, 'politically impossible and economically undesirable'.[120] The US Treasury and State Department agreed that further economic aid to Britain was unlikely to promote convertibility or non-discrimination in trade. In a frank assessment of US policy towards Britain, Treasury Department officials concluded that they could not see 'any basis whatever for believing that the British will ever voluntarily adopt convertibility themselves or even permit others to adopt it without the bitterest of struggles'.[121] For a 'dangerously long time' the major policy decisions of the US had been based on the 'delusion' that sterling would be made convertible if only the 'conditions were right'.[122] The Labour government's attachment to inconvertibility had proved 'unshakeable' and it was strongly suspected that the Conservatives would prove 'equally strong adherents of inconvertibility as both a latter-day version of Empire preference and the best possible bargaining weapon for shifting the burden of readjusting to a dollar-short world off of Britain and onto others'.[123]

Whilst the US Administration looked with dismay at the return on its 'investment', the view from London was somewhat different. In circumstances where the US continued to amass huge balance of payments surpluses, the curtailment of foreign aid simply exacerbated the world dollar shortage and ruled out a steady, progressive move to sterling convertibility (particularly at a fixed rate). As Rowan remarked in the run-up to the Robot debate,

> the results of the US actions – stoppage of Marshall Aid, tin and rubber policy, virtual abandonment of burden sharing, Battle Act, failure to find means to finance UK defence production, refusal to settle their Katz–Gaitskell liabilities, and the repeated change of front on the $300 million – would be more readily understandable if their purpose was to weaken the UK economy, rather than to strengthen it.[124]

The strained character of Anglo-American economic relations was noted in a reflective Treasury memo which concluded that the most striking feature of Anglo-US encounters, 'has been not merely their failure to achieve substantial results but, further, the failure of the representatives of the two countries to diagnose problems in the same terms or to reach a full and sympathetic understanding of each others' attitude and difficulties'.[125] In these circumstances it was considered that even in the midst of a new sterling crisis, Britain would struggle to gain substantial financial assistance from the US Administration for the financial year 1952.

The passing of the Mutual Security Act in 1951 combined economic aid under the European Recovery Programme and military aid under the Mutual Defence Assistance Act into one piece of legislation.[126] Aid would now be distributed through the Mutual Security Agency, which had at its disposal $1,022 million of economic aid and $4,879 million of military aid for Europe during the fiscal year June 1951–52 with the proviso that the President of the US had discretion to transfer 10 per cent of the total ($590 million) from military to economic aid.[127] In effect, this meant that for the year June 1951 to June 1952 the United States had set aside approximately $1 billion to relieve the balance of payments problems of countries fully committed to the NATO rearmament programme.[128]

In presenting the UK case to the US Treasury in November 1951, Butler indicated that Britain would require $600 million of economic aid in the first half of 1952 and 1.5 million tons of steel by December 1952 in order to carry out the proposed £4,700 million rearmament programme.[129] However, Butler's request for financial aid fell on deaf ears. Although the Chancellor stressed the serious outlook and the need for quick and effective action, the record of his meeting with the US Treasury Secretary indicates that 'Mr Snyder avoided discussion of economic aid under the Mutual Security Act', and on the question of boosting Britain's gold and dollar reserves, 'Mr Snyder did not respond'.[130] By the end of November, with the UK economic position deteriorating, Butler calculated that Britain would require not $600 million but $900 million for the first half of 1952.[131] After more detailed talks with William Batt, Chief of the Mutual Security Agency Mission to the UK, in mid-December, it was agreed that the maximum economic aid that could be granted to the UK under the Mutual Security Act was $300 million (and that even this would have to come from the virement from military to economic aid).[132] In the wake of Churchill and Eden's visit to Washington in January 1952, the Americans agreed to make available the steel required for the defence programme, but it was clear that any financial assistance from the US would be modest and drip-fed.[133] In a memo to the Cabinet on 11 February, Butler indicated that it was unlikely that more than $125 million would be received before the end of June, despite a projected deficit for the first quarter of 1952 of $750 million.[134]

From the viewpoint of the US Treasury continued large-scale assistance would simply encourage the maintenance of standards of living and investment somewhat higher than Britain could actually afford. Although it was important to help Britain meet its military commitments, Treasury officials had concluded that 'it is difficult to provide assistance to a country without tending to accustom that country to a standard of living which depends on the continuation of US assistance and in a sense tends to postpone the necessity for becoming competitive and earning its own way'.[135] Ironically these were the very arguments later deployed by supporters of Robot to justify the move to convertibility on a floating rate. As Otto Clarke, of Overseas Finance, would later emphasize, for the British economy to be successful, 'we've got to get through this stage of fighting our exports against the Americans, Germans and Japanese. There is no escape in restrictionism'.[136] This strategy, however, would only be possible on a floating rate since with fixed rates,

> the only way to get the reserves which are necessary to enable us to become convertible is to get a big loan from the USA, and if we had those reserves we should not use them as a fighting fund to cover inevitable losses while we were becoming more competitive but squander them on sugar and tinned salmon.[137]

By early January 1952 not only had officials in the Bank and the Treasury concluded that some form of emergency action, combining domestic and external measures, was necessary. The US Treasury had also arrived at the conclusion that a 'plan for British solvency' was required immediately 'to bring about a much closer balance in its external accounts'.[138] Two lines of action were possible. One approach would emphasize decontrol, 'in the hope that classical forces would force correction in the British balance of payments'.[139] The other approach would be to secure balance by strengthening certain controls. Whereas the former would run the risk of inviting 'large unemployment, unnecessarily low consumption and detrimental capital movements', the latter would simply freeze British economic activity at present levels and technically balance external accounts 'without securing any real reallocation of British resources'.[140] Whichever path was chosen it seemed clear to the US Treasury that only continuing pressure on the reserves was likely to force the government into action.

Two further events in early January focused attention on the 'decontrol' option and schemes for floating rate convertibility. On 4 January, Arthur Salter received a confidential Report on Sterling Area Policy that had been prepared by a study group at Chatham House.[141] The main thrust of the report was conventional. However, it contained a recommendation that the Treasury draw up a 'contingency plan' in case orthodox economic measures failed to deal with the deepening crisis. The essence of the contingency plan focused on blocking sterling balances and abandoning the fixed rate of exchange. The Chatham House Report found its way to the Bank where John Fisher, Advisor to the Governors, assessed the feasibility of blocking and confirmed that in the teeth of a crisis it would have to be accompanied by a floating rate, which would also entail the convertibility of non-resident sterling.[142] Finally, momentum for the consideration of floating gathered pace after the issue had been unexpectedly raised at the Commonwealth Finance Ministers Meeting which opened with a preparatory meeting of officials on 8 January.

IV The Conference of Commonwealth Finance Ministers

On 2 January, William Strath, Deputy Chief Planning Officer, indicated that the Chancellor should take full advantage of the conference to stress that without emergency action there was real danger of the complete collapse of sterling.[143] Strath suggested a plan of action comprising intensified anti-inflationary measures throughout the Sterling Area, import cuts and a clear policy on convertibility. The Sterling Area, he noted, 'cannot exist in the long-term on an inconvertible basis. If we don't take action, we shall be forced into convertibility in conditions in which we cannot hold the value of sterling'.[144] In language that would later be used by Clarke, Strath concluded, 'if we avoid unpleasantness now, we shall have chaos later. If we all take adequate action now, we have a fighting chance of getting through'.[145] Butler's response was to suggest that a Working Party be set up to look into the 'sort of convertibility we want'.[146] On 10 January, the Cabinet endorsed Butler's recommendation concerning the Working Party and agreed that it was necessary to develop a longer-term constructive policy to secure the viability of the Sterling Area.[147] Surprisingly the Cabinet concluded that 'whilst no steps could be taken in present circumstances towards greater convertibility of sterling, the ultimate aim should be to achieve total convertibility based, not on fixed rates of exchange, but on flexible and variable exchanges'.[148] Fforde attributes the mention of floating rates to Oliver Lyttelton, and this is perfectly plausible given Lyttelton's unswerving support for Robot, in both its guises, throughout 1952.[149]

In his opening address to the conference, Butler stressed the official line that it was a declared objective to 'steer a course away from perpetual inconvertibility'.[150] However, he added, 'it would not at present be possible to draw up a cut-and-dried programme to this end, since it was first necessary to right the present situation and restore reserves to an adequate level'.[151] This received a frosty response in particular from the Australian representative, Sir Arthur Fadden, who had been directed specifically by the Australian government to raise the issue of convertibility.[152] Australia would, of course, co-operate to the utmost to remedy the present situation, but it was clear to Fadden that 'the previous piecemeal approaches to the problem had been harmful to the long-term interest and health of the Sterling Area'.[153] To restore sterling to something approaching its previous strength and status it was 'essential that a more positive and radical approach to the sterling problem should be made'.[154] In short, the Sterling Area, from the Australian viewpoint, was at a crossroads: 'the alternatives were to mould its future intelligently according to our own desires and its basic needs, or to patch it up more in hope than in confidence of success. A patchwork solution would no longer serve'.[155]

Three days later, Arthur Salter replied on behalf of the government, inviting Fadden and other representatives to remain in London and participate in a Working Party on convertibility, development and other long-term problems.[156] In setting the terms of the Working Party, Salter indicated it would be necessary to seek to define convertibility; decide the relation between convertibility and non-discrimination; and, controversially, 'decide whether we meant convertibility at a fixed exchange ratio which we would try to keep stable, as in the years following the recent war, or at a freely fluctuating rate, as in September 1931 when sterling left gold'.[157] He stressed that both systems had dangers – fixed rates too often led to devaluation while freely fluctuating rates, when the trading position of a country was weak, could produce violent and chaotic exchange variations. In conclusion, Salter suggested that 'a fluctuating currency with the support of an Exchange Equalisation Fund might be the best solution'.[158] In the light of the subsequent Robot debates, it seems clear that Salter went beyond his brief with this final remark. The Commonwealth Working Party was not intended to provide a forum for general discussion of UK exchange rate policy. In fact, Herbert Brittain clarified to the British representatives that it would be best if the Working Party did no more than draw to the attention of Sterling Area governments the conditions necessary to make convertibility possible and 'set them thinking about these'.[159]

The preparations for the Working Party were significant inasmuch as they brought together Clarke, Bolton and Thompson-McCausland, who in their different ways were now convinced of the need for emergency action. In fact, Rowan, Bolton, Thompson-McCausland, Clarke and Brittain had been meeting on an informal basis since late November, after Cobbold had suggested that 'it might be valuable to have a round-table "free for all"'.[160] It seems likely that Clarke used the preparatory meetings as a sounding board for the ideas put forward in his memo of 25 January. Bolton and Thompson-McCausland both thought, firstly, that it was possible to devise a system in which free convertibility for current transactions could be combined with control over capital movements for residents of the Sterling Area; secondly, that convertibility could be achieved as a result of deliberate decision rather than force majeure, and thirdly, that the rate of exchange could in theory be flexible or floating.[161] Herbert Brittain also seems to have become a convert to floating rate convertibility during these discussions. Commenting on the best procedure to follow in relation to the vexed issue of fixed versus floating, Brittain noted, 'No decisions on such a point are called for yet and we do not wish to give rise to discussion of it all round the world.

When it arises it will be a matter for consideration and decision, in London, as a matter of secret high-level policy'.[162] This was sound advice gladly accepted by Butler, who did not wish to narrow his options in the face of the deteriorating situation.

Events moved swiftly in the second half of January and as the sterling crisis continued it seemed clear that traditional deflationary measures were failing to stem the drain in gold and foreign currency reserves. Butler was now less than confident that import cuts alone would prove effective. On 25 January, the Cabinet agreed to a further reduction of £150 million in imports and other expenditure in the non-sterling world in 1952.[163] This involved cuts in tobacco purchases from North America and reductions in cotton and soft wood purchases, in addition to cuts in wheat, flour, bacon and other foodstuffs. Quotas on products already 'deliberalized' were also reduced and the tourist ration was cut again to £25. In total the £150 million represented only 7.5 per cent of Britain's non-sterling imports and Butler was unconvinced that these measures would be sufficient to reach his declared objective of reducing Britain's deficit with the non-sterling world in the second half of 1952 to £100 million.[164] Britain could not, he noted, 'bear this great load without a massive expansion of our earning power – providing enough of the things which the world wants, at the world's prices . . . it will take a long and sustained effort to get these foundations of our economy right'.[165] Butler ended his January statement to the House on a sombre note indicating that, in view of the seriousness of the economic situation, the Budget would be brought forward from its usual late April slot to 4 March (it was later rescheduled for 11 March).[166] This, as later chapters indicate, was to have a decisive impact on the discussions surrounding the adoption of floating rate convertibility – compressing the time available for consideration of radical measures into less than a month. As Butler delivered his speech to the House on 29 January, Treasury and Bank officials were already contemplating Clarke's account of the merits of floating rate convertibility.[167] The secret, high-level policy process, alluded to earlier by Brittain, had now been set in motion and the Cabinet would shortly have to decide whether to accept Operation Robot and fundamentally restructure the global economy or reject the floating rate convertibility proposals and maintain a steady course in the hope of fair weather.

3
Operation Robot: Restructuring the Domestic and the World Economy

In the form finally presented to the Cabinet on 28 February 1952, Operation Robot comprised five elements which, the Chancellor hoped, would be introduced on Budget day, 11 March.[1] Firstly, 'overseas sterling' would be made fully convertible. In effect, this meant convertibility into gold, dollars or other currencies for all 'unblocked' sterling balances and new sterling earned abroad or acquired by Sterling Area governments (this was subsequently referred to as 'external sterling'). Convertibility would not be automatically extended to residents of Sterling Area countries. Secondly, the government would abandon its commitment to the fixed rate system and publicly accept the principle of a variable rate of exchange. It would, in modern parlance, be a 'dirty float' since privately the government resolved to use the Sterling Area reserves, via the Exchange Equalisation Account, to keep the rate initially within the limits of 15 per cent of the official parity of $2.80 (in effect between $2.40 and $3.20). Thirdly, sterling balances (net sterling liabilities of the UK) held outside the Sterling Area (except for American and Canadian accounts which were already convertible) would be frozen/blocked. Ten per cent of these balances would be classified as 'external sterling' and would be convertible at the current rate. Fourthly, not less than 80 per cent of sterling balances held by Sterling Area countries would be blocked/funded into long-term bonds and thus could not be used for current transactions. Finally, the London gold market would be reopened to provide a free market against external sterling. The price of gold would not be related to the official dollar price, but would fluctuate freely. However, residents of the Sterling Area, other than gold producers, would not be allowed to operate in the market without permission.

This complicated set of proposals was the result of an intense phase of covert activity carried out in the Treasury and the Bank. In the space of just over a month, Clarke, Rowan, Thompson-McCausland and Bolton hammered out a new course for Britain, and by implication the rest of the international political economy, based on accepting the principle of floating rate convertibility. Originally codenamed 'Operation Bolthole' (and intermit-

41

tently termed the 'External Sterling Plan'), the proposals were quickly retitled 'Operation Robot' – a code word which it was thought was connected with the names of its most active advocates, Leslie *RO*wan, George *B*olton and '*OT*to' Clarke.[2] The other possible derivation of the term is that it signified an intention to allow the price mechanism to regulate the economy, in the manner of an automatic pilot.[3] The logic informing the proposals was best outlined by Otto Clarke in a series of memoranda, beginning with his seminal 'Convertibility' paper circulated on 25 January.[4]

I Forging the Clarke/Bolton/Rowan alliance

Clarke proposed that internal action alone could not deal fast enough with the present crisis nor would it address the underlying problem of lack of competitiveness. Three approaches to external policy were posited. Firstly, the government could agree that sterling should stay formally inconvertible and make no attempt to move towards convertibility. This route was rejected as fundamentally escapist and against the long-term interests of the British economy. Bolton and Thompson-McCausland had already concluded that sterling in non-resident hands could not long be kept inconvertible and that the government was rapidly losing control of the value of sterling.[5] For Clarke, and senior officials of the Bank, it was clear that a choice had to be made between turning sterling into a domestic currency with little or no international use and allowing the Sterling Area to collapse, or retaining sterling as an international currency – which meant accepting convertibility for non-resident sterling.[6] It was also, thought Clarke, unrealistic to assume that a large bloc of nations would wish to be isolated from the rest of the world economy and in particular from the United States. The January Commonwealth Finance Ministers' Meeting had indicated to Clarke that South Africa, Ceylon, Malaya and the Gold Coast would probably not wish to long continue in an inconvertible Sterling Area system. In any case, he concluded, 'it *must* be in our interest to have sterling convertible . . . the restrictions which are necessary to maintain inconvertibility are not compatible with the development of the U.K.'s earning power'.[7]

Secondly, Britain could go all out to achieve convertibility on a fixed rate, although not necessarily at the level of $2.80. Unless this was achieved quickly, however, it was a policy virtually the same as formal inconvertibility. The three payments crises of the postwar period indicated that Britain could not rely on a calm course of years in which to steadily build up preparedness for convertibility. Britain could not, he argued, go to the first rung of convertibility (allowing overseas central banks to turn sterling balances into dollars) in 1953, the second rung in 1954, the third in 1955 and by stages reach full convertibility in, say, 1957. This was 'the fallacy of Bretton Woods'.[8] Events were bound to disrupt totally any idea of a smooth transition from a state of convertibility where a foreign central bank could turn sterling into dollars, to the last rung of convertibility where a British citizen could exchange sterling for dollars on demand. Furthermore, convertibility at a fixed rate would place intolerable strain on the gold and foreign currency reserves. In the fixed rate system, payments deficits are equilibrated through the loss of gold, and the extent of convertibility is determined by the size of the reserves. In the teeth of a crisis this policy would be suicidal. Convertibility at a fixed rate would only be conceivable with large gold reserves and it was now clear, thought Clarke, that the US Administration had moved away from offering large-scale assistance.

This left salvation through convertibility on a floating rate of exchange. In the floating rate system, the rate itself is the equilibrating factor, rising and falling to a point at which supply and demand for sterling cancel each other. Convertibility becomes possible, in principle, without large reserves. To Clarke, this seemed an attractive way of balancing trade. If imports exceeded exports, exports would be encouraged whilst imports would be choked off as prices rose. Moreover the floating rate system would set up tendencies to move the whole economy towards a more competitive position. If, Clarke argued, a floating rate had been introduced in September 1951, the pound might have fallen below $2.00. The consequent increase in food and raw material prices would have reduced consumption, increased unemployment and provided a real incentive for firms to seek new export markets. In short, structural economic adjustment would have been encouraged. With a fixed rate, the government could lose $1,500 million of gold without 'anybody noticing it at all – and no adjustment until the Government decrees it'.[9] The government is then perceived as inept, imposing artificial restrictions on the market whilst the real conditions of life go on as before. It is literally true, he noted, that 'after 31 January, no-one will have any more incentive to reduce his consumption of food or raw materials, or to export, than he had six months ago. Nor is it by any means obvious how this can be provided, except by complex fiscal measures, or by new controls, which take months to work out.'[10] The floating rate may make for instability and may be disliked by planners, but, concluded Clarke, when the pattern of prices, production, consumption, imports and exports is not the correct one for solvency, 'we cannot afford to have it stable; we must have some forces at work which will set up incentives which tend to right it and which act specifically on imports and exports'.[11]

Echoing both Fleming and Thompson-McCausland's early memos, Clarke emphasized that there was nothing sacrosanct about the fixed rate, 'the fact that floating rates are anathema to Mr Snyder and the IMF does not seem to me decisive. Nor do I think floating rates would be nearly as "bad for sterling" as doubts about a fixed rate.'[12] He did, however, pinpoint three 'formidable difficulties' about a floating rate. Firstly, the Sterling Area economies were in such a state of disequilibrium that the rate might fall to very low levels indeed, creating internal instability on a self-defeating scale.

Without large reserves it would be impossible to hold sterling at an artificially high level, and, consequently, 'our food prices and internal social and political structure would be at the mercy of the market'.[13] It was only fair to say, he added, that if this argument were true, we should in any case lose all our reserves protecting a fixed rate. Secondly, running a floating rate with exchange control would tend to increase the likelihood of big swings. Without considerable reserves it would be a very unstable market, and it was therefore probable that floating would inject major instability into the economy. Finally, he recognized the possibility that some Sterling Area countries might decide to float against sterling. This would disrupt the Sterling Area and force the situation 'in which we treated Rest of Sterling Area countries like foreigners'.[14] Nevertheless, despite the 'terrific risks', Clarke concluded that with a scarce money policy, and if the Sterling Area took it seriously, 'it might be a starter'.[15] Clarke's convertibility scheme thus comprised the following elements: a floating rate; the freezing and funding of all non-Sterling Area balances (except working balances); convertibility to all non-residents; the retention of exchange control on capital transactions; tight non-discriminatory import licensing in the UK and the rest of the Sterling Area on imports from the non-sterling world (and working deflationary action throughout the Sterling Area); and a policy of threatening 'foreigner treatment' to any Sterling Area country running an independent rate or not taking steps to put its 'house in order'.[16]

As Clarke's memorandum was being considered by Rowan, Brittain, Copleston and Flett in Overseas Finance, Thompson-McCausland and Bolton forwarded to Cobbold further notes arguing in favour of the restoration of convertibility for non-resident sterling.[17] In terms close to Clarke, Thompson-McCausland stressed that 'unless the effort to convertibility of sterling is made, the non-dollar world will be constantly tending to build price structures which divide the world into a low price dollar area and a high price non-dollar area. Convertibility must therefore be established'.[18] Bolton's 'Notes on Convertibility', which argued that the 'first step must surely be to make all sterling owned by non-residents convertible', was now seized upon by Clarke who reiterated that this was not possible on a fixed rate especially when the price system was not creating the right incentives.[19] For this reason, he concluded, 'the logic of Sir George Bolton's notes points irrevocably to a floating rate'.[20] In a further note to Rowan, Clarke explained that 'there is a very big issue underlying this. How are we to increase our earning power in static world market conditions?'[21] The answer was to 'force ourselves a bigger share of the world market, and in particular to cut out the Americans'.[22] The only lasting solution was to become so competitive that any contraction in the world market hardly affected British exports. Clarke concluded, 'Our standard of living may fall in the process, but that is not nearly as bad as having the planned chaos which is bound to result from cutting down our imports by decree to meet a declining export income.'[23]

Hard on the heels of his comments on Bolton, Clarke now drafted, at lightning speed, a note on 'Emergency Action' for onward transmission to Rowan and the rest of Overseas Finance.[24] It is important to recognize that Clarke's first draft, of 31 January, is wholly consistent with his conversion to floating rate convertibility.[25] The paper began by outlining that even after US aid, it was unlikely that the loss of reserves in the first quarter would be less than $750–800 million. This would bring the reserves down to below $1,600 million by the end of March, heading towards $1,400 million by the end of April. Previously, $2,000 million had been regarded as something like an effective minimum balance. The upshot for Clarke was that 'we must in practice work on the assumption that we shall have to take violent action of an emergency character – probably not later, in any event, than the end of April'.[26] The crucial question, he noted, was 'whether we should wait until we are forced to take this action or whether we should act earlier in anticipation of it'.[27] Of course, to Clarke, the answer was obvious. It was not at all clear that the measures taken by the government, and the Sterling Area, would be adequate to stop the drain. If the government acted now, it would have maximum freedom of manoeuvre, if it waited for three months, it would have none. In short, 'you can take much more prospectful emergency action with $2 billion than with $1 billion'.[28] Clarke then drew a distinction between emergency action which contributed to long-term recovery at the cost of heavy immediate sacrifices, and action simply to contain the current crisis. Filling the dollar gap by borrowing, whether from the IMF, the Exim Bank or loans from governments or private concerns (such as the Imperial Tobacco Company), might stave off the immediate crisis but, it 'sets up no pressures whatever in the UK (and even less in the Rest of the Sterling Area) to import less or to export more; it does nothing whatever to help our position in the second half of 1952 or 1953, and it creates serious liabilities for 1954 and 1955'.[29] Equally, devaluation to a new fixed rate would be a fundamental blow to sterling, 'in that it would then become believed that we were going the French road of the 1920's and 1930's'.[30] However, it was 'objectively true' that sterling was overvalued and that the

> present price/exchange relationships do not set up incentives to reduce imports and increase exports – and we have pretty well exhausted the possibilities of 'planning' import cuts and export expansion. Even less does the crisis have any impact on the Rest of the Sterling Area, unless the price system is made to operate on them.[31]

The solution, of course, was to adopt 'tough internal measures' and head in the direction of blocked sterling balances and a floating rate with 'attempts to increase and widen the convertibility of sterling'.[32]

The Bank plan for overseas sterling

After the paper 'Emergency Action' had been through a number of drafts, and in particular after the intervention of Robert Hall on 7 and 8 February,[33] the final version of 8 February was devoid of Clarke's radical solution, and offered a weak combination of external and internal measures to try to contain the dollar drain.[34] However, the ball was now rolling and on 5 and 6 February, Bolton and Cobbold discussed with Rowan some of the 'drastic ideas' circulating in the Bank on the idea of floating rate convertibility.[35] On 6 February, a single unsigned page containing eight bullet points was sent to Cobbold and Bolton, presumably by John Fisher, who had earlier made a positive assessment of the floating rate contingency plan contained in the Chatham House Report on Sterling Area Policy.[36]

The paper borrowed much from previous thinking in the Bank and from Clarke's latest memoranda. In summary form, it suggested the adoption of a tight money policy, including higher interest rates; the blocking of all sterling balances held by non-residents, and either an advance against such balances or the release of 10–20 per cent of the balances; the maintenance of exchange control over residents of the UK; the convertibility of all released sterling and new accruals held by non-residents of the UK; a widening of the existing parity ($2.80) to a $2.40 to $3.20 spread; the reopening of the London gold market to non-residents; an offer to the Sterling Area of a means by which the blocked balances could be used over a long period; and, finally, to sustain convertibility, a suggestion that the government could borrow against dollar securities in the Exchange Equalisation Account and try to persuade the Americans to put greater IMF resources at the disposal of the UK.[37]

On 7 February, Cobbold had a private discussion, 'at home after dinner',[38] with the Chancellor on the general sterling situation. Cobbold records that he 'set before him in some detail' the situation he had to face: either 'further tightening, increased controls etc., with sterling becoming a domestic UK currency or a complete and drastic review of exchange policy and relationships including a heavy freezing or funding of balances, a degree of convertibility and a degree of freedom in the rate'.[39] Cobbold's personal view was that 'we were bound to face up to the risks and dangers of the second alternative. They would certainly need to be supported by a strong Budget and a higher Bank Rate.'[40] With momentum now gathering, Cobbold asked Bolton to cancel a planned weekend trip to Basle, and work instead on a Bank plan for floating rate convertibility.[41] By the end of Saturday 9 February, Bolton had prepared the first draft of the key Bank memorandum, 'Plan for "Overseas Sterling"', which would be circulated to Rowan on 16 February and which formed the basis of Cobbold's personal note sent to the Chancellor on 13 February.[42]

Bolton's plan, which had been agreed in outline by the Governor,[43] built on the Fisher paper of 6 February. Radical action was now necessary to avoid losing control of the value of the currency, the break-up of the Sterling Area and in general the economic strength on which Britain's political position was founded.[44] A strong Budget was certainly required but this would not be enough without a major change in external financial policy. The Bolton paper therefore recommended a three-point plan of action.[45] Firstly, a clear distinction was to be made between 'home sterling' – in the hands of UK and Sterling Area individuals and institutions, and 'overseas sterling' – in the hands of people outside the Sterling Area and in the hands of Sterling Area central banks. Overseas Sterling was to be made fully convertible and the London gold and commodity markets were to be reopened. Secondly, it would be impossible to make sterling convertible without blocking virtually all of the £4,000 million of existing sterling balances. Hence there would a further type of 'sterling' in the blocked balances overseas. Ten per cent of non-Sterling Area resident balances would be transferred to new 'overseas sterling' accounts, and the remaining 90 per cent would be placed in 50-year Serial Funding Stock. A similar arrangement would apply to Sterling Area balances with the proviso that the remaining 90 per cent of the balances could be used for the settlement of prewar commitments, in exceptional circumstances for development purposes and the rest funded into Serial London Stock. Thirdly, the reserves were obviously insufficient to permit convertibility at a fixed rate and so the move would involve 'some measure of floating'.[46] Bolton proposed that the narrow margin of $2.78–2.82 be replaced with a wider unofficial margin of $2.40–3.20. As Cobbold clarified in his letter to Butler on 13 February, this did not contradict earlier Bank arguments against a floating rate. Hopes of additional US economic aid were slim and given the depth of the present crisis, 'a sterling–dollar rate floating over a much wider range than at present around a fixed parity might prove the best solution and might be a necessary protection for the degree of transferability and/or convertibility envisaged'.[47] Cobbold's preference for wider spreads around a fixed parity became, particularly in the eyes of the opposition, almost indistinguishable from Clarke and Rowan's general argument for a floating rate. However, it was a distinction never quite forgotten by Cobbold himself who would later claim that the final version of Robot placed too much emphasis on floating at the expense of a stress on stability.[48]

Whilst the Bolton plan was being polished in the Bank, Clarke refined his views on Robot and the problem of Britain's competitiveness.[49] To achieve economic stability and maintain overall balance worldwide, it was clear that Britain would have to move away from 'soft' trade in protected markets. 'We stand', Clarke noted, 'on our competitive power, with exchange rates as a safety valve . . . either we trade "hard" and are treated as a hard currency country, or we trade "soft". If sterling is an international currency, it must be "hard". This is the real issue about convertibility and sterling as an international currency'.[50] To achieve a balance Britain would, before long, have to cut into US exports of manufactures. In this sense, the dollar problem could only be met by Britain driving the United States out of its markets and here, 'the flexible rate is a great help, for it is a natural equilibrating factor'.[51] Although attempting to rush through a policy with such mind-boggling implications might seem contrary to civil service tradition, this, Clarke argued, was precisely what was required. If the government waited until the economy was in better shape (with larger reserves for instance) or tried to prepare the Sterling Area and the international economy more broadly, the impetus for change would be lost and Britain's slow economic slide would continue.

By the middle of February, the essential elements of the Robot plan were in place. It was already evident to Clarke that 'a departure of this kind in U.K. policy would have major effects upon the whole structure of the European economy'.[52] It was likely that membership, and adherence to the trade policies, of EPU would be incompatible with convertible sterling. The move would also represent a breach of many of the IMF Articles and pose particular difficulties for the United States in respect of their policies towards Europe. It would also throw formidable strains on Commonwealth relations, especially as the interests of the independent countries would tend to diverge from those of the UK.[53] Nevertheless, after extensive consultations with Overseas Finance, Bolton noted on 18 February that Rowan, Clarke, Flett and Copleston were 'more or less convinced' on the 'Plan for Overseas Sterling' and that 'zero hour' should fall no later than early April, when the government was due to publish official figures on the large fall in the central reserves over the last quarter.[54]

After a series of further meetings on 18 and 19 February, which now drew in Hall and Plowden,[55] Cobbold arranged a dinner on the evening of 19 February to discuss the plan with Churchill, Butler and Crookshank (Leader of the Government in the House of Commons).[56] The general conclusion, according to Cobbold, 'seemed to be that something on these lines, though disagreeable, was probably necessary'.[57] However, Churchill and Crookshank were anxious that if anything of the sort were contemplated, reference should be made to it in the Budget Speech, so that it would appear as one part of a whole solution. Cobbold replied that it would be impossible to refer to the proposals in the Budget unless the Chancellor actually did them at the same time – 'it was not a subject on which you could give 2 or 3 weeks' notice to the world'.[58] The deduction drawn from this was that if the new plan were to be put into force it would have to be done on Budget day, 4 March.[59] This news was relayed, the next day, to Robert Hall who was 'dumbfounded at the idea that such drastic steps were to be taken in such a short time'.[60] After a night's reflection, and a talk with Maurice Allen in the Bank, Hall penned a protest note to Bridges regarding the precipitate action. As a result, on 21 February, Butler agreed that the Budget would now take place on 11 March to allow time for further consideration and consultation (particularly with Eden who had flown to Lisbon late on 19 February to participate in discussions on the proposed European Defence Community).[61]

This delay did not dampen the enthusiasm of Overseas Finance and the Bank who now believed that the Chancellor was 'sold', the Prime Minister 'interested' and that there were 'great hopes . . . [of a] . . . favourable decision'.[62] However, as will be indicated in the next chapter, opposition to the plan began to take shape around this time and led to some of the most vociferous disagreements over fundamentals seen in Whitehall in the postwar period. Before documenting these battles, the rest of this chapter will detail in full the domestic and international implications of the Robot plan as seen by Overseas Finance and the Bank.

II Robot and the domestic economy

The Treasury and the Bank sought to justify Robot by pointing, above all, to the danger of the imminent exhaustion of the gold reserves and the disintegration of the external value of sterling. In emotive terms, Clarke and Rowan argued,

> the loss of the gold reserves is the one national disaster in peace-time which is comparable with the loss of a war. There can be economic crises which inflict hardship and want on the nation – unemployment, inflation, industrial strife. But these are all remediable. But to Britain, the gold reserves are rather like the Home Fleet in the first world war, or Fighter Command in 1940; if they are lost, everything else is lost, and the disaster would be permanent. With sterling reduced to a domestic currency like the franc or the lira, our entire standing and economic fabric would be permanently changed.[63]

In February this danger, of course, looked very real and therefore provided a powerful justification for consideration of the plan. However, although it was hoped that the plan would over time rectify the balance of payments, for Overseas Finance this was not its primary objective. Rather, the aim of the plan was to work on the long-term position of the economy, instead of applying short-term palliatives. As Clarke explained to Butler after the shelving of the first Robot scheme,

> I must make it quite clear that I do not regard the plan as a means of righting our current balance of payments. If adopted, it should in due course have favourable effects upon the whole Sterling Area's current balance of payments with the rest of the world, for if the pound falls this will tend to discourage foreign exchange expenditure of all kinds, not only in the UK but also in the rest of the Sterling Area. But I do not regard this as the sole purpose of the plan. The purpose of the plan is to change our external financial system in a way which will enable us to continue

without these crises – it deals with the capital position, so to speak, and not with the current position.[64]

This view was reiterated, on a number of occasions, by Edward Bridges who wrote to Butler that although the government had taken action which enabled the short-term position to be dealt with, 'the fact remained that this country was still trying to do too much, and that the decisions necessary to lighten the load had not yet been taken'.[65]

The real purpose of Robot therefore was to address the cause, and not the symptom, of the 'wasting disease' Overseas Finance identified as threatening the British economy: the slow decline in competitiveness. The plan would encourage costs to fall (particularly in relation to the United States), it would prompt a restructuring of business to widen the range of goods offered to dollar areas (plus eliminating 'soft' markets abroad and the 'soft' home market), and it would also check the growth in Britain's standard of living relative to the United States. Unless price incentives could be brought into play to encourage economic adjustments in the production and consumption spheres then even though, 'we may appear to be strengthening our position . . . fundamentally our position gets worse rather than better – i.e. time is not on our side'.[66] The view that Britain's competitive position was worsening had been suggested by a number of reports from the Board of Trade which drew attention specifically to the impact of German industrial recovery on British exports.[67]

In the immediate postwar years, German policy had concentrated on the re-equipment of factories and the building of new plants to replace war losses. The virtual disappearance of Germany and Japan from world export markets in the period 1945–48 therefore enabled British exports to expand rapidly. However, by 1951 it was becoming clear that German and Japanese recovery meant that these countries, once again, posed a serious threat to Britain's export trade. By the close of 1951, German steel output was within 5 per cent of the UK's output, and sulphuric acid output already exceeded production in the UK.[68] Motorcar production in the second quarter of 1951 was 25 per cent above the 1950 average in Germany, but 13 per cent below the average in the UK. Moreover, German producers were targeting the European market, sending 68 per cent of exports to OEEC countries in 1950, leading the Board of Trade to conclude that 'everything suggests that they will from now on exceed our exports to Western Europe, thus returning to their pre-war position'.[69] Although it was thought that world demand for metals and capital goods was likely to remain buoyant, at least in the short term, the considered view of the Board of Trade was that 'this comforting reflection does not hold good over the whole of the engineering field and in light engineering and much electrical equipment, there is a real risk that further expansion of German exports will be partly at our expense unless we can keep costs down'.[70] It thus seemed clear to Clarke and Rowan that without Robot, there were 'no compelling forces at work to drive manufacturers to seek export markets' – in conditions in which export markets were becoming increasingly competitive.[71]

Bringing the economy into balance

Robot would therefore achieve three objectives. It would stem the drain in the gold and dollar reserves, since reserves would be lost only to the extent that monetary authorities intervened to prevent the exchange rate falling too far. It would eliminate 'cheap sterling' operations since payment for exports would now be made in convertible external sterling, and by funding the sterling balances it would remove the greatest potential threat to the convertibility operation further strengthening confidence in sterling. Finally, and most significantly, since the strain of the balance of payments deficit would fall, not on the reserves but on the rate, the depreciation of the rate would have immediate and direct effects on the internal economy. In short, through its effects on prices and employment the plan would encourage structural economic adjustment and inject, what was perceived to be, a much-needed dose of 'market realism' into the domestic political economy. As Clarke explained to Rowan,

> The project of the floating rate, convertibility and blocking is therefore one and indivisible. It is entirely unavoidable. We cannot hold a fixed rate without reserves and we have not enough reserves and have no prospects of getting them. Once it is clear – as it overwhelmingly is – that the present and prospective reserves are not enough to maintain a fixed rate, the whole of the rest follows automatically.[72]

Overseas Finance was, of course, aware that the rate would have to fall to a point at which the world's supply and demand for external sterling achieved a balance and this would mean reducing expenditure and increasing income just as in the defence of a fixed rate. But, if the true value of the pound was somewhere between $1.00 and $1.50, then it was simply a 'Sisyphean task' to try to hold a fixed rate of $2.80.[73] Robot would not dispense with government measures to cut the volume of imports but, as Rowan and Clarke explained, 'the price system will be working in a constructive way, and will be bringing about all sorts of small adjustments which are far beyond the ambit of physical controls'.[74] For example, government payments, in dollar terms, would be greatly reduced by depreciation since they consisted largely of fixed sterling sums transferred to North America. So-called 'essential imports' from the United States into the rest of the Sterling Area might look less attractive, if the rate fell, than cheaper imports from the UK. The 'depoliticizing' aspects of using the price mechanism in this way were also considered by Clarke and Rowan. They noted, for instance, that cutting coarse grain imports was a very difficult decision for the government. But, if the price of grain imports went up 20 per cent, farmers would be encouraged to do what they steadily refused to do – grow more themselves. In this and other ways Robot would sidestep the 'great political difficulties in issuing government ukases'[75] and result in significant savings. A continuous process of change and readjustment would thus be set in train bringing into play forces which in the long run, it was hoped, would bring the economy into balance. Butler in particular was keenly aware of what he perceived to be the positive psychological consequences of moving towards greater reliance on market forces. As he explained to the Cabinet in the crucial February meetings:

> A moderate rise in the price of imports would have a salutary effect in bringing home to the people of this country the reality of the economic situation in which they were living. Under the planned economy the Government themselves assumed responsibility for varying the pattern of consumption by making adjustments in import programmes. There was something to be said, politically, for moving towards the system by which individuals were influenced, by the operation of the price mechanism to make their own adjustments to changing economic circumstances. This latter system had the further advantage that it enabled people to adjust themselves more gradually to changing circumstances and avoided the violent upheavals which seemed inseparable for Government planning.[76]

The adjustment process would, of course, entail a rise in the cost of living and, at least in the short term, a substantial increase in unemployment. The 'import content' of the cost of living index was judged to be about 20 per cent.[77] A 10 per cent depreciation would increase the cost of living by approximately 1.5 per cent, provided that sterling depreciated equally against all non-sterling currencies. However, the more effective the government's action to deal with the balance of payments deficit, the higher the rate would subsequently climb, stabilizing the cost of living.[78] The danger to employment would stem firstly from increased import prices (particularly raw materials) creating conditions in which goods could not be sold in the home market, and secondly from the loss of exports which would result from the elimination of 'soft' markets and the possible application of import restrictions across Europe following convertibility. Clarke calculated that approximately £200 million of 'soft' exports would be lost in the short term. This restructuring could well add between 300,000 and 500,000 workers to the unemployment register, possibly shooting the unemployment figure over the one million mark.[79] In Clarke's view the 'optimum' rate of unemployment lay somewhere between 3 and 4 per cent. This level increased 'flexibility', creating margins in industrial capacity, commodity stocks and manpower. Higher unemployment would also help contain the inflationary consequences of Robot by reducing pressure for wage increases. In the medium term, it was envisaged that unemployment would fall as the volume of exports to other destinations increased and industry became more competitive. Certainly a large increase in exports would be necessary to cover the gap in the interim and it would be difficult to judge how long the transitional period would last but it was hoped that high levels of unemployment 'would be of a temporary character, while the economy was becoming adapted to pay its way'.[80]

Opponents of the plan such as Lord Cherwell were rather less inclined to disguise the true meaning of economic 'adjustment'.[81] The Paymaster General argued that whenever exports failed to pay for imports, the pound would fall until imports diminished either because people could not afford to buy them or firms stop buying imports and closed down and those on the dole were forced to eat less thus further reducing the demand for imports. The process would be capped by a rising Bank Rate and steep unemployment. Cherwell concluded, 'If the workers, finding their food dearer, are inclined to demand higher wages, this will have to be stopped by increasing unemployment until their bargaining power is destroyed. This is what comfortable phrases like "letting the rate take the strain" mean, nothing more and nothing less'.[82]

In general terms, Clarke, Rowan and Bolton were of the view that this 'shock therapy' was necessary to tackle the 'creeping paralysis' which threatened to take hold of the British economy.[83] A continuation of present policy would both fail to stem the tide and result in much greater economic upheaval in the medium term. However, the case for Robot was made not simply in relation to the domestic political economy. It would also be 'major change in the world situation, which would have tremendous repercussions everywhere'.[84] The impact of the plan on the wider international political economy was thus crucial to its success at home and, as Butler indicated to the Cabinet, 'this series of proposals gives us the opportunity for taking a powerful initiative in the world economy, and the attitude of almost all foreign countries will be decided very largely by the way in which we seize this opportunity'.[85]

III Robot and the world economy

To assess in detail how the Robot plan would have restructured the postwar world economy this section will consider its impact on the Sterling Area, Europe and the United States. Initially, however, a useful insight can be gained into how British policy makers ranked the importance of governments and international institutions by reviewing the timetable produced by Overseas Finance for the implementation of the plan.[86]

Once through Cabinet, it was intended that Robot be announced in the Budget Speech on Tuesday 11 March. Commonwealth governments would be the first group to receive information about the plan via a Prime Minister's message delivered on the morning of Monday 3 March. They would be required to reply by Saturday 8 March, giving a clear indication that they accepted the conditions of the agreements governing sterling balances. Next, Colonial governors would be informed together with the Irish Republic on Friday 7 March. It is particularly significant that the US administration would not be informed 'before a fairly late hour' on Friday 7 March. At this point the UK Ambassador in Washington would be asked to notify Acheson, Snyder and Harriman. Selected OEEC countries, 'which we can trust, and whose action we particularly wish to influence' (including Denmark, Finland, Norway, Sweden and the monetary areas of Belgium, France and Holland) would be informed not later than the morning of Monday 10 March, whilst the rest of OEEC, BIS and the EPU would be notified later that afternoon. Finally, official notification covering only the new exchange rate system would be conveyed to the IMF on Tuesday 11 March.

In many ways, the timetable is a remarkable document. It displays British policy makers' disregard, bordering on contempt, for what many consider to be the key centres of power in the early postwar world – the United States, the European Payments Union and the 'twins' of Bretton Woods. Only Commonwealth governments were to be given time to reply (although Bolton later suggested that 'friendly' European countries could be approached a 'little earlier'[87]) and it was envisaged that none of the five proposals could be the subject of negotiation.

Robot and the Sterling Area

In a memorandum to the Cabinet on the eve of the decisive meetings on 28 February, Butler explained that Britain had lost $521 million since January, bringing the reserves down to $1,800 million – equivalent to three-and-a-half weeks' turnover of the Sterling Area's transactions with the rest of the world.[88] This demonstrated, on the one hand, the need for emergency action but, on the other, it was equally clear that there was no possibility of the world regarding sterling as a desirable currency with 'nearly £3,000 million overhanging the market'.[89] Hence the success of the plan, in relation to the Sterling Area, lay in convincing its governments of the need to block/fund the sterling balances. Butler and Overseas Finance had concluded that dissolving the Sterling Area as a means of reducing the dollar drain would be impractical. The Sterling Area was a source of both strength and weakness inasmuch as half of total trade was with other Sterling Area countries and the institution was of political as well as economic importance.[90] To go further than blocking the balances would destroy the whole structure creating, in Butler's words, a 'major dislocation which I do not believe we could stand'.[91] For Robot to succeed therefore it was important that Britain retain the confidence and co-operation of as many Sterling Area countries as possible.

Supporters of Robot believed that the plan would leave the basic structure of the Sterling Area unchanged, although some governments might indicate a willingness to leave. Gold reserves would still be pooled; there would be no exchange control between Britain and other Sterling Area countries and there would still be close co-operation on import and exchange control policy. Whilst prior to Robot there was a common interest in protecting the reserves, under Robot there would be a common interest in maintaining the rate between $2.40 and $3.20. However, it was acknowledged that the step of blocking/funding not less than 80 per cent of the sterling balances would create insuperable difficulties for some members. In detail, the objective of the proposal was to reduce the 'sight liabilities' on the sterling funds held by central banks of Sterling Area countries to 20 per cent of the total of the funds held by each country at the close of business on Tuesday 11 March. This was to be achieved by investing 80 per cent of the balances in special Treasury Funding Stock which would be non-marketable but redeemable and would carry interest of 2 per cent. The Stock would run for an initial five-year period at which time it was likely to be extended for another five-year span.[92] This action, Butler maintained, was an absolutely essential step, for although in some cases (covering India, Pakistan and Ceylon) a large part of the sterling was already immobilized under existing arrangements, 'the existence of the rest is a major cause of the dollar drain, for it enables these countries to run balance of payments deficits, the burden of which either falls directly on the reserves or on UK resources in the form of "unrequited exports" '.[93] Moreover, the size of the balances had a psychological effect tending to weaken overall confidence in sterling. It was essential therefore that the government could show publicly that its immediate liabilities had been drastically reduced. To this end Sterling Area governments were asked to agree to three 'firm propositions'.[94] First, that they would endeavour to meet the Commonwealth Finance Ministers' Meeting targets for their balance of payments with the non-sterling world and for their overall balance as quickly as possible. Second, that they would keep their local currencies (Australian pound, Indian rupee and so on.) at a fixed rate with sterling. Finally, that they would agree to the blocking/funding of 80 per cent of their balances.[95]

Overseas Finance and the Bank considered that most governments would agree to the proposals. However, it was clear that a number of Sterling Area nations would be anxious about, and possibly hostile to, some of the wider elements of the plan including the issue of why convertibility was extended to non-residents only; the impact of the plan on trade policy and their position in Europe should EPU collapse; and its impact on their ability to borrow from the IMF should that institution remain in existence.[96] Butler and Overseas Finance thought that Robot would pose particular problems for India, Pakistan and Ceylon given the renewal in early February of the Sterling Balances (Release) Agreements which allowed for a staged release of funds for development purposes.[97] To avoid a clash between the Sterling Balances Agreements and Robot's funding arrangements, Butler was to ask this group of countries to exercise restraint. However, if they could not accept this position they could leave the Sterling Area on good terms with the British government who would honour the release arrangements.

Concern was also expressed initially about the impact of the plan on Australia. Following the convertibility crisis of 1947, Australia had taken positive steps to support the pound and had agreed to sell its gold output to Britain for sterling.[98] However, this agreement had been terminated by the Australians at the beginning of 1951, and by December Australian gold was being sold for dollars on the premium market. In the eyes of the British Treasury this clearly cut across the Sterling Area dollar-pooling ethic. As holder of the second largest sterling balance and as a gold producer, Britain thought it crucial that Australia comply with blocking and remain within the Sterling Area.[99] Continued membership would also enable the British Treasury to persuade the Australians that they ought to surrender dollars from gold sales and draw on central reserves for dollar purchases. It later became clear, on the basis of discussions held between the Bank and Robert Menzies in June 1952, that British concerns were unfounded. Menzies clarified that Australia would have backed the Robot proposals (partly because they were concerned to enhance their credit rating in the US) and would have accepted blocking as part of a deal to introduce convertibility.[100] This was also the view of Mr Fussell, Governor of the Reserve Bank of New Zealand, who confirmed in mid-June that New Zealand would have accepted policy regarding the balances and followed the UK rate proposal.[101]

In respect of other Sterling Area members, Overseas Finance concluded in February 1952 that South Africa, Southern Rhodesia and the Irish Republic would accept the terms whilst Burma and Iraq would probably withdraw.[102] The position of the Colonies would remain largely unchanged. Colonial sterling resources would not be seriously affected and no change would be necessary in the banking machinery since none of the Colonial accounts would be classified as Overseas Sterling. Authorized dealers in the Colonies would continue to make sterling or foreign exchange payments to the non-sterling area, in line with existing exchange control procedure. A marginal tightening of exchange control might be necessary to avoid a leakage of sterling in Hong Kong and Singapore, but, on balance, Robot would not disturb existing arrangements and, as Oliver Lyttelton pointed out, the freeing of the gold market would help make the scheme palatable to the gold producing Colonies.[103]

The architects of Robot fully appreciated that the plan would be scuppered if it led to the wholesale disintegration of the Sterling Area. The proposals on blocking might prompt a restructuring of the Area with Pakistan the most likely to leave.[104] However, it was judged that the plan was likely to forge a stronger bond between Canada and the Area and might well encourage US investment in the Sterling Area. The measures, it was acknowledged, would impose some hardships but overall, Overseas Finance and the Bank concluded, 'it is reasonable to expect Sterling Area counties to be willing to cooperate in much the same way as they have in recent years'.[105]

Robot and Europe

Three issues dominated the Treasury and Bank's discussion of the impact of Robot on Europe. First, the consequences for intra-European and, by implication, world trade. Second, the effect of the plan on intra-European payments schemes and in particular the European Payments Union. Third, its impact on wider European schemes, including moves towards closer European integration and the future of the European Defence Community.

In the context of the world dollar shortage (with the United States running an annual surplus of $5 billion – very little of which was now offset by economic aid) Robot, in principle, threatened to produce a downward spiral of world trade and encourage the introduction of competitive import restrictions. Extending convertibility to all countries outside of the Sterling Area would enable these countries to earn dollars by earning external sterling. Moreover it was likely that such countries would maximize dollar earning by restricting imports from Britain and exporting as much as possible. This situation would be exacerbated by the fact that Britain's exports would now be thrown open to US competition. Butler's provisional assessment was that 'we must face the possibility that a substantial area of our export trade may be faced with conditions of great difficulty, and that we are bound to face a certain amount of dislocation as the world adjusts itself to the new situation'.[106] The adjustment process would not, it was hoped, prompt a return to bilateralism but it would certainly entail a tighter policy of discrimination in trade.

Wary of being seen to set in train a process of competitive import restrictions in Europe, Overseas Finance suggested that two principles inform import policy in the wake of Robot. First, it would not be in Britain's interest to discriminate generally in import policy (except, of course, in favour of the Sterling Area). Since everyone would now receive payment in convertible external sterling it would no longer make sense to buy from 'soft' currency countries at higher prices. Therefore basic food and raw materials should be bought in the cheapest possible market. Second, in order to relieve pressure on the exchange rate, less important imports would of necessity in the transitional period require restriction. Robot would therefore be accompanied by the 'deliberalization' of less significant imports. This, it was hoped, would guard against an immediate collapse of European and world trade whilst also avoiding the pitfalls of bilateralism. The implications of this strategy were developed further by Clarke in March 1952.[107]

Clarke's 'practical trade policy' to accompany Robot comprised three elements: first, the continuation of the Sterling Area in its present form until convertibility could be extended to the Area (still on a floating rate); second, the adoption of a non-discriminatory trade policy among the non-sterling countries with respect to trade in basic food and raw materials; and third, for imports of less essential foods and manufactures a division of the world into three camps: the Sterling Area from which Britain would admit imports freely; Dollar Areas which treated Britain as a dollar source of supply for which there would be a heavily restricted quota; and countries which gave as free entry to imports from Britain as they gave to imports from anyone else, which would be subject to a quota system on a less restricted basis.[108]

The success of this policy, to gain the benefits of general non-discriminatory trade without incurring its major risks, depended largely on how other European countries' exchange and trade policies developed in response to Robot. Two assumptions informed the British government's assessment of the likely impact of Robot on Europe's trade and payments systems. First, it was thought that the liberalization of intra-European trade was near to collapse. Second, that the European Payments Union (EPU), established retroactively on 1 July 1950 to oversee liberalization and encourage transferability in payments in Europe, was in terminal decline and would be killed altogether when sterling became convertible.[109] Overseas Finance judged that European countries would respond firstly on exchange rate policy and secondly on trade. The Treasury's principal objective therefore would be 'to get countries floating with us, in order to secure de facto exchange stability over the widest possible area'.[110] In this regard it was thought important, and highly probable, that Scandinavia, Belgium and France would join in floating convertibility. The world would therefore be split into three major units – US area (fixed convertible); the Sterling Area and associated countries (floating convertible); and the rest (fixed inconvertible). The greater the number of nations that could be drawn into the floating convertibility move, the greater the chances of arriving at a positive realignment of financial and trade policies thereby increasing the stability of the common rate.

Bolton's Payments Club

The most extensive analysis of how Britain might use Robot to restructure Europe was produced in the Bank by George Bolton in February 1952.[111] On the most superficial reading of the Overseas Sterling Plan, Europe would be placed in the Dollar Area, the EPU would collapse and, as a consequence, there would be a downward trade spiral. However, Bolton did not believe that these results would necessarily follow since it was not in the interest of most European countries to join their economy to the United States and peg their currency to the dollar.[112] The collapse of existing payments arrangements, he noted, would split Europe into two camps, 'those who are either under the influence of the US or who for political and other reasons cannot be regarded as moving in the orbit of the sterling system and the Commonwealth, and those whose trade and finance is to a large extent identifiable with sterling'.[113] In the first group he placed Austria, Germany, Greece, Italy, Spain, Switzerland and Turkey. The political and economic policies of these countries were likely to be dominated by Washington considerations and Germany in particular, it was thought, would defend fiercely her present parity and remain pegged to the dollar at the existing level. For these countries, Bolton proposed that the non-Sterling Area plans, regarding trade discrimination, would apply without prior consultation but without prejudice to any negotiated relaxations. 'List B' consisted of countries who had been closely associated with the sterling system, whose trade with the Sterling Area was important and where, in consequence, a community of self-interest could be said to exist. The list comprised Denmark, Finland, Norway, Sweden and the entire monetary areas of France, Belgium, Holland and Portugal. Although Bolton stopped short of suggesting that this group formally join the Sterling Area, he nevertheless recommended that they align themselves closely with the system. This move would help to maintain the stability of all the currencies involved, in particular against the dollar, and it would encourage the group to adopt a trade policy of 'mutual forbearance' reducing the need for high trade barriers. 'List B' countries would also be asked to conserve (rather than immediately spend) surplus earnings of external sterling to help prevent an undue depreciation not only of the value of sterling but of all the other currencies included in the association. As a measure of 'reciprocity' the Bank would relax stringent London Market credit restrictions in favour of any country requiring external sterling to finance trade. It might also be possible, noted Bolton, to pool surpluses of external sterling for the purpose of financing countries temporarily in need of external sterling. In order to diminish the disturbance to two-way trade, Bolton advised that there be 'full and frank' consultation with 'List B' countries at least seven days before Zero Day with the intention of 'offering certain advantages and relaxations in return for a promise to adhere to the new sterling system'.[114] Bolton was well aware that his suggestions might be represented as conferring greater benefits on the European members of a new sterling system than those enjoyed by full members of the Sterling Area. But, he noted, we should

> emphasise the advantage which the Sterling Area as a whole gains from securing the co-operation of a group of non-sterling countries which are similarly faced with currency difficulties against the dollar, and that, as none of the group owns substantial net sterling balances, no great price has to be offered for their co-operation.[115]

Bolton's paper was discussed with the Foreign Office and the Board of Trade on 28 February, and, as Beale reported to Cobbold, 'there was a general sigh of relief when it was appreciated how far our thinking had gone in the direction of doing something to keep trade between the Sterling Area and Europe moving'.[116] Although the Board of Trade and the Foreign Office made some suggestions regarding the inclusion of Germany in 'List B' (and the deletion from the list of Finland and Portugal), there was 'general acceptance' of the Bank memorandum.[117] However, Beale and Parsons now suggested that the proposals be split into two definite parts: interim measures to run for a period of weeks whilst a deal was struck, and the development of a payments mechanism on a relatively limited scale, not to replace the EPU, but to provide a workable mechanism intended to 'avoid throwing away all that has been good in the intra-European payments scheme and its successor EPU'.[118]

This latter point had already been considered in the Bank by Roy Bridge, who had anticipated that Robot would effectively terminate Britain's membership of the EPU and therefore be 'a straight repudiation of our obligations' leaving the Western Europeans 'high and dry and breathless'.[119] Two major problems confronted the EPU in early 1952.[120] First, its working capital of convertible currency was threatened by the existence of large creditor and debtor positions in the Union (UK and France principal debtors, with Belgium the main creditor). Second, Britain and France had already undertaken a substantial deliberalization of their imports from other members. However, despite its problems, it was by no means clear that Europe would welcome the termination of the Union and, as later chapters will indicate, the question of the EPU was to dog Britain's attempt to restructure the world economy until the introduction of convertibility at the end of the decade.

Bridge outlined two courses of action in relation to the introduction of Robot.[121] Firstly, the government could advise the OEEC that from Zero Day, Britain would no longer be willing to make sterling available to other EPU countries. Secondly, the government could take the decision to defer introducing the full new procedure *for EPU countries* until a later date, say four to six weeks after Zero Day. The second course of action would avoid repudiations; it would avoid leaving Western Europe bereft of all means of payment with the Sterling Area; and it would give a respite for further discussion on the development of trade policies in Europe. It would also, he noted, be welcome to the Foreign Office since it would soften the blow on American and NATO opinion. In addition, it would be a major gesture of co-operation with Western Europe without compromising the unilateral character of the Robot plan. In terms of operational principles, it was suggested that the introduction of 'overseas sterling accounts' (free transferability into dollars) would be deferred for EPU countries until the transitional period had ended. This would remove the risk of large amounts of sterling being drawn for conversion into dollars on Zero Day. Provisional EPU settlements could always be made on an interim basis until the final operational details had been agreed.[122]

Bridge's rather ingenious solution to one of the most difficult issues facing the Robot plan, would certainly have enhanced the attractiveness of floating rate convertibility to the Foreign Office and the Board of Trade. However, in the light of the problem of calculating EPU surpluses and deficits whilst maintaining convertibility outside of Europe, the Bank decided instead to opt for a more complicated version of the initial Bolton plan.[123] Following the suggestion made by Beale and Parsons, Bolton now devised a three-stage plan to prevent a breakdown in European payments. First, it would be necessary to put in place a seven-day stopgap arrangement during which time sterling could be made available on a one-month swap basis against local currencies. Strict individual limits would be fixed for each country. Second, for an interim period (possibly as long as two months), a bilateral swing arrangement would operate for those countries that had decided to link their currencies to sterling. Third, Britain would take the lead in forming a more regularized 'Payments Club' comprised of countries formally linking their currencies to sterling. It was thought that likely members would include Denmark, Norway, Iceland, Sweden, Holland and France, with Belgium and Portugal as possible adherents.[124] It was judged that Switzerland, Germany and Italy would remain linked to the dollar, whilst Turkey, Austria and Greece would be unsuitable for membership.[125] All members of the Club would have External Accounts and sterling would be freely transferable and usable for current payments on a worldwide basis. As in Bolton's initial plan, there would be some general understanding about forbearance from selling sterling for the sole purpose of increasing dollar reserves. All members would maintain proper cross-rates (fixed rates for other member currencies) and a fluctuating rate for the dollar in line with the dollar/sterling rate. The principal objective of the plan would be to keep a payments system alive, 'largely for the direct benefit of the others, but to which our adherence and support would be offered as a means of limiting and controlling their sales of sterling on the market'.[126] The Club would also provide an international forum for dealing with payments difficulties and, it was hoped, increase the usefulness and acceptability of sterling. Finally, it would provide a rudimentary mechanism, via limited credit margins, for the regular settlement of part or all of the residual positions without necessarily clearing the total accumulated positions as in the EPU (credit margins, compensations and monthly settlements would be conducted through the established Bank for International Settlements procedure). Under the control of the Bank of England, and with sterling as the main unit of account, Bolton's payments system would quickly re-establish the international supremacy of sterling, in the guise of assisting the currencies of the 'weaker' European countries.

The impact of Robot on Europe extended beyond finding a new basis for trade and payments in the wake of the demise of the EPU. The decision of each European country to float with sterling, float independently or remain pegged to the dollar at the current or devalued rate, presented governments with a series of choices which, thought Overseas Finance, 'may reveal important divergencies of interest which have been papered over during the last few years'.[127] In addition to terminating the EPU, it was considered that Robot would probably undermine recent moves made towards closer European integration embodied in the European Coal and Steel Community (which came into being during the spring of 1952) and might jeopardize discussions surrounding the signing and ratification of the European Defence Community Treaty. Faced with deciding fundamental policy, Robot would inject 'more realism into the world economy' and put the 'brave words about European economic unity to the test'.[128]

Anglo-French co-operation

In assessing the impact of the plan on Europe it is clear that Overseas Finance and the Bank were strongly influenced by reports from Paris on the attitude of the French government following the shift in the balance of forces in the French Assembly at the elections in July 1951, which strengthened the Right.[129] In early September 1951 the French Ambassador approached William Strang and the Foreign Secretary, Herbert Morrison, suggesting that British and French officials should meet, in secret, to review the state of Anglo-French relations throughout the world.[130] In particular, it was thought that the British and French governments should 'move along parallel lines' in order to exercise a moderating influence on the economic policy of the US government (to ensure that 'European problems are properly appreciated in Washington'[131]). This diplomatic initiative had its counterpart in meetings held between officials of the central banks, although there is no evidence that the Foreign Office was aware of contact between the Bank of England and the Bank of France.[132] In mid-February John Lithiby (Advisor to the Governors at the Bank) reported that the Bank of France under Wilfred Baumgartner, 'looks forward to a much closer collaboration in trade and monetary matters with the Sterling Area – with a view to creating a normal and not artificial mechanism through which West European economies would function'.[133] In 1949 and 1950 France had supported the idea of a 'little' Europe (Finebel) and, as Fforde notes, may have been sceptical of the 'big' Europe idea which underpinned both EPU and later European initiatives.[134] The main impetus for collaboration in early 1952, however, was to be found neither in the actions of the French Ambassador nor in those of the Bank of France, but in the set of circumstances which plunged the French economy into crisis in February.

In the spring and summer of 1951 it was already clear that inflation in France was much greater than in other countries. The deterioration in the terms of trade occasioned by the Korean war, the increasing burden of war in Indochina and, from July onwards, the withdrawal of economic assistance from the United States, produced a situation which led the Minister for Economic Affairs to state on 6 February 1952 that without measures to control imports, 'France would have had no hard currency left by 15 April'.[135] In summary, the French government faced a budget deficit of £765 million for 1952; a foreign payments crisis reflected in the exhaustion of foreign currency reserves; a deficit with the EPU of some $420 million; and a steady decline in exports and recurrent capital flight.[136] The response of the French authorities was to raise the Bank Rate twice (in October and November), to reduce imports from dollar areas, and, most controversially, to suspend liberalization measures and submit to quotas all goods originating from OEEC countries except for raw materials and certain essential foods.[137] The seriousness of the situation was aptly captured by Henry Labouisse (Chief of the Special Mission for Economic Co-operation in Paris) who wrote to Harlan Cleveland (at the Mutual Security Agency in Washington),

> In our view, the retreat of the French into a system of import restrictions and what are in effect export subsidies or a system of preferential exchange rates is a greater blow to the ideal of the creation of a harmonious and unified economic system to cover all of Western Europe, and of eventual political federation than the defection of any other country.[138]

In the face of such a severe financial and monetary crisis it is conceivable that Robot would have held many attractions for the French and that despite inevitable domestic opposition Europe could possibly have been restructured on the basis of Franco-British collaboration with sterling at the heart of a new monetary order. In the post-Robot world, with Germany pegged to the dollar, pooling within the Schuman plan and the EDC would be ruled out – 'it is impossible to take national decisions on location of production or allocation of financial burdens if one partner is floating and the other fixed'.[139] The British government's position regarding European integration had been clarified in the discussions leading up to the creation of the EPU when it was concluded that Britain should not involve itself in the economic affairs of Europe, 'beyond the point at which we could, if we so wished, disengage ourselves, and we should therefore treat with strict reserve any schemes for the pooling of sovereignty or for the establishment of European supra-national machinery'.[140] In this light Robot would enable Britain to capitalize on France's foreign currency crisis and French dissatisfaction with both the EPU and EDC and, as Fforde indicates, 'reorient French external economic policy in Europe so that it pointed in the opposite direction to the French defence commitment',[141] thereby further weakening Franco-German collaboration. In short, Robot could be used a wedge to divide France and Germany, enabling a British conception of European collaboration to prevail. In the view of Overseas Finance, 'if the talk of European economic unity has been a facade, it will collapse at the approach of Robot'.[142]

In many respects, of course, there must be some doubt, as Fforde points out, whether, come the day, the Governor of the Bank of France and his allies in the Ministry of Finance, 'would have won in Paris a battle analogous to that fought and lost by the Treasury and the Bank in London'.[143] Nevertheless for a short while in February 1952 circumstances existed which could justify the radical reorientation demanded by Robot and had the plan passed successfully through the British Cabinet it is at least plausible to posit French participation and consequently the establishment of Bolton's Payments Club in Europe.

Robot and the United States

Early assessments of the attitude of the United States to the Robot proposals suggested that although the Administration would applaud the move to convertibility and the blocking of the sterling balances, there would be objections to the floating rate and the reopening of the London gold market.[144] The United States, it was widely known, had long suggested the blocking/funding of the sterling balances. A diagnosis of the 'British problem' made by the State Department in December 1951 noted that Britain could not achieve external balance for four main reasons.[145] First, it was perceived that the government was not taking sufficient action domestically to eliminate inflationary pressures. Second, budgetary policy with particular respect to social services had fed inflation, with the consequence that the scope of the welfare programme had been expanded at a pace faster than the UK could afford. Third, restrictive practices of industry and labour were primarily to blame for low levels of productivity. Finally, it was judged that the Sterling Area, and in particular the sterling balances, had been the greatest source of Britain's postwar instability and weakness. With the balances topping $4.2 billion by June 1951, and Britain's policy dubbed 'weak and opportunistic', the State Department's diagnosis was that for sterling to regain credibility, the balances must be immobilized.[146]

The reopening of the London gold market and the adoption of a floating rate would, it was thought, cause particular problems for the United States and the IMF. The decision to link the reopening of the gold market to Robot had been taken primarily as a means of helping to stabilize sterling. As Rowan later clarified in discussions with Commonwealth ministers and the US Treasury, 'the claim of London to the market was manifest. Over 60% of world gold production originated in the Sterling Area and sterling is the natural and proper currency for the product to move in.'[147] Free gold markets would soon appear elsewhere and sterling when convertible could ill afford to dispense with the fortification which would come from a gold turnover of some £180 million a year. The existence of a gold commodity market in London would, like other commodity markets, increase the prestige of the City as a financial centre and, as Treasury ministers noted, 'why should a market providing profit, prestige and strength for sterling be abandoned to foreigners?'[148] Nevertheless the existence of a free market in gold would pose serious problems for US authorities pledged to trade gold at a fixed rate of $35 an ounce. As Rowan explained, 'it would mean that the central banks in Europe and elsewhere would be able to buy gold at $35 an ounce from the United States, sell it in the London market, obtain external sterling, thence go into dollars and return to the US Treasury for more gold at a profit'.[149] The Treasury's assessment that this aspect of the plan would be strongly opposed in Washington proved accurate. When the idea was floated again in 1954, the US Treasury indicated that the reopening of the market would inevitably produce a hostile political reaction in the United States. A unilateral British move of this kind, it was suggested, would have consequences for the US domestic economy and further weaken the position of the IMF. It would set up pressures for the restoration of the internal convertibility of the dollar and it might lead to the hoarding of gold in the United States forcing the Administration to adopt a tighter credit policy. The decision would mean the final abandonment of the IMF gold policy for which the UK and the US were jointly responsible and, as W. Randolph Burgess made clear, 'the Americans might therefore have difficulty in supporting a UK proposal of this sort if it came before the IMF'.[150] Despite these objections however, when the gold market was finally reopened on 22 March 1954, the US Treasury reacted with little more than a private note to the Chancellor expressing its displeasure.[151]

The US position on floating rates

Overseas Finance and the Bank judged that the adoption of a floating rate would, in particular, be disliked in Washington, since it would represent a breach of many of the IMF Articles and might jeopardize wider US political and economic objectives in Europe.[152] However, unknown to the British, the US Treasury was not fundamentally opposed to the introduction of floating rates. On 2 January 1952, Eddie Bernstein, Director of Research at the IMF, circulated, to the US Treasury, a memorandum on the European exchange rate situation.[153] Bernstein noted that recent monetary chaos in Western Europe had begun to reverse the important progress made since 1949 in multilateralization and the reduction of European trade barriers. In the circumstances there would, he suggested, 'seem to be a good case for much greater European exchange rate flexibility'.[154] Flexible rates would allow 'natural' market pressures to co-ordinate national financial policies without balance of payments strains and with a minimum of reciprocal impact. They were 'politically and economically preferable' to either centralized administrative or consultative coordination of national policy or the use of direct trade controls. In conditions of crisis, it was simply 'unrealistic' to expect OEEC countries 'to continue to fight disequilibrating forces with, in effect, one hand tied behind their back – and that possibly the most effective hand'.[155] Free or floating rates, he continued, would imply the full transferability of currencies, and under such a system the EPU's two primary functions, clearing and settlements, would disappear. But this, in Bernstein's view, would not necessarily set back the US policy objective of European unification. Whether or not Europe had a fixed or floating exchange rate regime prior to unification, he noted, 'probably does not matter much in terms of the unification objective, except as it affects the possibility of removing trade barriers. From this point of view, a floating rate may be the best interim choice, even though unification will presumably result in what amounts to a fixed rate (a unified currency system).'[156] Bernstein's conclusion, that there may be special merit to the adoption of flexible rates as an interim policy particularly as a transition to a later system of fixed parities, was, however, tempered with regard to sterling. The existence of the sterling balances posed a special threat to the stability of sterling and would require immobilization in a system with a floating rate for sterling and fixed rates within the Sterling Area.

In the US Treasury, Abramson and Willis discussed Bernstein's liberal view of the flexible rate and concluded that 'Judgments may differ concerning the contribution which such a rate could make to the solution of a country's financial problems, such for example as the Sterling Area, but the facts can never be so clear as to justify opposition to requests of responsible authorities in the affected countries'.[157] However, whilst it was thought that the Treasury should not oppose a request to use floating rates, particularly pending the establishment of a new fixed rate, it was considered 'unwise to announce in advance of requests to the Fund the receptiveness of the United States to proposals for the use of floating rates, or even to make this position known informally within the government'.[158] Furthermore, it was thought undesirable to seek a formal revision of Fund policies which would relax the limitations over the use of floating rates by easing the conditions under which they might be used or the periods for which they might be employed.

This view was later confirmed by Frank Southard, of the IMF, who noted that the Fund and the US Treasury were largely agnostic on the issue of fixed versus floating – 'genuinely flexible or floating rates rarely persist for a long period . . . our basic policy must and does admit the right of countries to adopt flexible rates under appropriate conditions'.[159] The difficulty, of course, was to decide when floating was warranted and if it would have an overwhelmingly negative impact on other countries or international institutional arrangements.[160] In making this assessment, US policy makers would have been guided largely by the impact of the new exchange rate regime on the IMF, on NATO and the defence of Western Europe and, crucially, on the EPU.

The achievement of a relatively stable international economic order (through the strengthening of GATT, the IMF and the World Bank) and the bolstering of the defences of Western Europe through NATO were two central US foreign policy aims in the early 1950s.[161] However, both aims had been called into question as the IMF and the World Bank had sought, somewhat in vain, to find legitimate roles in the postwar world and discussions continued regarding the funding of NATO. Since 1950 the British Treasury had been at variance with the United States over who effectively controlled the IMF, about the powers of the Fund and about access to its resources. The Treasury concluded by December 1950, 'it is clear that at the present time the Fund is not only failing to carry out the objectives for which it was founded, but it is also increasingly becoming a source of friction between the US and the UK'.[162] This view was echoed at the Bank of England by Bolton who wrote to Camille Gutt (Managing Director of the IMF), 'I am also sure that you will agree with my view that the Fund must find some means of earning a living and that it cannot increase the debit to its Profit and Loss Account indefinitely without endangering its existence'.[163] By 1952 the Treasury judged that the Fund's performance to date had been dismal. In a sharp assessment of the Fund, Treasury officials argued that the IMF Articles, Charter, structure and organization were not flexible enough to deal with changing circumstances; that there was a lack of internationalism among its members – most notably the US; that it was saddled with an outdated and rigid constitution and as a result had not made any worthwhile contribution.[164] If Bolton's Payments Club became a reality and a number of European states were drawn into a close association with the Sterling Area, the IMF would find its already precarious position weakened, and as Butler minuted in relation to Robot, 'unless they act cooperatively . . . it will be the end of the IMF'.[165] This eventuality had been partially acknowledged by US Treasury officials who had noted that the result of floating rates would be 'to take exchange rate matters largely out of the Fund while governments remained in a position to exercise effective control over exchange rates'.[166]

There was a further possibility that Robot would have disrupted NATO to the extent that the existing system of aid was based on dollar deficits (countries were allocated aid in relation to 'need' as reflected in dollar deficits). Britain and other countries adopting the floating rate would eliminate deficits, hence to continue beyond 1953 the US military aid programme would have to find new principles of operation. Secondly, it was concluded that a fall in the rate would endanger defence programmes inasmuch as it would increase their internal costs and instability of prices and employment would be much more readily attributable in public to defence. At the height of Pentagon concern over the 'containment' of the Soviet Union, it is likely that Robot would have been perceived as highly disruptive to the US defence effort in Europe, but no doubt that effort could have been continued albeit on a new financial basis.[167]

The US Treasury versus the MSA on the EPU

However, if the United States could live with the impact of floating rates on the IMF and its defence programme in Western Europe, there remained a question mark over how the Administration would view the almost inevitable demise of the European Payments Union. In this regard there was a clear division of opinion between the US Treasury (and the Federal Reserve) and the Mutual Security Agency supported by the State Department. On 13 February 1952, the Treasury produced a report on US policy in the EPU which concluded, in no uncertain terms, that the Union had failed to advance American objectives in Europe.[168] Despite early success with the liberalization of trade, the Union now faced a situation in which Austria, Denmark and Norway refused to liberalize beyond a maximum level of 60 per cent and Germany, France, Greece and the UK had deliberalized their trade after an initial phase of relaxing restrictions. The objective of trade liberalization within the EPU area clearly had not been attained. Moreover, the Treasury noted, there was no appreciable movement in Europe towards a reduction of discrimination against the dollar area and 'no clear evidence that the trade stimulated by the liberalization programme and the facilitation of payments by the EPU has actually resulted in an increase in efficiency or reduction of costs'.[169] In short, it appeared to the US Treasury that trade in Europe had not only moved away from the degree of liberalization attained in the earlier period, but that 'restrictions against the US have been intensified'.[170] In respect of movement towards the convertibility of currencies, the Treasury bemoaned that while the situation in 1950 gave some promise of progress, 'the situation now has been reversed and is much the same as it was at the beginning of the ERP'.[171] The EPU had clearly not facilitated progress towards convertibility. Similarly, as regards the issue of political integration in Europe, the Treasury concluded that 'we may be deluding the US Congress and the US people if we really claim that we are making progress towards integration in this way'.[172]

This negative assessment was rebutted, a week later, by the Mutual Security Agency.[173] On the issue of trade discrimination, the Agency noted that this was always seen as a gradual process and although the EPU suffered from, it nevertheless had withstood, the impact of renewed dollar shortage. Likewise, in respect of convertibility, the Agency suggested that the major obstacles to progress emanated from the economic consequences of Korea and the accelerated rearmament of the West. The effectiveness of the EPU was to be viewed, 'in terms of these obstacles as well as in terms of the absolute progress envisaged five months before Korea'.[174] However, the success of the Union was, for the MSA, to be found in the promotion of European integration. The establishment of the EPU, it was claimed, was a necessary and important step towards the ultimate goal of a single, large, competitive Western European market within which goods and currencies could move freely. There was no doubt that 'progress on this road during the first eighteen months of EPU's life has been greater than anticipated, despite the unexpected obstacles that have been met'.[175] In short, for the MSA, the Union had been an unqualified success and had laid the basis for further steps to complete economic and political integration in Europe.

This dispute between the Treasury and the Mutual Security Agency came to a head at a meeting of the National Advisory Council on International Monetary and Financial Problems held on 13 March 1952.[176] In a heated debate, Averell Harriman (MSA) and Leroy Stinebower (State Department) emphasized the importance of the continuation of the EPU to American political and economic objectives. Any indication, Harriman noted, that the United States was retreating from its support for integration would 'weaken the position of those who are battling for us and who have the upper hand at this time'.[177] Any move to disrupt the EPU would, he claimed, 'have a disastrous effect on United States policy'.[178] Against this view, John Snyder (Treasury) and William McChesney Martin (Federal Reserve) argued that the EPU was a 'transitory arrangement, and it had been hoped that it would be able to accomplish something'.[179] But at present it was simply building up an area that might exclude United States trade and therefore continued US sponsorship of the Union was simply misguided. In summary, claimed Snyder, 'the more the United States supports and encourages institutions such as the EPU, the more it solidifies the Payments Union and postpones the time when the United States can bring about better conditions with respect to the dollar and the US trade position.'[180]

This dispute rumbled on for some months until it was clear by the end of the year that the MSA and the State Department view would prevail. However, the significant fact is that in February 1952, again unknown to the British, official thought in the US was divided over the issue of the EPU. A move to adopt Robot, and thereby terminate the EPU, would not necessarily have been viewed as an economic disaster by the US Treasury.

Overall, the case for Robot as outlined by Overseas Finance and the Bank in the run-up to the February Cabinet meetings rested on three central planks. First, the plan would secure a future for sterling as a key global currency, thereby satisfying the concerns of Cobbold, Bolton and Thompson-McCausland. Second, it would employ market forces to encourage structural economic adjustment. In this respect, as Salter observed, 'Robot strikes at the heart of the philosophy of the Labour Party (and many outside that party). It subjects the general economy to the compulsion of a currency system, and expects the economy to be adjusted to the requirements of that system'.[181] It was not, primarily, a plan to solve the immediate balance of payments problem but rather aimed to deal with the long-term competitive position of the British economy. Finally, Robot sought to change the operation of the international political economy in significant respects. Once the government had 'taken the plunge into the freedom of the price mechanism'[182] postwar international trade and payments systems would be irrevocably altered. The effect of the plan on the Sterling Area, Europe, the United States, the EPU and the IMF meant that there could be no return to the complex, cumbersome international economic arrangements built by Attlee and his colleagues. This was, of course, potentially both a source of strength and a source of weakness. Once through Cabinet, domestic opposition to Robot could be resisted by pointing to the global changes set in train that could not now be recovered. The 'new look' international system could restore Britain's prestige, block early moves towards European integration and establish a working relationship on a new, more productive basis with the United States. However, by its very nature the plan carried a risk that Europe might not entertain floating rate convertibility and in particular that the Sterling Area might fragment at the approach of Robot. The success of the plan therefore rested initially on the compliance of key Sterling Area countries, and in February 1952 it seemed that this could be assured. It also seemed reasonable to assume that a sufficient number of European governments, including France, might agree to join Bolton's new Payments Club. Finally, although it was thought that sections of the United States Administration would have objections to the plan, these objections were not considered to be decisive enough to scupper the operation. However, the key question which still remained to be answered was whether the British Cabinet would give the green light to Operation Robot. The next chapter charts the manoeuvrings of the main oppositional forces and details the Cabinet battles which Macmillan, amongst others, described as one of the 'most extraordinary' moments in British political history.[183]

4
The Battle over Robot

Opposition to the Robot plan began to take definite shape following Robert Hall's letter to Butler which led the Chancellor to announce on 21 February that Budget day had been put back from 4 March to 11 March 1952.[1] Hall, as noted earlier, had initially thought the plan reasonably 'attractive', commenting that 'it certainly looks a great deal better when one thinks of alternatives'.[2] However, Hall found Butler's attempt to push the plan through Cabinet by 4 March, both alarming and ill-judged. In his view, Rowan and Clarke were behaving 'irresponsibly, in allowing the Chancellor to put forward something so drastic at short notice' since Ministers were not being given a chance to 'understand the thing'.[3] Hall's fears were not allayed by the decision to postpone the Budget. On 21 February, Rowan chaired a meeting of the Permanent Secretaries to explain the plan and to gauge reaction.[4] According to Hall, 'no analysis of the results of the action had been provided' and objectors were 'not given much chance to speak'.[5] Hall again protested at being 'bounced' in this manner and on 22 February, following another unsatisfactory meeting, he pressed Bridges and the Chancellor to recall Plowden (who had flown to Lisbon with Eden on 19 February to attend a NATO Council meeting) and to send officials to inform Eden who, he was sure, would push for a further postponement of the plan.[6]

As Head of the Economic Section of the Cabinet Office, Hall occupied a unique position of advisor not only to the Chancellor but also to other Ministers in Whitehall.[7] He was therefore perfectly placed to act as a link between the Section and other oppositional groups such as that brought together by the Paymaster General. Clarke and Rowan, he believed, were engaged in high-level 'intrigue',[8] and once it became clear that Cherwell, MacDougall and Maurice Allen (Chief Economist at the Bank) also opposed the plan, Hall began to push at the highest political level to slow the decision-making process and sever the link between Robot and the March Budget. This chapter will analyse in detail the main opposition to Robot, and the alternatives presented by the Economic Section, before turning to the role of the Cherwell, Plowden, MacDougall alliance in the run-up to the crucial February Cabinet meetings.

I Robot and the Economic Section

Between 19 and 28 February, six members of the Economic Section worked full-time on the Robot question. Nita Watts, Robert Neild, John Jukes, Jack Downie, David Butt and Peggy Hemming prepared a succession of papers for internal circulation, faster than Robert Hall could read them.[9] The Section, of course, did not play a major role in economic policy making and tended to be disregarded by the Treasury and Bank.[10] Nevertheless, it played a significant role in opposing Robot, partly through the ammunition it provided for Robert Hall and also through its link to Cherwell, who would later argue in Cabinet, somewhat disingenuously, that 'the economists in Government service who had been consulted about the plan were opposed to it'.[11]

The Section's first assessment, produced by Nita Watts on 19 February, identified two issues that would prove crucial in later debates.[12] First, Watts questioned the accuracy of the Bank's view that without emergency action, the reserves would soon run dry. It was at least plausible, she argued, that the action already taken, or to be taken in the next month or so, combined with natural trends, could stop the drain by the end of the year. Second, in choosing the type of exchange rate system (fixed versus floating) much depended, she noted, on the government's assessment of the causes of the present difficulties. If the problem were fundamentally that of an adverse balance of payments due to uncompetitive export prices and excessive demand for imports, then devaluation (or even letting the rate go completely free for a while) was an appropriate corrective. But if the main problem was caused by the physical shortage of exports that could be sold abroad in sufficient quantities to produce equilibrium (exacerbated by the demands of rearmament and home investment), then the Robot plan would be of little value. Without further investigation of the underlying causes of the present crisis, emergency action was simply premature. On balance, Watts concluded, 'it would seem desirable to do everything possible to maintain the existing exchange rate even at the cost of intensified controls over international trade and payments'.[13]

Watts had set the tone of the Section's response to Robot. Her analysis was now extended by David Butt who sought to clarify the principal points on which the Section and the Bank disagreed.[14] Everyone, he noted, shared the long-term objective of creating a convertible world with stable exchange rates and the least possible physical control over trade. However, Butt suggested, it was possible to move to this state gradually, introducing a number of controlled moves that would help tackle the present crisis. The government could drastically reduce dollar imports; expand dollar-earning capacity at the expense of home investment; and borrow as much as possible from the IMF to ease the dollar shortage and provide a buffer should Robot be pushed through Cabinet. Butt's principal objection to Robot focused on the likely impact of the plan on world trade. His argument here was later deployed with skill by both Hall and Cherwell. If Robot was implemented, all countries with a dollar deficit would, Butt suggested, adopt discriminatory and deflationary measures to defend their exchange rates and earn a surplus. The impact on international trade and payments mechanisms would be catastrophic and it was by no means certain that the United States would act to support the move: 'will the United States after we have unilaterally revoked the Bretton Woods Agreement, broken the EPU and so on, be prepared to co-operate in lending for the purposes of development in the non-dollar world?'[15] It was equally unlikely, he concluded, that Churchill would cut the defence programme sufficiently to increase resources for investment or that the government would revoke existing restrictions on East/West trade to enable fuller trade with the Soviet Union – one of the few areas where dollar substitutes (grain and timber) could be obtained on good terms.

On the basis of these perceptive contributions, Hall now asked the Section to turn its attention to developing alternatives to Robot. A bewildering array of alternative, and often contradictory, schemes soon emerged. The most bizarre, produced by John Jukes and quickly labelled 'Jukes' Folly', suggested the adoption of a floating rate with inconvertible sterling, if the controlled moves outlined above by Butt failed to stem the tide.[16] Jack Downie opted for a similar scheme, pointing to what he saw as the inherent contradiction of Robot – the impossibility of reconciling full employment with convertibility.[17] In a passage reminiscent of Cherwell's later remarks in Cabinet, Downie stated, 'I believe that the price and employment consequences will be so severe that there will be irresistible pressure on the Government to do something about it'.[18] The result would probably be a suspension of convertibility, leaving a confused system of inconvertible free rates. His own solution, 'Downie's Desperation', was to shortcut this circuit and jump immediately to an inconvertible free rate position in an enlarged Sterling Area with blocked balances and strictly limited transferability between non-sterling countries. Both schemes were heavily criticized by Butt and Neild on the grounds that Jukes' free rate without blocking was 'even more risky than the Bank's scheme', whilst Downie's proposal would be unworkable, creating a 'nightmare of central bank special accounts the world over'.[19] The Economic Section, in general, opposed a move to floating rate at this time for three principal reasons.[20] First, it would introduce a risk element into trading and encourage 'leads and lags'. Second, it could result in restrictive measures from trading partners seeking to protect their rates. Third, it was unwise to disrupt the entire fabric of fixed exchange rates and credit margins that had been created by prolonged campaigning and negotiation unless it was absolutely clear that the change was beneficial. Recalling Watts' earlier paper, Robert Neild concluded that he saw no reason why trading at a fixed rate with swings covered by credit and limited by import restriction operated bilaterally or internationally, could not be successful.[21] This critique opened the door for an amended version of the 'Watts' Plan' to emerge as the alternative favoured by the Section. In large part, it would be incorporated in Robert Hall's later lengthy response to Robot titled, 'The Future of Sterling'.[22]

The 'Watts Plan', circulated initially on 25 February, consisted of five main elements.[23] First, all leading currencies would maintain the fixed rate system. Second, among the leading currencies, a limited degree of convertibility would gradually be introduced. Third, a new and much broader sterling payments system modelled on the EPU would be formed. Four, non-Sterling Area balances would be blocked and could not be drawn upon for any purpose. Finally, Sterling Area balances would become freely transferable but only among residents of the Area, with each Sterling Area country to be given a sum in gold and dollars from the remaining reserves to provide a minimum convertible reserve to start life in the new system. The main advantage claimed for the proposal was that it would minimize loss of reserves without disrupting Britain's trade with the Sterling Area (and therefore would help minimize unemployment at home). Developed further by Neild it quickly became a justification for establishing a 'two-world' system based on extremely tight control of trade with non-sterling countries.

The 'discriminatory, almost Schachtian'[24] character of the scheme found few friends in Whitehall. The Section's overall conclusion that policy must move in the opposite direction to Robot and 'strengthen the defences against non-dollar countries trying to earn dollars from each other, while preserving the incentives to keep up a high level of mutual aid'[25] was shown, even by fellow-travellers such as MacDougall and Plowden, to be wholly unrealistic. MacDougall informed Hall that politically the scheme was 'naïve' and could 'easily play into the hands of our opponents'.[26] Economically it was judged that the plan would cause great resentment in the United States and place too many countries in severe difficulties by cutting out their capacity to earn dollars from other members of the system.[27] The Economic Section had provided some useful criticism of the Robot plan, but its officials had been unable to produce a coherent alternative.

II Cherwell and the Prime Minister's Statistical Section

Churchill's decision in October 1951 to rebuild the Statistical Section as an adjunct to government, and in particular to lure Cherwell, now 65, away from the tranquillity of Oxford, proved to be crucial in determining the character and outcome of the Robot debates. Appointed Paymaster General, with a seat in the Cabinet, Cherwell made Donald MacDougall his senior economic adviser and proceeded to recruit a small team which included Jack Parkinson, Maurice Scott and John Fforde.[28] A regular visitor to Chequers and Chartwell, Cherwell had privileged access to the Prime Minister. He accepted the offer of rooms on the top floors of No. 11 Downing Street, and, as Birkenhead notes, 'this was a convenient arrangement, for when summoned in the small hours by the Prime Minister, he had merely to walk through one of the communicating doors into No. 10'.[29]

As a member of the Economic Policy Committee of the Cabinet, Cherwell was first shown a detailed outline of Robot on 22 February, and he demanded, against Butler's wishes, to keep his copy for further study.[30] Branded by Fforde, an 'intellectual and social snob', averse to unquantified economic arguments expressed in emotive terms particularly if deployed by Civil Servants,[31] Cherwell immediately took against the plan. Over the weekend of 23 February he met with MacDougall and Hall, on one occasion on Hall's Oxford allotment, to prepare an anti-Robot memo for circulation to the Cabinet on 25 February.[32] Cherwell began the memo by reiterating the point made by Nita Watts, that it was too soon to conclude that existing measures had failed.[33] The fall in the reserves, he suggested, need perhaps only be regarded as a 'temporary emergency'. Instead of dealing with the crisis by reversing the policies of the past 12 years, he advocated a return to 'the fundamental verities: unless we can export more by volume or at higher prices or in the form of invisibles, we shall have to reduce our imports and therewith our standard of life. Nothing in the world can alter this'.[34] Cherwell thus recommended a five-point plan of action to be put into effect on Budget day. First, it would be necessary to cancel import contracts and licences for non-essentials. Second, the government should redouble its efforts to borrow dollars on the strength of the $300 million promised by the United States, the dollar securities held by the Treasury and the Sterling Area quota in the IMF which, he calculated, amounted to $2,000 million. Third, the government should offer inducements to, and exert pressure on, exporters to send their goods to countries prepared to pay high prices in hard currency and not to send out 'unrequited' exports. Fourth, the Bank Rate should be raised and budgetary action taken to prevent a fall in confidence. Finally, Sterling Area countries should be pressed to reduce their hard currency imports to avoid the need for rationing hard currency.

Robot, Cherwell concluded, was 'financial jugglery, some economic magic' luring us to the view that we can 'escape from our predicament without toil and sweat'.[35] Fundamentally, he argued, it would not correct the balance of payments problem. If the rate fell by 20 per cent Britain would have to export 25 per cent more in volume of goods to obtain the same amount of foreign exchange (and thereby imports). This might be feasible if exports were limited by price considerations. But, he suggested, this was not the case: 'the limitation is our inability to supply more, owing to shortage of steel and labour for exports, not high prices. Hence we cannot increase the volume of these exports and any devaluation would therefore represent a direct and immediate loss of foreign currency.'[36] Even if the volume of exports could be increased dramatically, this would take time and in the interval the deficit in the balance of payments would rise and the floating rate for sterling would fall. Accordingly it might well cost the Bank more reserves trying to support a falling pound than it would trying to hold it at its existing level. This was a powerful economic argument designed to appeal to the cautious members of the Cabinet. Cherwell now highlighted the political dangers of the plan, ridiculing the notion that automatically the 'rate might take the strain'. In plain English, this phrase simply meant allowing prices to rise to such a degree that people could no longer afford to buy so much food, manufactured goods or raw materials. Indeed, it had the 'specious lure of being automatic' and might even work through higher unemployment and suffering, but 'in a hard pressed community like ours this form of rationing imports by the purse can surely scarcely be promulgated as Conservative policy'.[37] Britain, he finally noted, would be pilloried throughout the world for Robot, causing consternation and chaos far beyond the Sterling Area.

Cherwell now sought to consolidate his opposition to the plan by convincing Churchill that it was 'reckless' involving 'appalling political as well as economic risks at home and abroad'.[38] Not only did he impress upon the Prime Minister that Salter and Swinton were 'strongly against' the plan, he also claimed the 'opinion in the Bank was divided'.[39] This, however, was far from the case since, as Fforde points out, there is no documentary evidence of divided opinions in the Bank beyond Maurice Allen's own dissent.[40] In fact, Cobbold had sought the advice of Edward Peacock, Sir John Anderson and Richard Hopkins and all favoured the adoption of Robot.[41] The views of Anderson, who had refused Churchill's invitation in 1951 to act as 'economic overlord',[42] and Peacock (former senior member of the Court) were particularly significant with the latter noting 'unless the action is taken I understand that creeping paralysis is almost inevitable. Creeping paralysis is practically incurable, so although the operation involves serious risks, the situation would seem to demand it'.[43]

As Cherwell applied continuous pressure to Churchill, MacDougall devised ways of persuading Ministers and officials to oppose the plan, in a contest in which he admits, 'no holds were barred'.[44] He was joined in this by the influential yet somewhat erratic figure of Edwin Plowden, who it seems played a particularly significant role in convincing Eden and Salter of the dangers of the plan. As noted above, on 19 February, Eden and a team of officials including Plowden, had flown to Lisbon to continue negotiations within the framework of NATO over the relationship between Britain's armed forces and the proposed European Defence Community (EDC).[45] The British government had made clear its intention not to join the EDC but nevertheless wished to maintain close links with it by extending the guarantee of the Protocol of the North Atlantic Treaty to the Community and participating as observers in the work of the EDC Interim Commission.[46] Robot would of course severely disrupt existing international arrangements and commitments, and so Churchill had decided on 21 February that it was impossible to go ahead with the plan without knowing the views of the Foreign Secretary.[47] Consequently, on 22 February, Herbert Brittain (Third Secretary in Overseas Finance) and Eric Berthoud (Assistant Under-Secretary at the Foreign Office) were dispatched to Lisbon to brief Eden. They arrived with letters and memoranda for Eden, and two letters for Plowden – one from Bridges, the other from Robert Hall.[48]

Bridges, somewhat naïvely, hoped that Plowden might nudge Eden in the direction of Robot. However, the Chief Planning Officer, as usual, sided with Hall: 'after reading Robert Hall's letter I saw that there were, to say the least, strong arguments against the plan and I set off from the hotel where I was staying to see Anthony Eden at the Embassy'.[49] Plowden records that on arrival he found Eden 'generally supportive of Robot'.[50] Churchill had painted a picture of the economy in the grip of a 'new financial supercrisis' and his letter stated bluntly, 'all the colleagues whom I have consulted think that the remedies now proposed are on the right lines. The Prof is the only exception'.[51] Likewise, Butler noted in his letter to Eden that although the plan raised difficulties, 'I feel that the European economy, which is strained and in flux, may out of this build a better and less artificial future'.[52] However, in the face of sustained counter-arguments presented by Plowden, Shuckburgh and Berthoud, Eden's enthusiasm soon cooled.

Plowden concentrated on the difficulties the plan posed to the middle class and the danger of antagonizing the organized labour movement.[53] Shuckburgh highlighted a number of 'political objections', and suggested that the only honest policy would be for the government to announce the plan and 'go to the country on it'.[54] Meanwhile Berthoud, it appears, strongly disliked the proponents of the plan, describing Rowan, Strath and Clarke as 'persons of an emotional character leading unnatural lives – divorced from their wives or otherwise emotionally unstable'.[55] Accordingly, Berthoud 'strongly advised the Secretary of State to oppose the plan largely because it seemed impossible to accept the serious external political consequences'.[56] Eden thus concluded, whilst in Lisbon, that the proposals were unacceptable. His personal diary entry is unequivocal:

I did not like them at all. They seemed to me ill thought out and I was by no means convinced that they would work. In such conditions I couldn't endorse proposals that would strike a grievous blow at some of our Commonwealth friends and send Europe into disarray and inflict increased unemployment (so I judged) on our own people.[57]

Eden expressed his anxieties, 'in brief and guarded form',[58] to Churchill by telephone from Lisbon and penned a note to the Prime Minister indicating that 'on first glance it is the operation on the home front that worried me most, and that not merely on a party view'.[59] Plowden returned from

Lisbon on 24 February to play a full part in the Robot discussions and prepare the ground for Eden's return.[60] After discussions with Cherwell and MacDougall, Plowden declared his opposition to the plan on three grounds: it would disrupt international trade, produce too much unemployment, and risk provoking a diplomatic crisis.[61] This last point chimed in with the view of Lionel Robbins (former Director of the Economic Section) who was asked to comment by Bridges and Hall.[62] Robbins saw two main dangers of the proposed course of action: direct economic dangers and indirect dangers to Britain's general economic and political standing. The chief economic problem lay in the threat of further wage inflation. Restraint would in any case be difficult to achieve but, he asked,

> do the authors of the plan think that it will be made easier if import prices are rising as a result of a falling pound? Do they think that the Chancellor's appeals for moderation will have much chance if the cost of living increases? Or are they prepared so to restrict credit that wage inflation is prevented by the creation of mass unemployment?[63]

Robbins' second, and decisive objection, centred on what he called 'the question of honour'. Although he was in no doubt that the plan had been proposed by 'men of the highest integrity and with the best possible intentions', the operation itself was 'not in fact strictly honourable'.[64] Britain's reputation as a custodian of other people's money would be destroyed and the decimation of existing international agreements would endanger future co-operation with Europe and the United States. However, unlike Plowden, Robbins thought that unless the current economic tide could be stemmed, a Robot-type operation might in any case become inevitable. But this day had not yet been reached. It was important therefore to try further resolute action at home to convince overseas holders of sterling that all options had been exhausted before considering Robot.

There can be little doubt that in the 'five days of battle'[65] leading up to the decisive Cabinet meetings, the 'gang of four' (Cherwell, Hall, Plowden and MacDougall) planted sufficient doubt in the minds of officials and Ministers to ensure that Butler could not rely automatically on the support of his colleagues. However, as Butler himself recalls, 'neither the Prof's private detective agency in economics, fascinating as it was to the Prime Minister, nor Salter's stream of sea-green memoranda would have sufficed to carry the day if the senior members of the government had been of a different turn of mind'.[66]

III The Cabinet decides: 28 and 29 February

On 27 February, with Bridges and Norman Brook anxious for a decision, Churchill announced that the Cabinet would meet to settle the matter 'within the next two days'.[67] At 12.30 p.m. the same day, he called a meeting of Ministers to gauge general opinion. In attendance were Butler, Cherwell, Woolton, Maxwell-Ffye, Lyttelton, the Marquis of Salisbury, Crookshank, Leathers, and Thorneycroft (Salter, Swinton, Brook, Bridges and Rowan were also present).[68] Butler opened proceedings, arguing that no alternative policy could be put forward which would save the currency. This received a sharp rebuttal from Cherwell who stressed that the Chancellor's scheme would lead to 'an appalling disaster'. Lyttelton predictably stood firm behind Butler, whilst Salter echoed Cherwell arguing for a stiff Budget and suggesting that 'if we had to take the step proposed by the Chancellor, we should only do so later as a result of force majeure'.[69] Thorneycroft leaned to the course proposed by Butler, indicating that although it would cause 'unpleasantness', it 'had the advantage of being quasi-automatic'[70] – a point also emphasized by Woolton. Swinton preferred to wait and see the effect of a strong Budget, whereas Crookshank and Maxwell-Fyfe were inclined to support the Chancellor. This left Leathers and the Marquis of Salisbury undecided, asking for further time for consideration. In short, it appeared that the pro-Robot camp was in the ascendant. Clear opposition had been expressed by only one Cabinet Minister: Lord Cherwell (Salter and Swinton were not at this stage full members of the Cabinet).

The Robot camp, however, was not as unified as this meeting appeared to suggest. A significant dispute had developed over whether a tough Budget should be introduced alongside Robot or whether it could be delayed to give time to judge the impact of the plan. Cobbold argued repeatedly that Robot could not be regarded as an alternative to strict Budget proposals and a rise in Bank Rate but on the contrary, made such measures 'all the more necessary'.[71] Moreover Cobbold had long been uneasy with Butler's presentation of Robot, which he thought placed too much emphasis on 'floating' and failed to stress that 'we must have a high degree of stability'.[72] In the Governor's view strong action was necessary in the Budget to help reduce inflation and pressure in the economy regardless of whether external measures were taken or not: 'External measures cannot be regarded as an alternative to a strong budget – this would mean nothing more than a new depreciation of sterling.'[73] However, Rowan and Butler were not convinced. Further import cuts and drastic action alongside Robot would, Rowan claimed, 'accentuate our difficulties with European trade'.[74] It was thus preferable to see the impact of the new plan before intensifying domestic measures. Butler agreed and, as he explained to the Cabinet meeting, 'under the external sterling plan we shall still need import cuts but we could – at any rate initially until we see what happens – avoid cuts which involve cancellation of contracts with our overseas suppliers, disruption of industry or really dangerous exhaustion of stocks'.[75] Savage import cuts along with the strict dollar rationing advocated by Cherwell and Plowden were, in Butler's view, 'politically, and in every way, far more onerous' than Robot.[76]

This division was not only unwelcome in respect of its timing. It also enabled opposition forces to claim that the Robot revolution was unnecessary given the alternative of a stiff Budget. To this end Plowden was asked to prepare a practical alternative to Robot which became known as the 'alternative plan'.[77] If Cobbold's suggestions had been followed more closely, the 'alternative plan' would have lost much of its appeal and Cherwell's argument much of its force.

Unperturbed by the lunchtime meeting of Ministers, Cherwell returned to his quarters and dashed off a note to Eden who was returning from Lisbon later that afternoon.[78] He implored Eden to study carefully his memorandum and reiterated that the plan would 'certainly do immense damage to our relations with Europe, the United States and many Commonwealth countries'.[79] He had little reason to worry. On return from Lisbon, Eden dined alone with Churchill and, as he noted in his diary, I 'told him my answer and its reasons'.[80]

The stage was now set for a day of drama on 28 February. In preparation, Norman Brook indicated to Churchill that the Prime Minister should talk privately with Butler and Eden before the Cabinet met.[81] He also suggested that when the Cabinet met, 'this could be a special meeting: if you wish, no papers need be circulated in advance and I would certainly recommend that no record should be circulated until after the decisions have been announced'.[82] At last the time had come to inform other members of the Cabinet who, remarkably up until this point, knew little or nothing of the plan. This meant drawing in Ismay, Simonds, Monckton and Macmillan.[83] The first meeting of the full Cabinet attended by all 16 Ministers would, Brook suggested, best be held after dinner on the 28th at 10.00 p.m.[84]

On the morning of 28 February, Churchill, Butler and Eden met for an hour to discuss Robot in advance of a meeting with the Governor of the Bank of England and Bridges.[85] Cobbold had prepared extensive notes for this meeting which argued that since 1945 the government had been moving rapidly towards losing control of the value of the currency, threatening the break-up of the sterling system and the loss of economic strength on which the political position was founded.[86] He explained how the Bank had advised remedial action in 1949 and stressed the gravity of the position prior to the General Election in 1951. International financial opinion, he argued, thought the burden on taxation and the productive economy was too heavy; the overseas liabilities were too large; and that there was no prospect of sterling being worth more but considerable prospect of it being worth less. Whilst it was, of course, impossible to predict at what point in time confidence would break, the Bank's view was that 'we are now at testing time and if real hope cannot be given in conjunction with the Budget, confidence may evaporate very quickly'.[87] In respect of Plowden's 'alternative plan', Cobbold counselled that it was 'most unwise and imprudent' to scrape the barrel by borrowing from the United States to finance further deficits on the Micawber principle – 'bad for credit, same old story'. Even with a strong Budget, 'the attack may be on us as soon as the March figures are published'.[88] In the circumstances would it really be easier to do all these unpleasant things, he asked, at a slightly later stage when it must surely be regarded as a move from weakness and a recognition of the failure of the Budget and earlier measures? In short, it was time to 'take the plunge now with all its admitted risks and dangers and show that we have constructive as well as restrictive ideas'.[89] The reaction of the rest of the world could not be predicted but Cobbold's personal view was that 'while Governments everywhere would be bound to protest, everybody who understands this, particularly in the countries whose life-blood depends on sterling, would heave a sigh of relief'.[90]

Eden's concerns, however, were not allayed by the Governor.[91] Sensing that 'nervousness was developing', Cobbold and Bolton took Butler to lunch to stiffen his resolve and discuss tactics.[92] Lyttelton meanwhile had produced a memo criticizing Cherwell's paper and sent it to Churchill, Butler, Woolton, Maxwell Ffye and Stuart.[93] As the evening meeting approached, the issue was still finely balanced. Eden's apparent opposition had dampened the high spirits of the Robot camp, yet Hall, Cherwell and MacDougall remained anxious, feeling that 'on the whole the party in favour of the Bank and Overseas Finance scheme is in the ascendant'.[94]

The 10.00 p.m. Cabinet

The remarkable character of the meeting of Ministers held at 10.00 p.m. on 28 February is well conveyed by Macmillan's diary entry for 29 February which reads: 'From last night's Cabinet till tonight has been the most extraordinary 24 hours I have ever spent.'[95] Whilst dining with Arthur Penn at the Turf, Macmillan received a call from Norman Brook's secretary at 8.30 p.m. announcing the Cabinet meeting at 10.00 p.m. A messenger duly arrived with secret papers for Macmillan at 9.00 p.m.[96] At this first meeting Ministers had before them copies of Butler's memorandum, 'External Action' and Cherwell's opposition paper, 'The Balance of Payments'.[97] When the meeting began it was clear to Macmillan that 'something quite unusual was in the air'.[98] Butler, who according to Macmillan seemed 'very exhausted', opened proceedings by stating that in the last eight weeks the reserves had dropped by $521 million and now stood at $1,800 million, which represented only three-and-a-half weeks' turnover of the Sterling Area's transactions with the rest of the world.[99] Internal action alone could not deal fast enough with the crisis situation, hence it was time to act 'in the most effective and drastic way which is open to us'.[100] In turn the Chancellor then rejected five alternative courses of action: devaluation to a fixed rate (who would believe this devaluation was final?); cancellation of import contracts and licences (it would destroy the basis for recovery); increasing controls on sterling (it would further impair the international use and standing of sterling); winding up the Sterling Area (not feasible politically or economically given Britain's trade with the Area); and further borrowing abroad (even if possible, this would simply defer the crisis for a few weeks or months). It was now time, he suggested, 'that we set a completely new course, stop the drain on the reserves immediately, stop the markets in "cheap sterling", rehabilitate sterling as an international currency and absorb some of the external pressures on the exchange rate instead of on the reserves'.[101] With a nod in the direction of the Governor of the Bank he added that this course of action was not a substitute for firm internal policies and that an increase in short-term money rates would be an integral part of the plan. Butler, somewhat falteringly,[102] then expounded his five-point plan. The fixed rate would be abandoned and the government would publicly accept the principle of a variable rate of exchange (although the Exchange Equalisation Account would be used to intervene constructively and keep the rate within the limits of 15 per cent either side of the official parity – this, of course, would not be made public). Secondly, all overseas sterling balances would be blocked, except for American and Canadian accounts already convertible into dollars. Ten per cent of these balances would be reclassified as 'external sterling' which, together with any sterling earned subsequently, would be freely convertible into gold or any currency at the current rate. Thirdly, the existing structure of the Sterling Area would be maintained. The UK and other Sterling Area countries would retain full exchange control and citizens who were permitted to acquire foreign exchange could buy it in the market. Fourthly, 80 per cent of sterling balances held by Sterling Area countries' central banks would be placed in funded form and could not therefore be used for current transactions. Finally, the London gold market would be reopened to provide a free market against external sterling. The price of gold would fluctuate freely but Sterling Area citizens (apart from gold producers) would not be permitted to operate in the market.

These measures, the Chancellor stressed, amounted to 'a reversal of the policies of the last twelve years'.[103] In remarkably candid fashion he informed the Cabinet:

> It would mean abrogating our monetary and payments agreements with non-sterling countries. It would be a shock to the Commonwealth members of the Sterling Area, and might bring one or two of them to the point of deciding to leave the Sterling Area altogether. It would disrupt the European Payments Union, and would therefore be viewed with mixed feelings by the United States Government. Finally, so far as concerned the internal economy of the UK, it would mean abandoning the principle of stability in internal prices and wages; there would in the initial stages be some rise in the cost of living and some measure of unemployment; and there would be a continuous process of change and adjustment, much of which would be painful.[104]

Despite all this, Robot, he stressed, was to Britain's long-term advantage. Not only would it eliminate 'cheap sterling' operations and significantly reduce the drain on the gold and dollar reserves, it would crucially 'bring into play forces which in the long run would tend to bring the economy into balance'.[105] Sterling could not continue indefinitely on an inconvertible basis and Robot offered an opportunity for the government to 'take a constructive and powerful initiative in the world economy' from a position of relative strength.[106]

At this point, Cherwell intervened to restate the arguments he had worked out with Hall, MacDougall and Plowden.[107] The remedial measures taken in November had not yet produced their effect and the Commonwealth Finance Ministers had not yet put into operation the further measures agreed in January. Economically, Robot was unnecessary and would probably make matters worse. Politically, there were grave objections both in terms of domestic governance and international relations. Rather than run the risks of Robot, Cherwell recommended a more traditional policy mix including further reductions in imports, an expansion of exports, further borrowing from the United States and the IMF, strong budgetary action to restore confidence in sterling and above all, renewed pressure on Sterling Area countries to reduce their imports from hard currency sources.[108]

Following the Butler and Cherwell presentations, Churchill turned to the rest of Cabinet and asked each Minister to speak in turn.[109] Predictably, the plan received strong support from Lyttelton who favoured an early move from a position of strength and thought that, by and large, the change would benefit the Colonial Empire since it had an overall surplus based on the export of raw materials.[110] Stuart, Thorneycroft, Crookshank, Ismay and Woolton also backed the plan. Crookshank feared that without Robot, 'we will have all this all over again in a month or six weeks time in a worse situation'.[111] Woolton was more emphatic. It was time to abandon the fixed rate and move back to floating since, this was 'the old tried method which has operated for many decades . . . it had the great advantage of working well and made London the financial centre of the world'.[112] Ismay tried to play down the impact of the plan on the Sterling Area arguing that 'it was unlikely that it would cause any great political upheaval in the Commonwealth'.[113] In fact, the plan, in his view, would help restrain Australia's use of its sterling balances, 'for her drawing rights were not at present the subject of any agreement and her overseas expenditure constituted the greatest current threat to the stability of the Sterling Area'.[114] Swinton seems to have been undecided in the meeting leading Cherwell to conclude that he had 'completely ratted'.[115] Monckton, Simonds and Macmillan 'refused to give a view at such short notice', although by the next meeting Macmillan had concluded, 'the more I think of it the more I feel that, in essence, the plan may be right'.[116] This line-up left Leathers 'doubtful inclining against',

Cherwell strongly opposed and Salter, Maxwell Fyfe, Eden and Salisbury unconvinced at this stage that the situation demanded such radical action.[117] The Cabinet adjourned at midnight with the issue still open, although Cherwell now sensed that after Butler's 'rather pathetic' showing, things were going badly for the Robot camp.[118]

Shelving the plan

At 9.00 a.m. on 29 February, Cobbold met Bridges and Rowan for a final briefing before the 11.00 a.m. Cabinet. Bolton recorded that the Cabinet had adjourned 'completely divided', that Eden's opposition was serious and as a result for Robot, 'looks as though failure'.[119] The Cabinet reconvened to continue their deliberations, with Stuart and Leathers absent.[120] Macmillan records that a 'general discussion of an elucidatory and explanatory character took place'.[121] Butler, who 'seemed very tired and uncertain of himself',[122] together with Lyttelton, Woolton, Crookshank and Thorneycroft, argued strongly for Robot. Macmillan, in partial support, said that 'the whole thing turned on whether the sterling leak could be stopped in any other way'.[123] However, at this meeting, Eden, with support from Salisbury, came out strongly against Robot and it quickly became apparent that the Prime Minister too 'had turned against the plan'.[124]

It is clear from the public records and private diaries, that Eden's opposition killed the February version of Robot. In advance of the meeting Eden had prepared notes on the implications of the plan which pointed to its 'grave foreign and domestic dangers'.[125] In terms of foreign affairs, Eden judged that Robot would be a blow to reviving confidence in Europe and the Middle East and would attract widespread criticism causing major trade dislocation. It would almost certainly split Europe into two camps and be regarded as a selfish action cynically indifferent to others: 'this at a time when Lisbon has given new hope for better European co-operation'.[126] Many Commonwealth countries might decide to resign from the Sterling Area (Pakistan, Ceylon, India and possibly Australia) and perhaps even from the Commonwealth itself. Furthermore it was not in Britain's interest to antagonize the United States whose 'support, if not approval, is necessary'.[127] On the domestic front, Robot broke election pledges, would increase short-term unemployment and lead to accusations of bad faith producing bitterness and possibly strikes. If, Eden concluded, the plan were necessary that there was no good alternative, then none of these points would justify its rejection. But, as Ministers and experts differed so profoundly, it was clear that before taking the plunge the Cabinet should opt for the alternative of cutting defence and imports, restricting credit and investment, increasing the Bank Rate and regaining full control over Commonwealth drawings on the dollar pool. Like Plowden, Eden was not opposed to the floating rate in principle, but he argued it was necessary to make these adjustments first and when stability was reasonably assured the floating rate could be introduced 'to provide an automatic regulator'.[128]

The decisive nature of Eden's intervention in the second meeting is confirmed independently by Macmillan, Cherwell and Berthoud – the latter writing at length,

> there is no doubt whatever in my mind from the atmosphere in London before my departure and the course of events afterwards that had it not been for the firm refusal of the Secretary of State [Eden] to take the plunge into the unknown, the Robot scheme would have been introduced within a matter of days after my visit to Lisbon.[129]

Salisbury added further fuel to the fire describing the Bank plan as too sudden and unexplained a change of front and comparing it with the Hoare–Laval Pact in the sphere of diplomacy.[130] In the light of the strong opinion of the Foreign Secretary, Churchill concluded the second meeting by noting:

> So long as there was so large a division of opinion within the Cabinet on the merits of the plan, it would be hazardous for the Chancellor to proceed with it. At the present time there was not within the Cabinet a sufficient body of support for the plan to enable the Chancellor to launch it with confidence that he had behind him the conviction, as well as the loyalty, of his colleagues.[131]

The Cabinet agreed to conclude their discussion at a further meeting to be held at 3.00 p.m., at which the Chancellor would present an alternative Budget plan.

As Eden walked with Macmillan from No. 10, he explained to the Minister for Housing and Local Government that

> the country are not ready to cast away the whole effort of years to return to "Montagu Normanism" without a struggle. For the plan is really one to restore solvency by bankruptcy, large scale unemployment etc. How could a huge armament programme survive the semi-revolutionary situation which would follow?[132]

Macmillan also noted in his diary that Woolton had told him, after the second meeting, that Eden had threatened resignation on the issue and that this explained Churchill's sudden change of front and abandonment of Butler.[133] Whilst this is difficult to verify, it is certainly clear that Eden's opposition was enough to sway Churchill. Out of the public eye, however, Eden was far from sure that he had made the right decision. He recorded in his diary: 'I was much troubled about all this. Later Roger Makins arrived back from the Middle East and I was greatly relieved when he told me that I had been 100 per cent right'.[134]

The Cabinet reassembled at 3.00 p.m. on 29 February with Stuart still absent but Leathers and Viscount Alexander (the new Minister of Defence) now in attendance.[135] Butler outlined his alternative plan. This consisted of an increase in Bank Rate to 4 per cent, substantial cuts in defence production, further drastic cuts in imports, action to cut investment and an approach to Sterling Area countries emphasizing the gravity of the situation.[136] In contrast to the earlier meetings this was a 'long and rather desultory' affair, although Churchill, who had been rather restrained, was now 'in tremendous and boisterous form, cracking every sort of joke'.[137] The meeting closed at 5.00 p.m. by which time the Cabinet had agreed the following conclusions.[138] First, although Ministers reaffirmed their desire to dispense with physical controls as soon as practicable and move swiftly towards convertibility, they 'were not satisfied that the present moment was opportune for the introduction of a plan, on the lines originally proposed by the Chancellor, for making some part of our sterling reserves convertible at a variable rate of exchange'.[139] It was agreed, however, that some action on these lines might be taken at a later stage – either if the circumstances became more favourable or if the government was compelled by a continuous drain on the reserves of the Sterling Area, to take urgent action to protect the currency. Second, it was agreed that the Chancellor frame his Budget in accord with the 'alternative plan' outlined in the third meeting, focusing principally on a rise in Bank Rate and further cuts in imports to the tune of £200 million.

The attempted coup had failed. Distressed and angry, Butler called a meeting of officials and 'practically upbraided Salter and Plowden'.[140] He then called on Cobbold who by this time knew that Eden's intervention had been decisive.[141] Undeterred, Cobbold concluded that the Cabinet had only staved off the inevitable and that 'it looked as if opinion was veering towards early consideration after the Budget'.[142] In an official capacity he wrote to Butler on 3 March that the Bank, having expressed its view, could only take note of the Cabinet's decision. However, he felt duty bound to place on record the Bank's opinion that, given the level of reserves and pressures on the currency, any improvement resulting from the Budget 'should only be regarded as a breathing space for urgent consideration of comprehensive and constructive measures in the overseas sterling field'.[143] On the same day he penned a note to Churchill requesting permission to bring a deputation of three members of the Court of Directors to No. 10 (termed by Robert Hall, 'Cobbold's stooges'),[144] to 'lay before you the grave view which is taken, not only by the Court of Directors of the Bank, but also by industrial and commercial circles in the City, of the state of our exchange reserves and the consequent threat to the economic and social life of the country and

Commonwealth'.[145] Sir John Hanbury-Williams (Chairman of Courtaulds), Mr Basil Sanderson (Chairman of Shaw Saville and Albion Line) and Lord Piercy (Chairman of Industrial and Commercial Finance Corporation) thus met with Butler, Cobbold and Churchill on 6 March. Discussions lasted over an hour and according to Cobbold, 'the Prime Minister appeared to take the points'.[146]

Butler's own assessment of the situation was that his rather poor showing in the Cabinet meetings had played into the hands of his opponents: 'my memorandum lost in strength by stating the difficulties so frankly that they were exploited by the Prof to great advantage'.[147] It was also clear to other members of the Cabinet that whilst Butler had been encouraged to pursue the plan by Churchill, once the Prime Minister sided with Eden, Butler was vulnerable as he had left it too late to woo the majority of his colleagues.[148] This, thought Macmillan, must explain Butler's 'lack of fight' – 'he really is too agreeable; too pliant; and too ready to go from plan to plan, accepting perhaps too readily the rejection of each. If he believed in his "Grand Design", he should have fought harder for it'.[149]

In the weeks following the shelving of Robot, the recriminations continued. Edward Bridges accused Plowden of behaving badly and 'intriguing against the Chancellor'.[150] Norman Brook confided to Butler that Churchill and some of his colleagues in Cabinet did not really understand 'the difference between the measures necessary to deal with the short term position and those necessary to deal with the long term'.[151] Bolton considered resignation but was persuaded by Cobbold that Robot, in some form, still had a future.[152] However, despite the protestations of the Robot camp, it was clear that their disregard of normal Whitehall procedures had been a tactical gamble which had played into the hands of their opponents. Berthoud noted the reaction in the Foreign Office and elsewhere to the way in which the Treasury and the Bank had tried to bulldoze the plan through Whitehall without proper consultation with other Departments at formative phases. This, he claimed, 'showed signs of autocratic and ill-considered action and was contrary to all the traditions of Whitehall'.[153] Lack of consultation and discussion gave rise to the view that the Robot camp was 'hysterical' and 'panic-stricken'.[154] According to Macmillan, what shocked the Cabinet at the first meeting on 28 February was the recollection that the Commonwealth Finance Ministers had only left London a few weeks earlier and neither the Bank nor the Treasury seemed to have contemplated such drastic action then.[155]

Amongst Ministers, the reputation of the Bank was also damaged by the episode. Cherwell, Hall and Eden were quick to levy the charge of 'banker's ramp' and in turn allow themselves to be portrayed as 'gallant knights saving the country from the grasp of misguided conspirators'.[156] Nevertheless, the charges of 'hysteria', 'volatility', and 'recklessness' could not disguise the fundamental importance of the questions that had been raised in the

Cabinet meetings. The Robot camp had 'lost the day' and had failed to link floating rate convertibility to the March Budget.[157] However, the underlying crisis, of both the British and the international economy, remained unresolved and, as the next chapter details, it was not long before Robot walked again.

5
Robot Walks Again

It was widely rumoured that the Budget of 11 March would be as severe as those associated with Stafford Cripps in the early days of postwar austerity.[1] It had also been suggested, following the communiqué from the Commonwealth Conference in January, that the Budget might provide for a further devaluation of the pound or even the adoption of a floating rate.[2] However, in the wake of the Cabinet decision not to proceed with the Robot plan, the most pressing issue facing Butler was how deflationary should the Budget be to tackle the short-term dollar drain? Since radical action in the external field had now been sidelined, two issues in the domestic field dominated Budget committee meetings: how high should the Bank Rate be pushed and should cuts in food subsidies be accompanied by a new tax on coal?[3]

After consultation with Niemeyer and Bolton, Cobbold advised Butler to go for a Bank Rate of 4 per cent on the grounds that the exchange situation was so parlous that the government could not neglect any action that might remedy it.[4] According to Butler, this sharp rise was 'an unusual course which left the country, and the foreigner, in no doubt that I was prepared to make a thoroughgoing use of monetary as well as fiscal policy in controlling the economy'.[5] The action, predictably, was applauded by Robert Hall who suggested that 'it enables one to take a less severe look at what is needed elsewhere'.[6] In this he was supported by Bridges, who persuaded Butler that in the light of the Rate rise it was unnecessary to both reduce food subsidies and introduce a tax on coal.[7] Thus on 11 March, Butler announced a Bank Rate of 4 per cent; a cut in food subsidies to produce a saving of £160 million; an increase in petrol duty; GPO increases (letters and telephone rentals); changes in purchase tax to encourage exports and a proposal to impose an excess profits levy on public companies (beginning in earnest in 1953). Finally, on the external front, Butler announced further cuts in imports of around £100 million, bringing the total cut since November to £600 million.[8]

In general the Budget was well received both at home and from monetary authorities and markets abroad.[9] Labour leaders were unable to make much political capital out of the measures and Gaitskell's only riposte was that Butler seemed unsure whether his main objective was to guard against inflation or deflation. A Gallup Poll taken on 12 March showed that 62 per cent of those polled thought the Budget was fair, including 42 per cent of Labour Party supporters.[10] More significantly, the Budget seemed to have succeeded in slowing the rate of loss of reserves. Butler's assessment was that it may have helped stem the outward flow of short-term capital as much by what it did not do as by what it did.[11] The pound, which had been at $2.78 since early January, rose to almost $2.81 on 14 March.[12] But it was far from clear that the immediate emergency was over. The Robot camp was still guided by Cobbold's assessment that any improvement resulting from the Budget should only be regarded as a breathing space for urgent consideration of radical measures in the overseas sterling field. Overseas liabilities were still too large, the burden on the productive economy too heavy and the position of sterling still precarious. This was also the view taken by US State Department officials who observed that the Budget was 'not sufficiently deflationary for a fiscal-monetary solution to the resource allocation problem facing Britain'.[13] Balance of payments forecasts suggested that the scale of the loss of reserves could once again increase and, as Cobbold noted in discussions with Butler, the authorities were still very much at the mercy of an ill wind, such that 'we might find ourselves rushed into unfavourable decisions with little warning'.[14] This assessment provided the backdrop for continued work on the Robot plan by the Bank and Overseas Finance. Throughout the spring and early summer, Clarke, Cobbold, Bolton and Rowan sought to modify Robot I to make the new plan, at least in principle, acceptable to the Foreign Office and the Board of Trade. Fully aware that they would never convince Cherwell (or even Hall) of the merits of the plan, the Robot camp now tried to marginalize the Paymaster General and the Economic Section. In this regard they were helped significantly by the emergence of various 'two-world' plans emanating from the Economic Section which received little or no support from officials or ministers. This chapter begins by outlining the plans developed by the Economic Section, before analysing the 'new look' Robot constructed by the Bank and Overseas Finance in the run-up to the decisive meeting of Ministers on 30 June, called to discuss, once again, whether the Robot plan should be adopted.

I Sterling Union: paving the way for Robot II

Prompted by MacDougall and Plowden, in early March Robert Hall instructed the Economic Section to prepare more material against the External Sterling Plan. Clearly alarmed by rumours that 'the Prime Minister had been much impressed by the deputation of Cobbold's stooges which he had brought along after the Cabinet turned the plan down for the first time',[15] Hall was now convinced that the best alternative to Robot was to take the initiative in the formation of a new and much broader non-dollar payments union with fixed exchange rates.[16] This would halt the drain on the reserves, resulting from the dollar deficits of the Sterling Area, by rendering sterling completely inconvertible. Henceforth Sterling Area countries would have to meet their dollar requirements out of their own gold and dollar earnings and reserves. The most cogent of these 'two-world' solutions was the 'Sterling Union' plan put forward initially by Robert Neild drawing on the earlier Watts Plan.[17]

The centrepiece of Neild's new system would be an international Sterling Union, 'which would enable trade, production and employment in the non-dollar world to be maintained at as high a level as possible irrespective of the world dollar shortage'.[18] The Union would offer the attraction of relatively free trade at fixed rates of exchange over, it was hoped, a large area of world trade. Since Union countries would give preference to each other's goods (over dollar area goods) production within the Union would be stimulated and in time this would help eliminate the chronic dollar shortage.

MacDougall reacted with horror to the plans of the Section and, according to Hall, thought they were 'almost worse than those of the Bank'.[19] However, Hall was not to be deterred and, working closely with Downie, Neild, Hemming, Watts and Butt, he refined these initial thoughts to produce his ultimate two-world manifesto, 'The Future of Sterling' on 25 March 1952.[20] Framed in opposition to Robot, the document advocated greater insulation from dollar areas and the reform of the Sterling Area and the European Payments Union. Automatic gold payments from the mutual trade of non-dollar countries should cease. Fixed exchange rates would be preserved, but in Hall's vision there would be no automatic convertibility of Sterling Area or transferable account area sterling into dollars. The dollar-pooling mechanism of the Sterling Area would be abandoned, the reserves divided up and each Sterling Area country left to balance its own dollar trade bilaterally. Existing sterling balances would be left unblocked and free intra-Sterling Area trade encouraged. In respect of the European Payments Union, the government would insist on amendments to reduce and hopefully eliminate automatic gold payments, increase credit margins and revise the rules about non-discrimination to allow greater trade between debtors (such as France and the UK). Eventually, thought the Section, the Payments Union could be absorbed into a larger trading bloc focused around a reformed Sterling Area – 'a Sterling Union in which each member is responsible for balancing his accounts with the dollar area'.[21]

Predictably, Hall's scheme based on the effective insulation of sterling from the dollar was roundly criticized for its impact on the competitiveness of British industry and the City, and its effect on US policy and the Sterling Area. MacDougall redoubled his criticism and tried to persuade Hall to restrict the circulation of the paper, whilst Plowden judged that the naïvety of the scheme 'might actually play into the hands of our opponents'.[22] In the Bank, the Economic Section's work was derided as the construction of 'visionary worlds'. It ignored the need, in the non-dollar world as a whole, for further deflation and the expansion of exports to dollar markets.[23] Butler was unimpressed and Bridges pointed to the 'considerable' political difficulties of the plan.[24] However, it was left to Otto Clarke to completely demolish Hall's paper and in so doing convince Ministers and officials of the necessity of a 'one-world' solution (whether gradualist or 'plunger' in the form of Robot).[25]

The limits of a 'two-world' solution

Through a careful analysis of the composition and distribution of US exports, Clarke began his response to Hall by asking how sense could be made of the trade figures for the fourth quarter of 1951 when US imports totalled $9.8 billion whilst exports had again risen to above $15 billion.[26] In 1947, when the notion of a 'world dollar shortage' was introduced, US imports were $5.7 billion and exports $15.3 billion. It was widely thought at the time that exports were greatly inflated by the need for 'abnormal' reconstruction goods abundant only in the US – coal, grain and equipment – and that as production elsewhere was restored the demand for US goods would fall. This indeed was the case, to some extent, and Clarke even conceded that the US authorities had done what they could to help curb inflation and reduce demand for raw materials. Nonetheless it was a fact that US exports had increased from $10 billion at the end of 1950 to $15.1 billion at the close of 1951. This movement moreover could not represent an increase in the world's *need* for US exports since all countries were producing more than two years ago. The inescapable conclusion reached by Clarke was that the main reason for the great expansion of US exports was the superior competitive power of the US and the 'failure of other countries' competitive power'.[27] A review of the composition of US and UK exports indicated that the export of specialized machinery available only in the US could not account for more than a small proportion of the increase. Hence, the bulk must consist of products in which Britain could be fully competitive, 'if we had enough production of the right kind'.[28] Here Clarke reflected the concerns of the 'Rootes Report' and other studies into the low levels of productivity found in British industry and the poor export penetration of British goods in dollar markets.[29] Bilateral trading and tariff preferences simply exacerbated the competitiveness problem. Whereas US exports of finished manufactures had risen by 25 per cent between 1950 and 1951, British manufactured exports increased over the same period by only 3 per cent. In contrast, wages and prices in Britain rose by 10–15 per cent in 1951 compared with a mere 5 per cent rise in the US. In summary, Clarke argued the dollar shortage was a clear result of the inadequacy of British (and other non-dollar) competitive power. Only by strengthening competitive power could Britain hope to increase prosperity and correct balance of payments problems. Costs must fall, the range and quality of goods increase and, in the short term, Britain must suffer a fall in its standard of living. This 'economic reality' could not, he argued, be sidestepped by 'two-world' devices designed to isolate the US from the non-dollar world. Without the productive power to supply goods and the competitive power to sell them, Britain had no counter attractions to offer. If, Clarke suggested, 'we were strong enough to build up a two-world system, we should be strong enough to live quite happily in a one-world system'.[30] In short, the main task facing the government was to find an external economic policy which would set up pressures to move the economy onto a sounder, more competitive footing and abandon policies which would conflict with that objective. In Hall's 'two-world' solution, the dollar problem would be exacerbated and 'we shall gradually find ourselves isolated and unable to conduct an effective international trade policy to maintain our standard of living and our status as a Great Power'.[31]

Clarke's tour de force was well received in Treasury and Bank circles. Although Hall tried to dismiss Otto's paper – 'it was a very dishonest reply as might be expected from both the author and the occasion'[32] – he was later forced to admit that the two-world plan was a mistake and 'not very acceptable to anyone'.[33] MacDougall and Plowden had been proved right. Hall's fanciful scheme had played into the hands of the Robot camp. Clarke and Cobbold could now, with some justification, dismiss the Economic Section as 'two-worlders', and concentrate on revising those aspects of Robot that had provoked most opposition from Eden. Overseas Finance and the Bank identified three such areas. First, Robot II should place greater emphasis on the stability of the operation, hence the 15 per cent spread on either side of the parity should be reconsidered. Second, attention should be given to softening the impact of the plan on the Commonwealth. Finally, it was judged that the single most important task would be to give detailed thought to how the plan could be made more compatible with existing intra-European trade and payments arrangements.

II Towards the 'new look' Robot

In the Bank, Thompson-McCausland, Bolton and Cobbold spent the first weeks of March working to produce a new more positive framework for Robot.[34] Perturbed by Butler's lacklustre performance in the February Cabinet meetings, Thompson-McCausland stressed that 'there must be none of the deplorable apologetics which appeared in the first Treasury drafts, presenting the proposals as a regrettable necessity unwillingly accepted by us in the face of crippling adversity'.[35] Cobbold was sure that the first version of the plan had placed too much emphasis on floating and that in its next presentation, 'we must have a high degree of stability'.[36] This opinion was also now shared by Clarke who noted that 'stability is very important – provided that one doesn't try to hold a rate which is obviously too high'.[37] The considered response of the Bank, accepted by Overseas Finance, was to amend Robot I so that the new plan would involve a commitment to widening existing spreads on the dollar to 10 per cent (rather than the original 15 per cent) on either side of parity.[38] The Exchange Equalisation Account would accordingly be used to smooth out fluctuations and maintain the rate within the range $2.50 to $3.10. However, although the Equalisation Account would operate to maintain as much stability as possible, neither the Bank nor Overseas Finance wished to see reserves seriously diminished to fight for a rate under heavy pressure. The reserves would thus be used primarily to provide support at the beginning of the operation after which time the rate would have to find its own level. As the Bank summarized, 'it must surely be accepted that our intervention must largely be confined to ironing out fluctuations rather than determining the level'.[39]

In an attempt to minimize Ministers' fears over the issue of floating, Robot II would now be presented as emphasizing stability on rate policy. In private, however, Clarke envisaged sterling depreciating sharply. His assessment was that initially, 'we shan't get a decent equilibrium much above $1.50–1.75, although I can readily envisage our building up quite a long way from that'.[40] The sterling–dollar rate would be determined above all by the world dollar shortage (that is, by the US balance of payments). Until British industry became more competitive – the only lasting solution to the dollar problem – the process of balancing the dollar area with the rest of the world could only be accomplished with a major change in the world price structure. It is 'obviously uneconomic', Clarke maintained, to do lots of things at $2.80, which at $2.00 would be highly profitable and which would contribute to a solution.[41] In short, the dimensions of the structural adjustment needed had been completely concealed by US aid which had enabled exchange rates to be kept far above the levels required to create equilibrium. Robot would result in a substantial fall of the pound over an initial two- or three-year period. Following this depreciation however Clarke believed that, 'we should gradually build the rate up again as fundamental forces making for a recovery in our economic strength reasserted themselves. Indeed if conditions in the US tended to be inflationary over a long period, and provided always that we kept our internal house in order, we might find the rate becoming very strong indeed'.[42]

Rethinking the problem of the Commonwealth sterling balances

The second aspect of the New Look considered by the Bank and Overseas Finance in early March focused on the treatment of the Sterling Area under Robot I. In retrospect, Clarke now concluded that Robot I was 'entirely unsatisfactory in its treatment of the Sterling Area because it tried at one and the same time to destroy the Sterling Area and to keep it in being'.[43] The Bank, during pre-Budget discussions, had also expressed reservations about the feasibility of outright and uniform blocking of official sterling balances held by members of the Sterling Area.[44] Bolton and Cobbold now turned their attention to revising the blocking and funding of Sterling Area balances and suggested that it would perhaps suffice if each country made a declaration identifying a 'hard core of balances that would not be drawn down except after prior consultation with London'.[45] This would render some £800 million of balances harmless for purposes of foreign opinion. By mid-June, the Bank and Overseas Finance had concluded that there could be 'no question of further drastic measures of funding or blocking Sterling Area balances. Politically this is impossible to contemplate'.[46] One question, however, remained unanswered: how to convince foreign opinion that Britain's true sight liabilities were £1,000 million or less out of the total balances standing at £3,430 million in May 1952? The Bank considered two options. First, adopt the formula used by the IMF to decide whether countries were justified in asking to repurchase borrowings from the Fund. Second, adopt a new scheme whereby Commonwealth countries would endorse an 'agreed analysis' of balances and thereby reduce sight liabilities to an absolute minimum with no funding or blocking required. Following this second route the Chancellor would be able to announce on D-Day that, after discussion with the balance-holding countries and with their concurrence, the government 'intends to publish forthwith an analysis of the various categories of balance which will show that of the gross total of Sterling Area balance only £X million can be regarded as representing sterling immediately available for expenditure'.[47] On 27 June, Overseas Finance agreed that this solution was far superior to the immobilization measures of Robot I, and accordingly Butler was able to state in his key paper, 'External Financial Policy' delivered on 28 June, that 'the main difference between this and the former plan is that the present one contains no provision for the formal funding of the sterling balances of Sterling Area countries, since this does not now seem to be necessary'.[48] This amendment, it was generally acknowledged, would be very helpful to Commonwealth countries and create much less friction than the blocking measures of Robot I. The Bank and Overseas Finance were confident that the Sterling Area would co-operate with Britain in producing an agreed assessment of the extent to which the balances represented a 'sight liability' upon the UK economy. This would help convince overseas monetary authorities that the exchange value of sterling would not be subject to constant depreciation under the weight of an excess of sterling since the statement would show that the effective liability of the UK was only a small proportion of what was generally believed. The sterling release agreements with India, Pakistan and Ceylon would remain unchanged under the new proposal.

Bolton and Cobbold seemed to have overcome one of the major stumbling blocks to the implementation of Robot. Declaratory identification of minimum balances, as Fforde emphasizes, at a time when total balances had already been heavily run down towards minimum working levels, should not have been difficult to achieve and would certainly have been helpful internationally.[49] Cobbold continued to lay the basis for the success of this aspect of the plan in secret discussions with a number of high-ranking Commonwealth Ministers and officials, including the Australian Prime Minister, Robert Menzies, the Governor of the New Zealand Reserve Bank, Mr Fussell, and Mr Coyne and Mr Towers of the Bank of Canada. All seemed to suggest that they would welcome Robot II. After his meeting with Coyne on 29 May, Cobbold recorded, 'I feel certain that Mr Towers (Governor of the Bank of Canada) and Mr Coyne would welcome any step in the direction of which we are thinking.'[50] The response from the Australian Prime Minister was even more enthusiastic:

> Mr Menzies was clearly in favour of a step on these lines and would probably favour it sooner rather than later. It fits in with his general conception that the Commonwealth should take positive steps along a definite road and put themselves in a position to negotiate jointly with the USA on a constructive basis.[51]

Heartened by Menzies' support for Robot, Cobbold now approached the Governor of the Reserve Bank of New Zealand. Fussell thought the ideas 'sensible and constructive' and saw 'no difficulty about a statement that New Zealand regarded the bulk of her sterling balances as a minimum reserve'.[52] Cobbold was left in no doubt that Australia, New Zealand and Canada would follow Britain's exchange rate policy and Bolton enthusiastically recorded 'sudden action now possible'.[53]

By early June it seemed that the Bank and Overseas Finance had addressed, and largely rectified, two of the main weaknesses of Robot I concerning the stability of the rate and the immobilization of Commonwealth sterling balances. They now turned to focus on the issue that had proved to be the major stumbling block in the February Cabinet meetings – intra-European trade and payments and, in particular, the impact of Robot on the European Payments Union.

Robot II and European trade and payments

It was now widely recognized and accepted in the Robot camp that the 'most serious difficulty' of the original plan had been its impact on Europe and the apparent incompatibility of floating rate convertibility and the continuation of the European Payments Union.[54] As early as 11 March, Clarke had begun to distance himself from Bolton's proposals to incorporate most of Western Europe in an enlarged Sterling Area bloc, and cautioned,

> it may well be the most important thing, however, not to find new formulas at the outset for intra-European trade and payments, which are

bound to go through a period of flux, but to seek to devise means by which the genuine co-operation which has been possible, particularly on the financial side, can continue.[55]

This was good advice in light of the hostility of the Foreign Office to Robot I and given that in mid-March Butler was scheduled to confirm UK support for an extension of the European Payments Union for a further year from 30 June.[56] Clarke's revised approach, that 'we must find a new basis for co-operation with Europe',[57] meshed with work in the Bank conducted by Roy Bridge who, since late February, had been looking at schemes for Britain's withdrawal from the European Payments Union.[58] As noted earlier, in an effort to avoid a straight repudiation of Britain's obligations towards the European Payments Union (EPU), Bridge had suggested a strategy whereby the UK would defer introducing automatic convertibility for EPU countries until a specified later date. This, he suggested, would be a meaningful gesture of co-operation towards European countries and 'would give a respite during which they could make up their own minds on the possibility of continuing EPU in any form (very doubtful)'.[59] Bridge, and other Bank officials, continued their work throughout March and towards the end of the month devised a new strategy, accepted by the Treasury in April, in which Robot II would be applied in full from D-Day, but which also enabled the UK to continue in the European Payments Union providing interim finance for a period of two to three weeks.[60] In its new guise the scheme allowed for the UK to withdraw from the monthly settlements mechanism and add all or part of its accumulated EPU debt to the working capital of the Union. As Fforde makes clear, sterling would, at least in part, be made acceptable as a means of discharging 'gold' payments to the EPU by the remaining members at the monthly settlements.[61] The contribution which this would offer to the Union, would, according to Bridge, be of great value to Europe since 'it would provide a means for the granting of temporary sterling finance to EPU countries under joint European supervision'.[62] The Bank had thus seemingly squared the EPU circle, enabling Robot to be implemented whilst maintaining meaningful contact with the Union as an associate member. Of course, if other important members (such as France or Belgium) were to join Britain in introducing a floating rate system, then, as Bolton concluded, it was 'improbable that EPU could be continued in its present form'.[63] If this occurred the best that could be envisaged was that settlements between France, Belgium and Britain could be made in gold, from time to time, and that the countries could agree to hold modest amounts of each other's currencies.[64]

By the end of June, the Bank and Overseas Finance had agreed a scheme that would provide a transition between EPU settlements and the new system, should Britain act in isolation. The government would offer 30-day swaps against local currency (renewable for a further thirty days) to coun-

tries in difficulties, to be repaid through the EPU. In addition, and depending on which countries floated with Britain, the government would consult
with the OEEC regarding continued membership in the Union.[65] Butler and
Cobbold may have accepted these transitional arrangements in principle
(and for presentational purposes in Cabinet), but it is clear that in private
they believed the arrangements would not be required. The EPU would collapse, not simply as a result of unilateral British action, but because

> it is very likely that France and Belgium at any rate, and perhaps others,
> would follow any lead given by us. There may be indeed a possibility of
> concerted action over quite a wide field in Europe, and if the plan were
> adopted by us, it would be possible to have prior consultation with the
> French, Belgians and Scandinavians in time to permit them to concert
> with us.[66]

Combined action with a number of key European countries would in addition greatly reduce the problem of trade discrimination against Britain. In
arriving at this assessment Butler and Cobbold, as noted in Chapter 3, had
been strongly influenced by reports from Paris on the attitude of the Pinay
government and the Banque de France as revealed in particular in discussions with its Governor, William Baumgartner.[67]

III Anglo-French collaboration

In the week before the March Budget, Cobbold had written privately, and
somewhat indiscreetly, to Baumgartner indicating the likelihood of the
interest rate move to 4 per cent and noting 'it looks to me as if we are going
to have to do a lot of thinking about European payments arrangements (and
other things!) in the next month or two, and I am becoming very doubtful
whether the present EPU structure will hold for long'.[68] Acting independently of the Chancellor, Cobbold suggested that in order to discuss recent
developments 'we had better perhaps meet somewhere not at our respective
banks'.[69] A week later Baumgartner visited Cobbold at Knebworth during
which time, Cobbold records, 'I had a long talk with him about the French
situation and also gave him a hint in very general terms that we were thinking about exchange questions here'.[70]

In many respects the French economic crisis was deeper than that in
Britain. The new Pinay government faced a budget deficit of £765 million
for 1952; a payments crisis reflected in the exhaustion of foreign currency
reserves; a deficit with the EPU of £420 million; a steady decline in exports
and a constant flight of capital.[71] In response the French authorities had
tightened monetary policy (the Bank Rate was raised in October and November 1951), cut imports from dollar areas by 40 per cent and suspended
liberalization measures, thereby submitting to quotas all goods from OEEC

countries except for raw materials and food. However, by early March it was clear that without further action the French quota in the EPU would soon be exhausted.[72] Consequently on 14 March, the OEEC Council approved an emergency loan of 100 million units of account from the EPU to France, effectively relieving the government of an obligation to pay $60 million in gold to the EPU (which it was rumoured the French Equalisation Fund would have been unable to meet).[73] This measure coincided with a slight improvement in the position of France's gold and foreign currency reserves in April and May, but it was clear to monetary authorities that any adverse movement would bring on a new crisis.

Given the precarious position of both economies, Cobbold widened his discussions with Baumgartner and arranged for Butler and Rowan to meet with Pinay and Guillaime Guindey (Official Head of the French Finance Ministry). On 6 June the British group flew to Paris to discuss collaboration on external financial policy.[74] Butler was intrigued to hear that the French authorities had concluded that the only way out of the current crisis was to make some change in external financial policy, and that they were actively considering the adoption of a fluctuating rate of exchange.[75] At a subsequent meeting between Guindey and Rowan it was further clarified that although the French Treasury had not given a great deal of thought to the issue of convertibility (of current earnings for non-residents), they did not think this would involve much risk to the French position. Moreover the French team suggested that whenever either side had made a definite decision to change policy it would be fruitful to have talks, 'perhaps three weeks before action was taken'.[76]

Butler, Cobbold and Rowan were particularly heartened by the French view of the impact of Robot on Europe. In general, Baumgartner thought that the major European countries would 'welcome a change to a fluctuating rate'.[77] Belgium and Italy would respond positively, but if Germany remained fixed this would of course create difficulties for the EPU. However, if the EPU was thought a political necessity, it might be rescued if all members jointly floated against the dollar while retaining fixed rates between each other.[78] As regards the impact of Robot on wider European schemes, the British group's fears were somewhat unfounded as the French, 'did not even mention the Schuman Plan or E.D.C. in this connection'.[79]

On his return to London, Butler called for a series of meetings with Overseas Finance, the Foreign Office and the Board of Trade to discuss the merits of further collaboration with the French.[80] By mid-June, the Bank and Overseas Finance were of the view that 'it was much more likely than six months ago that other European countries, for example, France, Belgium and even West Germany, would become convertible on a floating rate, in some cases perhaps regardless of whether or not the UK were to set an example'.[81] The French had even indicated that they thought a move in late July would be most advantageous. This assessment of the situation in Europe had an important bearing on the method by which Robot II was to be launched. Britain would no longer be acting alone and would not be held solely responsible for creating chaos in Europe. If several other countries were ready to adopt a similar plan then the situation would demand that there be consultation with at least France, Belgium and West Germany, 'as long as possible beforehand with a view to the launching of a multilateral, cooperative plan'.[82] On the basis that France, Belgium, Switzerland, Denmark, Sweden and possibly Germany would welcome convertibility (even on a floating rate), the Bank set about devising a 'swing' arrangement for the stability of intra-European rates.[83]

The position on Europe had now been clarified sufficiently for Bolton to circulate a new timetable for the implementation of Robot II.[84] The effective date of the operation would be Monday 21 July 1952. This was based on the assumption that a Cabinet decision would be obtained on Thursday 3 July and that the Chancellor would make a broadcast outlining the operation on Saturday 19 July.[85] France and Belgium would be informed of the plan on 10 July (four days before the US administration) and West Germany, Holland and the Uniscan countries on 15 July. As Bolton circulated the timetable, Cobbold arranged for a final meeting with Baumgartner and made plans for himself and Butler to dine with Ivar Rooth (Managing Director of the IMF) before the end of the month.[86] Baumgartner now pledged Cobbold his full support. The Bank of France had advised Pinay that he should take action before the end of July. However, whilst it was uncertain whether the French government would move by themselves, Cobbold was now sure that 'they would certainly move with us if we did something'.[87] Fearing a new crisis in late summer, Baumgartner now conveyed to Cobbold that he was 'most anxious to make a move while the Government have the initiative and not wait until they are forced into precipitate action'.[88] He also confirmed that he favoured a move sometime between 20 and 27 July and that he would be quite prepared to introduce convertibility to allow overseas holders of francs to buy any currency in Paris (that is, the same treatment as proposed by Butler for overseas sterling). Furthermore, for an initial period of two months after the introduction of Robot he suggested managing a steady cross-rate and stable rates between sterling and the franc without disclosing any formal link. Baumgartner's parting shot was to ask Cobbold to inform Ivar Rooth of the proposals. This occurred on 1 July and Rooth's personal and preliminary opinion, as relayed by Cobbold, was that 'if we could make a good story about general financial measures, there should be reasonable prospect of substantial IMF support, both morally and materially'.[89] Somewhat to Cobbold's surprise, Rooth seemed less worried that he had anticipated about the introduction of a floating rate. If Britain was prepared to take drawing rights in a number of currencies, rather than dollars only, and if other Sterling Area countries made similar arrangements at the same time, then there was a good chance that IMF facilities could be made available for a comparatively short period of time (one year renewable for a further twelve months). Provided the US was not asked for new money and Britain did not exercise the waiver in respect of loan payments to the US and Canada, Rooth thought that overall the proposal would most likely be seen as 'a major measure consistent with the objectives of the IMF'.[90]

Cobbold's note on these discussions arrived too late for it to be fed by Butler into Cabinet Ministers' deliberations on Robot II. The new timetable called for a Cabinet decision by Thursday 3 July. In preparation for the decisive informal meeting of Ministers on 30 June, Butler circulated on Friday 27 June, 'in most secret fashion',[91] the memorandum, 'External Financial Policy' outlining the case for the new plan.[92]

IV The fate of Robot ii

Prefaced with a message from Cobbold indicating the parlous position of sterling, Butler's memorandum restated the case for the 'new look' Robot which would now comprise the following five elements. First, 'external sterling' (sterling earned by countries outside the Sterling Area) would become convertible into any foreign exchange or gold through the London market. Second, the fixed rate of exchange with the dollar ($2.80) would be abandoned. No attempt would be made to maintain the existing margin of $2.78–$2.82. Instead, the objective of the operation would be to allow sterling to find its own market level. However, the Exchange Equalisation Account would be used to intervene constructively to keep the rate between $2.50 and $3.10. This intention would not, of course, be made public. The effect of this change in policy would be that the gold reserves would cease to take the full strain of the deficit on the Sterling Area's balance of payments. In theory, the strain would be taken instead by the exchange rate unless the reserves were used to maintain the rate. Third, the London gold market would be reopened and gold would be traded against external sterling, dollars and other currencies at prices fluctuating according to supply and demand (and not in any way tied to the official US price for gold). Newly mined gold from the Commonwealth could be sold in the market but Sterling Area residents, including governments and monetary authorities, would not be permitted to purchase gold in the market. Fourth, sterling balances of non-Sterling Area residents (except American and Canadian accounts) would, at zero hour, be renamed 'Old Sterling Accounts' and would be frozen to prevent any appreciable offerings of such balances on the London market in exchange for dollars. However, a small proportion, to be negotiated, could be transferred to external sterling; some pre-zero commitments could be met from the balances; foreign commercial and central banks could transfer agreed sums to an external sterling account as working balances; and the remainder of the balances could be invested in quoted securities with a life exceeding ten years (such securities being then blocked as at present). Fifth, the present structure and operation of the Sterling Area would be maintained and, of course, Sterling Area balances would not be blocked but, by negotiation and release, the sight liabilities of the UK would be drastically reduced.[93]

If Ministers now decided to adopt Robot, Butler would also attempt to secure a line of credit (in the region of $600 million) from the IMF to be announced, if possible, concurrently with the plan. Finally, in order to reduce the load on the domestic economy the plan would be accompanied by 'definite and effective reductions' in the Defence Programme; reductions in imports and revisions in the investment programme putting greater emphasis on productive industry and less on social investment including housing. The Bank Rate would remain unchanged.

Butler's relatively brief memo stressed once again that the purpose of Robot II was not primarily to right the UK's balance of payments problems. Rather, it was to act as a stimulus to increase competitive power and exports and in this sense it sought to 'change our external financial system in a way which would enable us to continue without these crises'.[94] In summarizing the efficacy of the plan, the Chancellor concluded,

> Despite all its dangers, one great advantage of the plan is that it has strong constructive possibilities and offers hope of fruitful collaboration with our partners in the Commonwealth and in Western Europe on lines which can lead, with American co-operation, to making sterling an effective currency.[95]

The memorandum was sent to Churchill, Woolton, Cherwell, Lyttleton, Thorneycroft, Lord Salisbury, Macmillan and of course Edward Bridges and Norman Brook.[96] It was scheduled to be discussed by this informal group of Ministers (plus Crookshank) at a meeting arranged for 10.00 p.m. in the Prime Minister's room at the House of Commons on 30 June, prior to consideration by the full Cabinet later in the week. Cherwell and MacDougall, somewhat predictably, produced a 'counterblast' over the weekend which was circulated on the morning of 30 June.[97] Those opposed to the plan rehearsed three, now-familiar, arguments. First, Cherwell stressed that despite recurrent doom-laden forecasts from the Bank predicting the exhaustion of reserves (in February, April and June), the economic situation had not worsened appreciably. In fact, with intensified efforts further improvement was possible without incurring the dangers of Robot. Second, it was still not clear whether Robot would correct or worsen Britain's overall economic position. Cherwell repeated his earlier view that a move to a floating rate would not necessarily increase exports because 'our exports are not limited by price. Metal goods are limited by lack of steel; soft goods by the world slump in demand for textiles'.[98] Thus it was likely that the trade gap would actually widen and increase the drain on the reserves – 'this is the overriding objection to letting the pound slide while our position is weak'.[99]

In addition, although a falling rate would increase the cost of imports, against this would have to be set the 'certain disadvantage' that any rise in prices would lead to a demand for increased wages. This would be much harder to parry, Cherwell suggested, when the rise could not be blamed on external causes but 'is attributed, not without reason, to a Conservative surrender to the "banker's ramp"'.[100] The thought that the plan would increase inflationary pressure in the economy had also been raised by Lionel Robbins who was shown Butler's memorandum by Bridges and Rowan on 30 June.[101] Robbins still distrusted the floating rate (until the pound was stronger) and was disturbed at the effect on overseas confidence of the move to block newly earned sterling. However, the chief danger to the economy lay, he argued, in the threat of further wage inflation. Although an international comparison of price levels did not suggest that the UK's present rate of exchange was inappropriate, Robbins feared that 'another round or two of wage increases might change this position and knock us off our perch completely'.[102] Sceptical that wage inflation could be prevented by a return to mass unemployment, he stressed that at this juncture any upward movement in prices would render much greater the dangers of wage inflation. Thus, in present circumstances, 'any fall in the exchange ipso facto, creates a new inflationary danger'.[103] To this, Robbins added his now-familiar objection that Robot endangered Britain's reputation as a custodian of other people's money. The plan was fundamentally dishonourable: 'Ever since I was first shown the original papers, the thing that keeps me awake in the middle of the night if it comes into my head, is the conviction that what is proposed, although proposed by men of the highest integrity and with the best possible intentions, is not in fact strictly honourable'.[104]

To these objections, Cherwell added his final 'economic' difficulty with the plan, 'the fact that convertibility will be a tremendous incentive to people outside the United Kingdom to send us imports and refuse our exports'.[105] Every pound earned overseas would, he suggested, be converted to gold, 'this terrible handicap to our exports is probably the strongest long term economic argument against the Bank's plan'.[106] In short, Robot II would end in disaster whereas an extension of the current measures to redress the trade balance, by selling more abroad and buying less, would probably see the government through the autumn without collapse. Cherwell ended his memo in typically emotive fashion: 'The Bank has been wrong before. It may be now'.[107]

Predictably, Arthur Salter and Edwin Plowden joined forces with the 'doubters' to argue against the plan. Salter emphasized what he saw as the harmful consequences for the Conservative Party if unemployment reached 6 or 7 per cent. If substantial unemployment followed Robot,

> the political chances of a Government falling would seem to be considerable; and a General Election on such an issue would probably bring in a Government which would, a/ be determined, as they would put it, to

end the tyranny of the Bankers and the City and b/ be committed to causes which would render the restoration of the country to anything like what it has been impossible.[108]

Plowden reiterated his preference for 'holding the current situation' through a combination of further defence and housing cuts, deeper import cuts, opting for use of the waiver on US loan interest repayments and increasing the Bank Rate to 5 per cent.[109] This was preferable to the government taking a 'leap in the dark' along the lines proposed by Butler. The simple issue to decide, both Salter and Plowden agreed, was whether further deflationary measures should be taken first, ahead of a decision on Robot, or whether the measures and Robot should be introduced simultaneously. Posed in this manner it seemed likely that the majority of Cabinet Ministers would reaffirm the status quo.

This outcome had indeed been anticipated by Clarke and Rowan, who since March had sought to convince Ministers that the strongest case for Robot was the initiative it gave the government in the external field – 'a new deal in external affairs'.[110] It was recognized that the Budget and the positive response of the Commonwealth to calls for renewed economies had made it more difficult to convince doubters of the merits of Robot. Privately Rowan agreed with Cherwell's analysis that it was possible to 'scrape through' another year without a major disaster, but, he added, 'this is not the whole argument'.[111] Without Robot II, Britain might conceivably see out 1952 but would spend the next few years without a long-term policy, with little hope of avoiding open crisis in the wake of adverse events and with no real chance of reaching convertibility in the short term. Robot II would allow the government to seize the initiative rather than be forced to adopt a similar policy at a time when it could not be presented as a logical continuation of existing strategy and hence would be seen as a 'confession of the failure' of policy.[112] The external sterling plan was the one policy that would confront what Edward Peacock had termed 'the creeping paralysis' which threatened to undermine the British economy.[113] Balance of payments problems were a symptom of a deeper malaise which required a radical change in the external financial system to enable Britain to continue without recurrent crisis. Robot held out an opportunity for the government to break free from the domestic and external constraints which its supporters thought sapped the competitive strength of the economy.

On 30 June, the select group of Ministers met to consider the memos from Butler and Cherwell.[114] Macmillan records that 'it was a terribly hot night and very oppressive. The Prof had a hand-fan, which we felt must be running on atomic energy.'[115] Butler opened the discussion with a 'grave statement' and, according to Macmillan, 'showed an unusual emotion' which indicated that 'he had clearly been under a very great strain'.[116] There was a sharp exchange between Butler and Salisbury, who objected to the Chancellor's continual reference to wishes of the Bank of England. Churchill, anxious for unanimity and apparently unwilling to impose a view, asked everyone in turn for an opinion. Lyttleton supported Butler. However, once again, 'the general view was sceptical of the possibility of success and almost universal against the timing'.[117] Eden, apparently, had sent a message from his sick bed that the 'Opposition must not have this "gift"', and Cherwell had threatened resignation if the plan went ahead.[118] Soon after midnight the meeting broke up with Butler still pressing for a decision to be taken by the full Cabinet on Thursday 3 July. However, Churchill made it clear that he doubted whether the scheme should go forward at all, and early on 2 July, Brook announced that Butler had withdrawn Robot II and the scheme would not now be placed before the full Cabinet.[119]

In the Bank, Cobbold and Bolton felt both dejected and humiliated.[120] Bolton, upset that certain Ministers had complained that his actions suggested disloyalty, offered his resignation to Cobbold. He explained to the Governor that as a Bank official he had 'no loyalty to politicians', and in any case, his 'passionate advocacy' of the plan was 'known all over Whitehall'.[121] Cobbold acknowledged that there was 'much bad blood about Robot', but refused to accept Bolton's resignation. In this, the Governor was supported by Otto Niemeyer, who sided strongly with Bolton and argued that if anyone was to resign, it should be Rab Butler.[122]

On 4 July, Cobbold met Butler to review the general situation.[123] According to the Governor's diaries, he made it clear that there would be high-level resignations in the Bank if the crisis deepened and the government did not take appropriate action. In short,

> the Court would feel bound to make noises if the reserves looked like going below $1500 millions, and that, if they were to fall as low as $1400 millions without effective action being taken, I thought that many members of the Court, including myself, would wish to consider their position.[124]

Despite Butler's repeated failure to convince Ministers of the merits of Robot, neither the Bank nor Overseas Finance saw this necessarily as the end of the external sterling plan. Before taking his vacation, Cobbold contacted Bridges and indicated that if some accident occurred over the summer on the exchange front, the Bank's view was that Robot was still the best line of emergency action.[125] He also wrote to Butler expressing both his disillusionment with government policy and the opportunity afforded by the upcoming Commonwealth Economic Conference in November: 'If HMG can show a strong and constructive policy and give a definite lead to the Commonwealth, then it might be the most fruitful occasion since the end of the war for the future of the Empire and of sterling.'[126]

The second rejection of Robot meant that unilateral British action to restructure the world economy would not now be attempted, barring a deep and sudden economic crisis in the summer of 1952. However, Robot II had indicated to the architects of the plan that prior consultation on policy with the Commonwealth and some Western European states could possibly remove some of the political and economic obstacles to the introduction of floating rate convertibility. The next chapter shows how Overseas Finance and the Bank finally outflanked Cherwell and the 'doubters' to produce a collective plan for floating rate convertibility accepted as official policy by Ministers in the run-up to the November economic conference.

6
The Collective Approach to Freer Trade and Currencies

The reluctance of Cabinet Ministers to make a definite move on the external economic policy front began to create serious credibility problems for the government in the latter half of 1952, committed as it was to the pursuit of convertibility and non-discrimination in trade. Since February, Cobbold had argued that the government should express a clear view in order to maintain overseas confidence: 'at least to the extent of saying whether our aim is the North Pole or the South Pole'.[1] It would not be possible, he noted, to 'go on for long with an inconvertible currency and differing rates of exchange, and under the threat of recurrent "devaluation" crises, without doing permanent damage to the standing and utility of the currency and risking a progressive break-up of the Sterling Area'.[2] The visit of the Australian Prime Minister, Robert Menzies, to London in mid-June highlighted that there was a degree of concern in the Commonwealth regarding the direction of external policy. Invited to the Cabinet on 17 June, Menzies indicated that Australia, Canada and New Zealand attached special political importance to the Conservative manifesto pledge that a Commonwealth Economic Conference be held before the end of 1952.[3] It was essential, he suggested, that Commonwealth countries 'concert their economic, financial and commercial policies', and there was everything to be said for holding a meeting on these subjects as early as possible. Furthermore, he proposed to the Cabinet that to prepare for this Ministerial-level meeting, a separate gathering of senior officials from the Commonwealth should be held prior to the main event. This would allow clarification of technical issues and provide 'a reasonable opportunity of reaching fruitful decisions' at Prime Ministerial level.[4] Australia, New Zealand and Canada were keen to hold the main conference in the second half of November. Caught somewhat off-balance, but unwilling to lose face, the Cabinet accepted Menzies' proposals despite protestations from the Commonwealth Secretary that the government would not be fully prepared until January.

The decision to convene the Commonwealth Economic Conference in London in mid-November was, according to Hall, greeted 'with the greatest alarm among officials'.[5] It was, of course, generally accepted that the Government take a lead in discussions and use the occasion (the first for over twenty years) to present a clear, confident and definite external economic programme to gain the conviction and support of the Commonwealth. However, the debate on external economic policy had been so dominated by Robot that the shelving of the plan now left the government without a clear programme. It would not suffice, as Thorneycroft pointed out, to continue to talk in abstractions or 'fruitless metaphysical discussion of terms'.[6] Rather, it was necessary to put forward a 'policy for concrete action' detailing the internal financial policies required of the Sterling Area; policies for the development of Sterling Area countries; steps leading towards convertibility; and an approach to the US on commercial policy.[7]

For some months Thorneycroft, as President of the Board of Trade, had led an Official Committee on Commercial Policy, looking at the problems of trade with particular reference to the future of the GATT.[8] Clarke and Thompson-McCausland feared that Thorneycroft was intent on using the Committee as a vehicle to conduct a major examination of external economic policy, outside of Butler's immediate purview.[9] Commercial policy, Clarke argued, must follow financial policy, and it was therefore a complete waste of time to discuss Britain's long-term commercial policy until the Cabinet had decided finally on whether or not to implement Robot.[10] Accordingly, from April to June, the operation of Committee had been severely hampered and by the time of Menzies' visit, it was almost defunct.

Exasperated at the Cabinet decision to convene a Commonwealth Conference in November, Bridges decided to 'get the whole thing' into the hands of Overseas Finance, proposing that Clarke write a draft report on external economic policy by 25 June.[11] Bridges would then chair a meeting on 30 June to instruct a new drafting group, to be called the Working Party on External Economic Policy (headed initially by Hitchman), to consider Clarke's memo and place alternatives before Ministers on 14 July. In this way, the Working Party (and Clarke in particular) would act as the brains behind the Ministerial Committee on Preparations for the Commonwealth Economic Conference (PEC), to be chaired by Eden.[12]

I The development of the Collective Approach

The first meeting of the Working Party took place on 1 July 1952.[13] In addition to Alan Hitchman as Chair, it consisted of representatives from the Treasury (Clarke and Edgar Jones), the Bank (Thompson-McCausland), the Economic Section (Christopher Dow), the Paymaster General's Office (Donald MacDougall), the Board of Trade (Leckie), the Commonwealth Relations Office (Snelling) and the Cabinet Office (Morland). Clarke's initial draft of 25 June soon expanded into three separate reports covering 'The Economic Background', 'External Economic Policy and the Commonwealth', and the key policy report, 'Problems of External Economic Policy'.[14] In a memo sent to Rowan, Clarke explained the rationale behind the reports which were to be considered by Eden's PEC committee on 30 July.[15]

Clarke's revised approach to floating rate convertibility

It was now clear, began Clarke, that the Cabinet would not 'take the plunge' and adopt Robot unless there was a major crisis or unless the case for the plunge were based on quite different considerations. The idea that convertibility could be regarded as an independent step taken by the UK, whatever the reaction of other countries, would have to be reassessed. A new phase was now beginning in the international consideration of these subjects and it was likely that floating rate convertibility would only be introduced as a result of combined action by the Commonwealth, Western Europe and the United States. To this end, Clarke suggested, the question of convertibility

> now has to be treated in a very much more dispassionate manner, unrelated to precise timing and precise operational dates. We have to argue about it and discuss it internationally without any of the aura of secrecy which has surrounded the discussions in the last six months. We have somehow got to get the whole discussion on to a more reasonable and practical basis and to consolidate Whitehall behind the forces which we think right, rather than seek quick decisions from the Cabinet on timed operations.[16]

Clarke put forward a three-point plan to outflank the forces opposed to a quick move to convertibility. Firstly, it was necessary to 'shoot down a lot of alternatives to free-world multilateralism'.[17] This meant convincing the Cabinet to finally dispose of any remaining 'two-world solutions' such as those favoured by Thorneycroft or Amery.[18] Permanent discriminatory groups, whether focused on the Commonwealth, or the Commonwealth in association with the OEEC, would not address the problem of the UK's dependence for essential supplies on the outside world. With some 30 per cent of UK exports directed to countries outside the Sterling Area and Western Europe, the UK would be seriously exposed to retaliatory action should the government attempt to form a permanent bloc. Moreover it was also becoming clear that most Commonwealth countries would stop short of action which permanently restricted US investment and trade. In Clarke's view, these ill-thought-out strategies simply amounted to 'adding a lot of weak brethren together, all of whom need the USA (and Canada) in the hope that together they will make a strong brother who does not need the USA'.[19]

Bilateralism, on the model of the German system of the 1930s, was also judged to be ill-adapted to the needs of the UK economy, offering no solution to recurrent balance of payments problems. As the Working Party clarified in its third report, so far as our imports of essentials are concerned, access to the UK market is a bargaining counter of limited value in present conditions when basic foodstuffs and most raw materials are scarce: our overseas suppliers can dispense with our markets longer than we can afford to forego the imports we must have from them.[20]

It was equally inconceivable that the UK would pursue policies to deliberately break up the Sterling Area or endanger the possibility of future co-operation with the United States. Hence it was thought that UK policy must be consistent with a 'one-world' solution, must gain Commonwealth support, and enable Britain and the United States to work co-operatively to seek modifications to the IMF and GATT. This last point, of course, presented great difficulties, but the Hitchman group concluded that it would be premature to embark on long-term policies which precluded co-operation with the United States, before events had shown that this attempt was impossible.

Clarke's first objective therefore was to coax Ministers into accepting that Britain's long-term policy should be consistent with the co-operation of the Commonwealth, the United States and Canada (and, in principle, Western Europe) and should aim at establishing a multilateral trading and financial system covering the 'free world'. This, he thought, a fairly easy task although it would involve 'the rejection of a number of highly prized specifics' on the part of some members of the Cabinet.[21]

Secondly, Clarke used the opportunity afforded him, as author of the background paper, to emphasize that whatever form the multilateral system took it would need to address three 'facts' of external economic policy.[22] In order to pay its way without a recurrence of crisis the UK must first, either acquire substantial resources to strengthen the gold reserves or alter the external financial system to reduce the strain on the gold reserves (or do both). Second, the UK must strengthen its competitive power and expand exports and invisible earnings. Third, policy should be oriented to providing an effective basis for the elimination of the UK's £500 million deficit with the dollar area. On the basis of these considerations the Hitchman group concluded, the UK should continue to apply strict internal financial policies, take steps to increase industrial production (and develop import-saving production) and above all move to make sterling convertible 'sooner or later'.[23] This decision, after all, merely reaffirmed the conclusion of the Commonwealth Finance Ministers' meeting in January, which read: 'Accordingly it is our definite objective to make sterling convertible and to keep it so. We intend to work towards that goal by progressive steps aimed at creating the conditions under which convertibility can be reached and maintained'.[24] Clarke saw great significance in renewing Ministers' commitment at this stage, in light of the second rebuttal of Robot.

The third stage in Clarke's plan was to smooth the path for an early move to floating rate convertibility. The events of February and June had shown that this could not be achieved by forcing Ministers to a quick decision. However, it might be possible to persuade Ministers that as part of a major process of international consultation, definite steps could be taken towards floating rate convertibility. It would be necessary, as Clarke conveyed privately to Rowan, to 'expunge the old Robot from our vocabulary'.[25] Unilateral action was out, but Clarke clarified, 'there are plenty of people who hate the idea of Robot who would feel quite differently about a proposition that we should try to get American support in association with the Commonwealth and Western Europe, for an operation, say, next spring – and who would prefer this to a policy of going on as we are'.[26]

Robot in disguise?

This new route to floating rate convertibility was not, contrary to Cherwell's initial reaction, simply Robot in disguise. Above all else, Robot was a plan for unilateral British action – an independent step taken by Britain with forewarning to other countries but not in any way dependent on their reaction to the plan. By contrast, the new route would be taken only after full discussions with the Commonwealth and 'limited talks' with OEEC nations. If Ministers could agree on the need for early convertibility by the time of the Commonwealth Conference, then the decision on how to proceed could take one of two forms: to take action immediately after the conference (thus gaining two or three months experience of the new regime before opening discussions with the Americans) or attempt to persuade the Americans to provide as many of the prerequisites as possible with the ultimate decision on 'the plunge' dependent on the outcome of the American negotiations. At this stage, Overseas Finance clearly favoured the first course of action.[27] If the Treasury and the Bank remained in the driving seat of the Working Party, then thought Clarke, it would be a fairly straightforward matter to 'argue about the great difficulties which we should encounter in going into a negotiation with the Americans on this issue and thus work up a case for an early step being taken before the American negotiations'.[28] If all else failed, Overseas Finance and the Bank would insist on a return to Robot.

The success of this new strategy rested initially on Ministers endorsing the Hitchman group's third report on 'The Problems of External Economic Policy'. Eden's Cabinet Committee on Preparations for the Economic Conference consisted of Salisbury, Lyttelton, Thorneycroft, Butler, Macmillan, Cherwell and Swinton.[29] At its crucial meeting on 30 July, Thorneycroft and Macmillan criticized the report of the officials for paying lip-service to the notion of multilateralism whilst failing to suggest steps to improve the UK's real economic position. However, Eden, Butler and Lyttelton strongly supported the Working Party's conclusion that the government's primary objective should be the development of a worldwide multilateral trade and payments system. Accordingly, it was decided that officials now prepare 'concrete proposals, based on the theory embodied in the conclusions, which they could discuss with a view to communicating them to other Commonwealth Governments'.[30] As a result, a number of special Working Parties were set up to look in detail at short-term balance of payments; commodity policy; development policy; and of course trade and finance with particular reference to sterling convertibility. Chaired by Herbert Brittain, the Working Party on Sterling Convertibility was dominated by Overseas Finance with Clarke and Frank Figgures responsible for the drafting of reports.[31] Lucius Thompson-McCausland represented the Bank, whilst MacDougall and Dow formed the main opposition in the meetings to the floating convertibility camp.

The first step in Clarke's revised plan for sterling had been achieved. It now fell to the new Working Party to report on the 'steps which should be taken towards the convertibility of sterling', with a view to proposing a clear course of action for the British government.[32] However, the forces opposed to Overseas Finance and the Bank were not to be so easily outmanouevred. On 1 August, Cherwell circulated a memorandum on external economic policy that threatened to sideline the new floating rate convertibility scheme. The solution to current difficulties, he argued, lay in the formation of a new payments union and trade liberalization system incorporating the United States, Canada, the Commonwealth and the OEEC.[33] On the instruction of Eden and Butler, the attention of the Working Party thus shifted temporarily away from 'steps towards convertibility' to the analysis of the Cherwell plan.

II The Cherwell/MacDougall plan for an Atlantic Payments Union

Donald MacDougall claims that the idea of a new payments union arose in discussions he had with Robert Marjolin and Harry Lintott, Secretary-General and Deputy Secretary-General respectively of the OEEC, in late Spring 1952.[34] In Marjolin's view, the US Presidential Elections provided an ideal opportunity for Western European governments to press the new Administration to transform the European Payments Union into an Atlantic Union with convertible currencies, incorporating the US and Canada. The attraction of such a scheme to MacDougall and Cherwell was that it provided a 'possible half-way house between the extremes of Robot and two-worlds', although they were strongly against offering convertibility at the outset.[35]

The Paymaster General presented the plan to Eden's Cabinet committee as a compromise that would satisfy the main schools of thought on international economic policy. It would

> provide for co-operation with the United States and Canada; retain the Sterling Area and Imperial Preference; automatically reach convertibility

at the earliest safe moment; avoid the dangers of premature convertibility and non-discrimination; and recognise that the dollar problem exists and must be solved.[36]

In detail the proposal consisted of four main elements. First, there would be created an Atlantic Organisation for Economic Affairs to deal on a practical basis with the 'economic difficulties of the free world'.[37] Its members would be drawn from the Commonwealth, the OEEC and the United States. For the modern world to work, Cherwell noted, every kind of weapon was useful to help restore balance in international payments – internal financial policy, use of gold reserves or international credit, exchange rate variations, import and export restrictions and discrimination. The art of international economic co-operation was to ensure that these instruments were used in the right circumstances and in the right proportions. Virtually no economic problem would be beyond the terms of reference of the organization. Regular meetings would be held at the highest level to discuss such issues as international investment, military aid, trade policy, business activity (particularly in the US), economic development and commodity policy. In this respect, Cherwell's idea foreshadowed the later meetings of the G5, G7 and G10 that emerged in the 1960s, 1980s and 1980s.[38]

Second, under the umbrella of the Atlantic Organisation for Economic Affairs, an Atlantic Payments Union (APU) would be set up on lines similar to the EPU. Membership of the APU would include the present members of the EPU plus the United States and Canada. The proposed Union would differ in certain respects from EPU, but retain those aspects of the system that had proved successful. In particular, at the end of each month the central bank of each country would report its position vis-à-vis the other central banks and the net position of each country would be worked out with settlements to be made in gold and credit (the proportion of gold varying as the country's credit or debit position changed).[39] There would also be a general understanding (as in the OEEC) of the importance of liberalizing trade, with a let-out clause for countries in severe balance of payments problems. Third, the APU would differ significantly from the EPU and the OEEC in respect of the issue of discrimination between members. In a move drawing heavily on the thinking behind the 'Scarce Currency' clause of the IMF, Cherwell and MacDougall proposed that the APU would have the power to declare as 'scarce' the currency of a 'persistent creditor'. It would follow that other members would have permission (and incentive) to discriminate immediately against the goods of the 'persistent creditor'. In this way, the United States could join the system and the dollar would be kept harder than other currencies so long as the dollar shortage persisted. However, when the shortage eased and the reserves of the other members rose, there could be progressive relaxation and finally a controlled move to non-discrimination and full currency convertibility. Finally, as an incentive to balance trade, the APU would operate a new 'gold tax' arrangement. Deficit countries would pay a gold tax to a 'persistent creditor' whilst those in surplus with the creditor would receive a gold bonus.[40]

The Robot camp's response to APU

As Robert Hall predicted, Cherwell's proposals were immediately considered unworkable by Brittain's Working Party on Sterling Convertibility.[41] Clarke questioned whether the Union could operate with a combination of convertible and inconvertible currencies.[42] The EPU could only function adequately because all currencies were inconvertible. Would Cherwell expect the Americans to make the dollar inconvertible? In addition to this 'technical' difficulty, Clarke pointed to the political problem of excluding Latin America and Japan from the Union. Frank Figgures reaffirmed Clarke's technical objection and added that if the United States were to enter such an arrangement it would be necessary to make a fundamental change to its banking and currency laws.[43] New exchange control regulations would be required in the United States in order to hold the currency of other members, or give short-term credit on an automatic basis for the other members, between monthly settlements. The exclusion of Latin America and Japan would 'create trading difficulties for us and the rest of Western Europe and political difficulties for the United States'.[44] Congress would almost certainly object to increased discrimination against the United States, and Canada and Belgium would not easily accept that they too should discriminate against the dollar. Finally, Figgures raised the important consideration that it was difficult to judge whether the proposal was a serious step towards convertibility. Herbert Brittain, on these major points, agreed in full with Clarke and Figgures.[45]

At the Bank, Thompson-McCausland produced a ten-point rebuttal of the Cherwell/MacDougall plan.[46] Among the 'considerable difficulties in the proposals put forward', he identified that Congress would have to pass legislation to set up an agency to accumulate foreign currency on the scale required, and that in general, 'it would be a great mistake of tactics to base our approach to the Americans on what would inevitably seem to them yet another ingenious scheme for getting dollars out of them without any adequate concession in return'.[47] The system of monthly settlements would, he surmised, only be possible on the basis of fixed exchange rates. Cherwell was therefore clearly attempting to predetermine a matter on which Ministers were as yet undecided. Thompson-McCausland's major criticism, however, was that the APU would inevitably lead to the break-up of the Sterling Area. If the Sterling Area were to be treated as a single unit, the result would be 'fruitful of friction between the individual countries' in the Sterling Area'.[48] A country in dollar surplus would have to accept the consequence of other countries dollar deficits. The pressure generated by this situation would be intensified under the rigid rules governing the Union and possibly lead independent members of the Area to abandon sterling as their general currency for external payments.

These preliminary assessments were brought together at the end of August when the Working Party produced its final report on the Cherwell/MacDougall plan.[49] It was accepted by Brittain's group that the creation of a forum to discuss international economic policy was desirable and should be incorporated in future plans drawn up by the government. However, on the debit side it was judged that the proposal would provide no move towards convertibility; it would prove unacceptable to US authorities; Canada would be unable to join unless it abandoned its floating rate and introduced exchange control on Canadian dollars held by non-Canadian residents; and the 'gold tax' would give foreign governments a direct incentive to encourage dealing in the export of Sterling Area raw materials to the USA (that is, encourage cheap sterling transactions). For these reasons, as Figgures reported to Brittain, 'the whole Working Party except the Paymaster General's representative is agreed in rejecting the proposals on technical grounds'.[50]

Brittain now endorsed the recommendation that the Chancellor ask his colleagues to agree that the proposal be dropped. In addition to the technical difficulties, he noted that 'the plan would be a poor affair to put before the Commonwealth governments who are no doubt expecting us to contemplate some positive plan which will take us further toward convertibility than we were in January'.[51]

The Convertibility Working Party had been busy throughout August – meeting for three hours every evening in a basement room in the Treasury – drafting the 'positive plan' initially requested by Ministers on steps towards convertibility.[52] The Working Party report sought to convince Ministers that early action was required and that floating rate convertibility would best be achieved in a concerted move of the key European currencies backed by a Special Assistance Fund provided by the United States. This 'collective approach' to convertibility was the perfect vehicle for Clarke's new strategy since, in principle, it could be easily distinguished from Robot crash convertibility programmes which it seemed would never gain Foreign Office or Board of Trade approval.

III The adoption of the Collective Approach

In late August 1952, the Convertibility Working Party began its final re-draft of the 'Steps towards Convertibility' report which recommended that Ministers adopt a new 'key currency' or 'collective approach' to trade and payments.[53] The report proposed collective action on the part of countries whose currencies were deemed to be fundamental to the operation of the international economy. A move would be made in concert to make key currencies convertible, and a small management group would be formed to operate at high level with few written rules and a minimum constitution to achieve two objectives: to maintain convertibility with the help of a dollar stabilization fund provided by the United States, and to constitute a steering committee for the IMF and GATT whose roles would be confined to meeting the needs of smaller countries.[54]

It was at this point in the re-drafting that Cohen of the Board of Trade suggested that as part of the collective move it might be possible to strike a deal on quantitative import restrictions and thereby minimize the risk of a contacting spiral of world trade.[55] This issue had, of course, figured largely in the Board of Trade's decision to reject the Robot proposals. Hall records that Overseas Finance now saw a great opportunity to win round the Board of Trade and the Foreign Office, and 'leaped in' at this point to

> work up a plan for an approach to France, Germany, Benelux, Canada and the United States on the basis that we should all go convertible together, and all give up quantitative import restrictions except against the United States who would agree to everyone discriminating against her (including Canada) and who would put up an exchange stabilisation fund of 5 billion dollars.[56]

In this form, the Collective Approach was now endorsed by officials from the Commonwealth Relations Office, Colonial Office, Board of Trade, Foreign Office and, of course, the Treasury and the Bank. Only Donald MacDougall, the Paymaster General's representative, opposed the plan with Robert Hall undecided.[57] The report of the Working Party was finalized on 1 September for onward transmission to Eden's Cabinet Committee.[58] The main question now facing the Ministerial Committee was relatively straightforward: should it accept the majority view to go ahead boldly with an international plan for convertibility or the minority (Hall and MacDougall) view to carry on with existing policies? Although Robot seemed no longer to be on the horizon, the report in the hands of the committee warned that if the Cabinet opted for the minority view and reserves began to disappear, 'the least objectionable course open to us would be to allow newly acquired sterling in the hands of non-residents to become convertible at a floating rate'.[59] If the Collective Approach proved impossible or unattainable within a reasonable period, the majority on Brittain's Working Party were of the view that Robot would be the only alternative. However, as Brittain clarified to William Armstrong, at this stage the majority would still not support Robot as an immediate policy.[60] The Foreign Office still feared that independent action would have an unfortunate political effect in Europe, and the Board of Trade felt that it would seriously expose the economy, if others retained import restrictions. For Overseas Finance and the Bank therefore, the collective approach represented the 'one hope of going out strongly for convertibility in the next twelve months or so with the full support of the Foreign Office and the Board of Trade'.[61]

PEC considers the 'Collective Approach'

The Collective Approach considered by Eden's Cabinet Committee on 4 September comprised five main elements.[62] First, a number of countries whose currencies were considered to be 'key' to the maintenance of the global economy would collectively and simultaneously move to convertibility. This move would be made at some point in the second half of 1953. Each member would be free to adopt a fixed or floating rate. The UK would float sterling against the dollar. The nucleus would consist of the UK, the United States, Canada, France, Benelux and Germany (as indicated below, Germany was later removed from the nucleus). Second, import restrictions would be abolished among the countries of the nucleus, except the United States, who would immediately acquire the status of a 'persistent creditor'. Restrictions could be reimposed in situations of extreme balance of payments difficulties (if authorized by all the other members). This proposal would relate only to quotas, not tariffs or imperial preferences. The abolition of quotas would, of course, increase the significance of tariffs and make it more important for the UK to obtain concessions from the United States and GATT on imperial preference. Third, the nucleus would attempt by negotiation to induce other important trading countries to adopt a similar commercial policy on a reciprocal basis. This would require modification of the IMF and GATT and make the new trade rules worldwide in their application. Four, the United States would be asked to make available a fund of $5 billion to be used as an Exchange Support Fund to back the convertibility operation. Drawings could be made by any member experiencing balance of payments difficulties in the transition period. In the case of the operations undertaken by the UK, convertibility would also involve some freezing of the sterling balances of non-residents of the Sterling Area, largely along the lines discussed in the plans for Robot II. Finally, there would be continuous consultation on economic questions between members of the nucleus who would adapt their policies and use their influence in the IMF and GATT to secure 'a satisfactory and expansionist trade and financial system'.[63] This would not require the creation of a new organization; rather the nucleus would become in effect 'the Economic Steering Committee for the Free World'.[64]

Eden was aware that the Governor of the Bank of England had commended the proposals to Butler with two important provisos. First, that the Cabinet should not rule out Robot – 'we must keep our hands free to make an earlier move by ourselves if it seems either necessary or in the general interest'.[65] Second, Cobbold cautioned that it was *sterling* convertibility that counted. The idea of a nucleus was fine but 'we must retain the initiative and the power to make our own decisions, and not get too much tied up in committees and rules which may easily suit others but not us'.[66] This issue was also keenly felt by the Working Party who pointed to the risks involved in any approach to the United States. Not only might the United States refuse the stabilization fund and baulk at continued discrimination but, Brittain warned

> we should not underestimate the dangers of finding ourselves at the end of any negotiation, with a choice between accepting something much less satisfactory than and perhaps even different in kind from that we had proposed ourselves, and breaking off a negotiation which we had ourselves initiated.[67]

Questions, of course, remained over the commitment of European countries to convertibility and their willingness to forego import restrictions. Nevertheless, as Clarke doggedly reminded the doubters, 'On the present basis we are thrown into crisis as soon as there is the first sign of a storm and nobody has yet been able to think up any line of policy which has a ray of hope in it'.[68] A policy of inconvertibility and bilateral negotiation would not lead one fine day to a convertible and multilateral world but might well make these ends progressively unattainable.[69] In the circumstances, the tactics of handling the Collective Approach and dealing with the difficulties of operation could wait. The first and most important task was to convince Ministers to proceed with the plan and secure Commonwealth agreement, before approaching the United States and the OEEC.

The Ministerial response to the plan initially resembled the full Cabinet's reaction to Robot. Despite the majority recommendation from Brittain's Working Party, only the Chancellor and the Colonial Secretary gave the plan unconditional support.[70] Eden and Maxwell-Fyfe were non-committal, whilst Thorneycroft, Swinton, Salisbury and Macmillan echoed Cherwell's criticism that floating rate convertibility, at this stage, placed too much strain on the economy. However, with Eden in the chair, the doubters were not to win the day. Discussions were continued on 9 and 10 September, by which time Brittain's Working Party had agreed a definite plan of action. Germany was now omitted from the nucleus pending negotiations leading up to convertibility. The United States would be asked to give a firm commitment on financial support before the convertibility operation. In addition, the rules relating to drawing on the Exchange Support Fund were clarified and it was decided that the Fund itself would come under joint management.[71]

By 12 September the Collective Approach had been clarified sufficiently for Ministers to reach a decision and agree policy on the convertibility of sterling.[72] It was generally accepted that convertibility in the context of a one-world multilateral system was desirable. However, there remained a clear difference of opinion on the form and timing of any convertibility operation. Cherwell, fighting a rearguard action, still favoured the Atlantic Payments Union scheme, although this now received little support. Lyttelton remained wedded to Robot and suggested that the Collective Approach should only be tried if independent action failed. Predictably, this line was strongly criticized by the Foreign Office and the Board of Trade.[73] With both extremes sidelined, the time seemed right for the adoption of the Collective Approach. Macmillan and Maxwell-Fyfe had now softened their earlier criticism and were prepared to agree that the scheme be remitted to the Preparatory meeting of Commonwealth officials.[74] Eden, with strong backing from Butler, finally suggested a line which was endorsed by the Cabinet Committee. The primary objective remained convertibility and the development of a system of multilateral trade and payments throughout the free world. However, before the step to convertibility could be taken there must be effective internal financial control, action for the development of resources to increase competitiveness and agreement on the use of discrimination to protect trade. The scheme for a collective approach to convertibility offered a possible means to this end. It would therefore be put forward in this light, carrying the endorsement of the Cabinet Committee (whilst recognizing the criticism of Lord Cherwell). However, this was only a Cabinet Committee and Eden was careful to include the following important rider: 'This scheme, which would not in any way bind Ministers, would enable the UK officials to take the lead in the discussions. They should not, however, declare themselves as inflexibly wedded to it, but should invite other Commonwealth officials to propose alternatives, if they so desired'.[75]

This decision marked something of a watershed in the discussions surrounding exchange rate policy that had begun in earnest in January. For the first time in these discussions Cabinet Ministers had endorsed a proposal for floating rate convertibility. Admittedly this was not a meeting of the full Cabinet and this was not a plan for unilateral British action. Nevertheless it constituted a victory for Overseas Finance and the Bank. Cherwell concluded that Ministers had at last surrendered to the 'bankers' ramp' and now placed his faith in Commonwealth officials rejecting the plan.[76]

IV The Commonwealth Economic Conference

The Preparatory Meeting of Commonwealth officials began on 22 September and closed on 15 October.[77] It was hoped that the real negotiations would take place at this meeting, allowing a more relaxed atmosphere to prevail at the full Commonwealth Prime Ministers' Economic Conference in November. Cobbold advised Rowan, who was leading the British team and preparing the opening statement, to 'cover up a bit on floating rates and talk more in terms of flexibility within wider exchange points in the initial stage'.[78] Accordingly on 23 September, Rowan addressed the first meeting of officials outlining in very general terms the government's thinking on convertibility. The main objective of the Collective Approach, he noted, would be 'to get some protection against some of the risks of independent action and make a beginning in a co-operative effort by the major trading countries to bring about an effectively working multilateral trade and financial system'.[79] Bolton reported that the UK initiative caused a 'buzz of excitement' and over the next few days Rowan and his team outlined the scheme in full.[80]

Conclusions of the Preparatory Meeting

Three conclusions were evident by the close of business on 15 October. Firstly, there was no real support for moving towards convertibility through the mechanism of an extended payments system along the lines suggested by Cherwell and MacDougall.[81] Jayawardena, the Deputy Governor of the Central Bank of Ceylon, had expressed some support for this proposal but no other delegation spoke in its favour and the Canadian team emphasized that it would present insuperable difficulties for them. Secondly, it was clear that in general terms the collective approach had been well received. Taken as a whole, the Preparatory Meeting concluded that the approach 'had substantial merit and constituted an imaginative and constructive approach to the problem'.[82] In respect of individual delegations, Canada, Australia, New Zealand and South Africa wholeheartedly endorsed the proposals. The views of officials from Pakistan, Ceylon and Southern Rhodesia were somewhat harder to divine although the British team were sure that these countries would fall in line with the majority view.

The main stumbling block was represented by the Indian delegates who were under strict orders from Nehru. Raghavan Pillai (the new Secretary of the Ministry of External Affairs) explained to Frank Lee that fundamentally the Indian government could not agree, for political reasons, to anything which might look as though it involved 'subjecting India's economic destinies to the control of Western Powers, or that might be represented, by however wild an exaggeration, as a device by the Western Powers to re-establish "colonial domination" in Asia'.[83] India's exclusion from the 'nucleus' would, for this reason, cause Nehru great political difficulties. In addition, Nehru had issued instructions that India would not support the extension of Imperial Preference in whatever form (principally because it posed a threat to further US investment). In addition, amid the general disappointment that only non-resident sterling was to be convertible at the initial stage, the Asian Dominions and Southern Rhodesia were 'troubled' by the flexible rate, and India and Pakistan opposed the removal of quantitative restrictions and questioned the absolute right of discrimination against the United States. In light of these remarks, the final conclusion drawn by the Cabinet Committee, at the end of the Preparatory Meeting, was that the British Government could move forward in one of three directions. It could ditch the Collective Approach and revert to the gradualism so heavily criticized by Brittain's Working Party; it could ignore the points raised by Commonwealth officials and put forward the original proposal at the November Conference; or the Cabinet could agree to modify its proposals and put forward an amended scheme for discussion in November. Eden pressed for the latter solution and throughout the second half of October, Overseas Finance, the Bank and the Board of Trade produced the Collective Approach – Mark II.[84]

The new 'Collective Approach'

Following revisions by Overseas Finance and the Bank, the new collective approach was now more practically oriented and Clarke believed that he had a 'packet which would certainly command the support of the R.S.A., Canada, the United States and probably Europe' inasmuch as it contained better safeguards than the old scheme.[85] It was decided that there could be no concessions on the flexible rate or on limiting convertibility to non-residents. However, modifications were suggested in respect of quantitative restrictions, the Exchange Support Fund and the 'nucleus' group of key countries. On the issue of quantitative restrictions and discrimination in trade, Clarke now agreed with Hall that the original plan was 'never realistic'.[86] It was now proposed that the United States, Europe and the Commonwealth reach agreement on the *long-term objective* of removing quantitative restrictions and discrimination as the world dollar problem was solved. The speed of the removal of restrictions would not necessarily be the same for all Commonwealth countries given their different interests and trading arrangements. The new plan would give countries the right to impose restrictions and discriminate when in balance of payments difficulties, but there would be an obligation to justify the action to a joint committee of the IMF/GATT. The United States would no longer be labelled a 'persistent creditor' but would be asked to adopt 'good creditor policies' as part of the grand plan to abolish restrictions and discrimination.[87] This policy would thus safeguard British interests (the aim was to extend liberalization from 45 per cent of total trade with Europe to 75 per cent) and allow other Sterling Area countries greater freedom to import dollar goods.

In revising the Collective Approach, Clarke further strengthened the hand of the government by suggesting that the idea of the Exchange Support Fund be dropped. Whilst it was important that funds be made available, it was equally important that no strings were attached (such as a fixed rate stipulation or a non-discrimination clause) and that the UK had assured access to the funds. Instead of the Exchange Support Fund it was therefore proposed that each country make its own arrangements to draw funds through the IMF. The IMF would, of course, require an increase of funds and to this end the United States would be asked to put substantial new money at its disposal. If this proved difficult, the government would seek credits bilaterally with other North American institutions such as the Federal Reserve Bank or the US Stabilisation Fund (the former, of course, would avoid the need for Congressional action).

This new funding suggestion also cleared the way for resolving problems surrounding the establishment of a 'nucleus' group of key countries. Instead of a Managing Board limited to nucleus countries, a joint committee of the IMF and GATT could be constituted to gather at prearranged intervals. Membership could be extended to representatives of between ten and twelve countries and if possible meetings would be held in London – 'nearer the scene of operations of the countries primarily concerned in the convertibility operations'.[88] Finally on the matter of Imperial Preference it was decided that the government must stand its ground. Concessions could not be granted to India. The Sterling Area would increasingly need to rely on tariffs and preferences to defend and preserve intra-Commonwealth trade as quantitative restrictions were reduced.

On 30 October, Eden's Cabinet Committee met to consider whether to recommend to the full Cabinet that the Collective Approach Mark II be put forward by the Government at the upcoming Prime Ministers' Conference.[89] In advance of the meeting Bridges sent an emotive memo to Butler supporting the Collective Approach and emphasizing the need to adopt an external policy which would result in a stricter internal policy: 'I regard the next twelve months as absolutely crucial, not only for Her Majesty's Government, but for the economic life of the country in this matter.'[90] Despite Cherwell's stubborn resistance,[91] the Cabinet Committee endorsed the view that the modified proposals should go forward to the Cabinet meeting on 3 November.[92]

The Cabinet and the Commonwealth endorse the Collective Approach

The Cabinet's discussion of the proposals on 3 November turned principally on the effects which a return to a system of multilateral trade and payments were likely to have on domestic policies in Britain.[93] Butler, mindful of Bridges' note, stressed the need to cut public expenditure and move the economy on to a more competitive footing through the adoption of the collective approach. However, several Ministers continued to share Cherwell's apprehensions of the risks involved in a premature move to multilateralism. Nevertheless, Eden and Butler together managed to convince the doubters that the Collective Approach should be put forward as the basis for discussion at the Prime Ministers' Conference. The government would reserve the right to make the final judgement, when the time came, on whether conditions were right for the plan to be put into operation. On this basis, the Cabinet agreed that the Collective Approach to a system of multilateral trade and payments be put forward with conviction as the best plan the government had been able to devise. Cherwell, in private, claimed that the decision 'did not seem to represent the general tone of the Cabinet debate', and regarded it as 'a put-up job between Butler and Churchill'.[94] However, agreement had now been reached and on 4 November telegrams were sent to Commonwealth High Commissions outlining the Cabinet's decision and specifying the modifications to the collective approach.[95] Commonwealth governments now had three weeks to determine their stance before the Prime Minister's Meetings opened in London on 27 November.

The Prime Ministers' Conference itself was somewhat of an anticlimax. The major differences of opinion had been hammered out in the preparatory gathering of officials and only one difficulty emerged in the Prime Ministers' meetings, although it was serious enough for Eden to ask the advice of the Cabinet. It was integral to the scheme that members of the Sterling Area would maintain fixed rates with sterling after the pound had become convertible at a flexible rate. However, in the course of discussions it became clear that India, Pakistan and Ceylon would not give a firm undertaking that they would maintain a de facto link with sterling (reserving the right to link instead to the dollar).[96] Butler explained that pegging on the dollar would be incompatible with full membership of the Sterling Area and had received assurances from the representatives of India, Pakistan and Ceylon that there was 'a ninety-five per cent likelihood' that they would decide to link their currencies with sterling. It was perceived that this uncertainty created a serious difficulty in negotiating the next stage of the collective approach. As Eden explained to the Cabinet on 8 December, 'any ambiguity in our approach might well influence the attitude of the Governments and the organisations concerned to our plan and might affect the extent of credit we were able to obtain'.[97]

On closer investigation it transpired that the problem facing India was once again political rather than economic. For technical reasons legislation would be required in the Indian Parliament to give effect to the link with sterling. In passing such legislation the Indian government would lay itself open to the charge that it was reversing a step taken after the transfer of power. This potentially serious issue was resolved by Cobbold, who managed to secure a compromise with his old friend Deshmukh, the Indian Finance Minister. If, at the time of the operation, the chances of success and stability were reasonably good, then it would be rational and convenient for Sterling Area currencies to keep in step with sterling. But, Cobbold continued,

it would be for the Sterling Area countries and other countries associated with the collective approach, in the light of conditions then ruling, to decide on the precise exchange techniques to be adopted. The Treasuries and the Central Banks of the Commonwealth countries should continue to consult together for the purpose of establishing practicable techniques, in accordance with these arrangements, designed to prevent trade and payments from being hampered.[98]

On 8 December the Cabinet concluded that this formulation would suffice for the moment. The plan would now be put formally to the US government on the supposition that all members of the Sterling Area would remain tied to sterling. If the response from Washington looked positive, the Asian members of the Commonwealth would be asked to take a definite decision on exchange rate policy before final Ministerial discussions began. If, Churchill clarified, the Asian members of the Area at this point refused to link their currencies to sterling, then the collective approach 'would have to be abandoned in order that the unity of the sterling Commonwealth should be preserved'.[99] Accordingly, on 11 December, at the close of the conference, a communiqué was issued, outlining in very broad terms the Commonwealth's commitment to the Collective Approach Mark II.[100]

Robot and the Collective Approach

A clear programme of action had now been formulated, but its implementation proved somewhat problematical. Officials had agreed that the ideal arrangement would be to hold talks with the Americans immediately after the conference. Eden could then make a very general statement to the Council of the OEEC in December before holding confidential discussions with selected European governments and further detailed discussions with the United States thereafter.[101] It was now clear, however, that Eisenhower's inauguration would not take place until 20 January 1953. It would be four to six weeks after this date that the new President would, even in principle, be ready to open talks on international economic policy. Equally it would be fruitless (and possibly dangerous) to disclose too much to the current administration. In the circumstances it was decided to send a message to Washington with the conference communiqué on 11 December indicating that the UK was keen to proceed with international action but acknowledging that the new US Administration required time to 'bed-in'.[102] This approach was well received. Following Eisenhower's inauguration, Randolph Burgess of the US Treasury suggested that exploratory talks could be held in the first week of March.[103] On the Europe front, Eden and Butler convened private meetings with representatives of European governments in Paris on 14 and 15 December.[104] Although the Italians seemed sceptical of the success of convertibility, Pinay and Baumgartner were more receptive and simply cautioned that they would 'prefer to concert a line with us before we talked to the United States'.[105]

As 1952 drew to a close, a number of awkward political and economic questions remained unanswered. Hugh Ellis-Rees, reporting from the OEEC, indicated that European governments might be less than enthusiastic about a move to convertibility before the 'structural disequilibrium' in the world economy had been corrected.[106] On the other side of the Atlantic, it was conceivable that the United States might refuse to play its part in the Collective Approach or that the scheme might be successfully negotiated but then run up against a severe US recession which, in Clarke's view, might mean that the United States would 'lose the cold war'.[107]

If, for whatever reason, the Collective Approach failed, three lines of policy remained open to the British government. First, a 'two-world' solution could be tried in which Britain and the Commonwealth attempted to 'live without the Americans'.[108] This state of affairs would, Clarke pointed out, verify in a remarkable way the Russian Communist Party's analysis of the developing international situation.[109] It would not, however, be in Britain's political interest nor would it help resolve any of the pressing economic problems. Second, the government could pursue independent action along the lines of Robot II. Clarke was convinced that if the original Robot proposal had been put into operation, it would have been highly successful. If the United States would not now co-operate, the case for Robot was even stronger: 'we should need the cushion of the flexible rate; we should need to make certain that sterling would be an acceptable currency for our vital supplies; with no hope that anyone else was going to pull our chestnuts out of the fire, we should have to clear decks for action ourselves'.[110] But the government would have lost the advantage of surprise and initiative. It would be known that Britain had failed to secure American support and in this sense it would be clear that the government was acting from a position of weakness. In the circumstances, it might be best to opt for the third route: continue with present policies and work towards convertibility. The danger here, of course, was well known. The level of gold reserves was altogether inadequate in relation to the level of transactions in sterling and the slightest downturn could create severe crisis. This would more than likely force the government into a choice between a fixed devaluation and Robot.

On all counts, Overseas Finance judged that the Collective Approach offered the best future for Britain and the Commonwealth. However, if Plowden's suspicions proved correct and the United States failed to offer sufficient support, Clarke believed that he had now devised the best fallback position.[111] Present policies would continue whilst Robot was readied for action. It would be best, however, to 'wait until the puff of wind came before doing Robot, for what we should really want to do would be to remain inconvertible for as long as we reasonably could in the hope that the United States attitude would change'.[112] The Cabinet had taken a year to accept the argument for floating rate convertibility. Whether Britain would lead the restructuring of the world economy along the lines of the Collective Approach now depended on the outcome of the Anglo-American talks which were due to open in Washington on 4 March 1953.

7
Anglo-American Negotiations and a New Bank Route to Convertibility

The official text of the Commonwealth Economic Conference communiqué published on 11 December 1952 indicated in very broad terms that international action was required to create the conditions for the expansion of world trade and production.[1] The aim would be to secure agreement on the adoption of policies by creditor and debtor countries to restore balance in the world economy on the basis of 'Trade, not aid' and by progressive steps to create an effective multilateral trade and payments system covering the widest possible area. The restoration of sterling convertibility was judged to be an integral part of this move to multilateralism but the achievement of convertibility would depend upon three conditions: firstly, the continuing success of the internal action taken by sterling Commonwealth countries to curb inflation and correct the deficit in the Sterling Area balance of payments; secondly, the general adoption of trade policies conducive to the expansion of world trade; and thirdly, the availability of adequate financial support through the IMF or otherwise to accompany convertibility. As regards procedure, the communiqué was deliberately vague, merely indicating that 'it is proposed to seek acceptance of this plan by the Governments of the United States and of European countries whose co-operation is essential, and to work as far as possible through existing international institutions dealing with finance and trade'.[2]

Between December and late February 1953, when Eden and Butler left London to hold talks with the US Administration, Overseas Finance and the Bank battled to maintain domestic momentum for the Collective Approach and contain criticism emanating from the OEEC that Britain 'was going to play with the USA on their own, and the Europeans must therefore look after themselves'.[3] As early as 19 December 1952, Clarke had feared that although Overseas Finance had 'got what it wanted out of the Commonwealth Economic Conference', there was a very real danger that momentum would be lost and the whole project would 'go sour'.[4] This danger was all the greater since, as Clarke acknowledged, 'there are plenty of Ministers and Officials in Whitehall who are half-hearted about the plan' and the new US

Administration will have a lot to do and may not be inclined, early on, to take a big international initiative.[5] In addition, he recognized that discussion could easily become bogged down with the Europeans, that there was endless scope for argument and controversy, and 'unless there is some pressure of external events to press the matter forward the discussion can become interminable'.[6] Clarke, Rowan and Cobbold therefore pushed ahead with the 'Epistle to the Americans' – as they christened the memorandum submitted to the US Administration on 3 February 1953 – despite mounting pressure from Europe indicating that the procedure outlined for carrying forward discussions would be 'the worst possible for collective action in the OEEC'.[7]

The Treasury clearly acknowledged that European governments were anxious about the future of the EPU, were concerned that convertibility could inadvertently lead to increased levels of bilateralism and a descending spiral of trade, and were disturbed by reports that Britain might scoop up almost the whole of available US resources in financial support for sterling convertibility. Nevertheless, as Overseas Finance made clear to the Cabinet, the government could not allay the fears of the Europeans until it had opened talks with the Americans. Britain could not assume, even in principle, American acceptance of the two most delicate and potentially controversial features of the plan – the flexible rate and financial support – hence, 'it would be impolitic to float these ideas in Europe before we have made sure that the Americans will not reject them out of hand'.[8] In the Bank, Cobbold was less concerned about reports that the Europeans were restless. He had been assured by Baumgartner that the Bank of France, and the 'more responsible parts of Government', welcomed the plans and recognised that Britain must talk first with the US Administration.[9] Baumgartner even suggested that the British government 'need not be too concerned about the fuss that has been made in EPU' and that it would 'probably shake itself out after the Washington visits'.[10]

I The Epistle to the Americans

On 3 February 1953, the Cabinet agreed that the 'Epistle to the Americans', formally titled 'A Collective Approach to Freer Trade and Currencies', be made available to the US Administration.[11] The document, written by Clarke and revised by Brittain and the Bank,[12] developed the principal theme of the Commonwealth communiqué and urged the United States to look ahead and set in train positive policies, since 'the longer the delay, the greater the danger that the restrictive policies which were inevitable for dealing with the initial postwar problems will become permanently embedded in the world economy'.[13]

To appeal to the Americans, Clarke framed the memorandum in terms of 'Trade, not Aid'. The world dollar shortage, he noted, could only be solved by concerted international action. Since the beginning of the Marshall Plan, the rest of the world had run up a current deficit with the United States averaging $4 billion a year, in spite of stringent attempts to restrict US exports. The deficit had been funded by US government grants of approximately $4 billion a year, in addition to US government loans and private long-term investment of the order of $1.5 billion a year.[14] The United States had been 'unprecedentedly generous' but this was 'not a sound or permanent basis for a healthy world economy'.[15] In fact, it simply shored up the real problem, the failure of competitive power elsewhere. Hence, Clarke argued, there was a need for policies to develop competitive power in the context of supportive 'good creditor' action by the United States. To this end the Americans were asked to consider an approach to multilateral trade and payments consisting of four main elements: freer currencies, freer trade, increased capital for development (both inside and outside of the Commonwealth), and the creation of an international forum cutting across the IMF and GATT, in which problems of finance and trade could be discussed in the context of the world economy as a whole. The crux of the approach hinged, of course, on the first element and in particular on the conditions necessary for the convertibility of sterling. Convertibility, it was outlined, would be approached in stages, the pace of which would depend on the success of the first step, and on the progress made under all the elements in the proposals. The first step would be that on a given day, all sterling accruing to individuals and institutions outside the Sterling Area would be designated as 'External Sterling' and could be freely exchanged in the market for gold, dollars or any currency. Given the UK's limited dollar resources, this move would not be possible at a fixed rate of exchange hence the government would introduce a flexible rate. To support a convertibility operation of this scale, Britain would require substantial financial support. This, it was stressed, was needed not to fill continuing balance of payments deficits, but to deal with short-term exchange rate fluctuations and pressures which might arise from converting existing sterling balances held by non-residents of the Sterling Area. Above all, financial support would provide confidence that the UK had at its disposal sufficient reserves to protect sterling even in the face of economic downturn. It was hoped that such funds could be made available from the IMF on a 'stand-by' credit basis, to be drawn on as required for a period of not less than twelve months, with agreed provision for extension thereafter. Although the memorandum did not state an actual figure, it was made clear that the present unexhausted balance of the UK's normal drawing rights in the IMF ($1.3 billion) would not be sufficient. The US government would therefore be required to provide additional funds to enable the IMF to offer a larger 'stand-by' credit (a figure of $2.5 billion had earlier been mentioned in confidential discussions with Ivar Rooth, Managing Director of the IMF[16]). Finally, the memorandum acknowledged that whilst convertibility would probably end the

European Payments Union, it was hoped that leading European countries would move in step with the UK on convertibility and evolve working arrangements to secure exchange stability and facilitate intra-European co-operation both in trade (through the removal of import restrictions) and finance.

In the run-up to the crucial Washington meetings, evidence began to mount that negative European reaction to the idea of abolishing the EPU was beginning to influence the US Administration. Ellis-Rees reported from Paris that the Belgians were 'very interested in the establishment of a common market for the ECSC (through which the Belgians will receive some large payments) and the European Payments Union is ideal for supporting it'.[17] The US Administration now sent the government a long list of questions – termed in Bank and Treasury circles the 'American examination paper'[18] – raising a number of internal and external policy issues including the future of the EPU. On this point, Robert Hall admitted 'our hands are quite empty'.[19] However, by 26 February (the day Butler, Plowden, Rowan, Clarke and Stevenson left by sea for Washington), Clarke had circulated to Rowan and Brittain an 'Epistle to the Europeans' outlining a way forward on the EPU front.[20] The memorandum indicated that it would be 'technically impossible' to maintain the current Union if some currencies were convertible and others not. Convertible currencies would not, of course, present a problem with regard to multilateral settlements. The real problem would arise in respect of those countries that had not felt able to make their currencies convertible and which would no longer have available credit margins in the EPU. Clarke therefore proposed to use the residual assets of the EPU to provide a fund at the disposal of a 'Managing Board' in the OEEC, for the purpose of providing short-term credit for countries in this position to enable them to continue the liberalization of trade. Clarke summarized, 'the possibility of use of a fund of this kind together with borrowing from the IMF could in the opinion of the UK government be worked into a satisfactory scheme, especially if the number of countries which did not become convertible was relatively small'.[21] This did not, however, address the geopolitical concerns which, it soon became apparent, were now uppermost in the minds of the US Administration.

II The Washington Talks and US foreign economic policy

The Collective Approach came as no surprise to the US Administration. In fact, unknown to the British, Gifford had sent a telegram to Dean Acheson on 16 October 1952 indicating that Commonwealth Officials were considering plans to introduce convertibility in 1953.[22] Gifford also revealed that moves were likely to be made in the direction of a flexible rate and that the United States would be expected to adopt 'good creditor' policies and provide financial support should sterling be made convertible. This information arrived as the State Department, in collaboration with the MSA and the Treasury, began a thorough re-examination of American foreign economic policy in early October 1952.[23]

Neither Bretton Woods nor the American loan

The mere continuation of postwar economic policy would not, the State Department argued, bring about sufficient and rapid enough progress to meet the economic problems of the 'free world' to the extent required by the United States' overall political, security and economic interests. It was clear, noted Leddy, that

> we are at the end of the 'transitional period' of emergency economic policy, and the post-transitional world of economic equilibrium and stable economic growth envisaged in the Bretton Woods instruments and ITO-GATT has not emerged. Continued economic aid is not the long-run answer. But neither are the programs to promote world trade and financial objectives which were evolved almost ten years ago.[24]

In addition to the failure of the Bretton Woods model, political developments had forced a reorientation in the US approach to the international political economy. In particular, the threat of Soviet aggression had led large sections of the US Executive to favour the development of a common regional approach to economic and political problems in Western Europe.[25] It was now no longer clear that the State Department and the Mutual Security Agency viewed convertibility as necessarily compatible with the wider security interests of the United States. To the dismay of Treasury officials, who had by now lost the battle over the continuation of the EPU, Harlan Cleveland of the MSA began to question whether the objective of convertibility, 'might not be an objective which was *competitive* with defense and other policies of the United States Government'.[26] The response of the Executive was to call for the creation a number of in-depth Staff Papers, and in December the Treasury Department produced a highly significant survey of the most 'important financial aspects of relations between the Sterling Area and the Dollar Area'.[27]

In a review of Britain's exchange crises since the war, the US Treasury noted that 'internal demands in the Sterling Area were still placing such a heavy strain on production, resources and manpower that exports competitive with the dollar area were not being increased in a way that would give real competitive strength to the Sterling Area'.[28] Although Britain's gold and foreign currency reserves had increased since March 1952, the Treasury expressed 'strong doubts' that the Sterling Area had made significant strides towards a stronger competitive position with the dollar area. In such circumstances, convertibility would either 'have to be restricted very severely through bilateral understanding or the countries given the privilege of converting sterling would rapidly drain away British reserves to buy their needed goods in cheaper markets'.[29] The US government, of course, had a keen interest in helping to develop the competitive strength of Britain and the Sterling Area. A stronger position would avoid the recurrent and disturbing fluctuations of reserves and 'provide a much better basis for the political and strategic role which the United States would like to see the British countries play'.[30] At the same time, the US Treasury recognized that the postwar policies of the United States had 'tended to encourage the maintenance of standards of living and investment which may well have been somewhat higher than could have been maintained without continuous US aid'.[31]

In considering approaches to the discussions with the British in 1953, the Treasury therefore proposed that the Administration give some assurances with respect to the liberalization of trade policies, investment, customs procedures, acceptance of price support programmes for Sterling Area commodities and similar measures, whilst offering 'no substantial financial commitments to the Sterling Area on the part of the US Government either directly or through the International Monetary Fund'.[32] In this way, negotiations could be carried on without causing major embarrassment to either party or giving rise to political repercussions in the Sterling Area. It would, the Treasury continued, be foolish to become involved in the provision of a bilateral stabilization fund of several billion dollars, since this would 'in effect be a repetition of the Anglo-American Financial Agreement of 1946'.[33] The reconstitution of British reserves through large dollar credits would 'very likely result in their dissipation through general imports and the postponement rather than the expediting of the fundamental readjustments in the Sterling Area's international accounts which would make it self-reliant and competitive'.[34]

In a conclusion which could have been penned by Otto Clarke in the run-up to the February Robot debates, the US Treasury finally noted that unless the British economy could become more competitive, and the volume of goods sold for dollars increased substantially, technical attempts to make progress towards convertibility would simply be reflected in drawings on British reserves. The temporary replenishment of these reserves by stabilization credits merely provided a breathing space and did not deal with the long-run problem. In short, only if the exchange rate depreciated significantly to a point at which the Sterling Area was in balance or earning a real surplus with the dollar area, without any dependence on discriminatory restrictions against the dollar area, was there a basis for lasting convertibility. The only practicable road to convertibility would therefore lie in 'the acceptance of flexible exchange rates generally during a period in which restrictions are gradually removed, and in this way the price system gradually restored to its pre-war role in adjusting the volume and composition of international trade'.[35] However, in the context of the Cold War, with the National Security Council still fearful that the Soviet Union could overrun

Western Europe by mid-1953,[36] it was agreed that any radical or destabiliz-ing moves were to be avoided. Accordingly, the Treasury recommended, for political and economic reasons, that in the forthcoming negotiations the United States should 'restrain British desires to move forward rapidly'.[37]

By the time the Washington talks began on 4 March, the American posi-tion had been hammered out in detail by the Treasury, the Mutual Security Agency and the Department of State. On the first day, following an opening address by Eden and Butler, the US team whisked the British party off to the Federal Reserve to receive lectures on the Budget and the economic outlook in the US.[38] Rowan observed that 'these were both designed to show us how difficult it would be to do anything on trade policy and to emphasise the enormous Budget problem which faces them'.[39] On 5 March, Dulles clari-fied the view of the US Administration:

> The President was following the talks with interest and took the view that convertibility mirrored a sound and healthy society. The British propos-als, however, raised some substantial issues such as the size of the Support Fund needed, the effect of the proposals on Western Europe and the nature and timing of the discussions with Western Europe. There were also questions as to whether the UK economy was sufficiently strong and flexible to sustain the proposed operation.[40]

On the final day of the main talks, a disappointed Butler said to the assem-bled group that 'it seemed clear from the course of the discussions so far that the United States regarded the United Kingdom proposals as prema-ture'.[41] He therefore 'doubted the usefulness of continuing the talks on the existing lines at this time'.[42] Randolph Burgess, Deputy to the Secretary of the US Treasury, hoped that the UK proposals would be 'treated as in sus-pense rather than abandoned' and stressed that the US side agreed with the UK objectives and wanted to end the discussions on a note that the two governments were working towards these objectives.[43] This upbeat message was the key theme of the joint communiqué issued on 7 March which noted that:

> The Government of the United States welcomes the initiative taken by the United Kingdom Government in connexion with these problems of common concern. The two Governments believe that there is reason to hope for continued progress towards better balanced, growing world trade and toward the restoration of a multilateral system of trade and payments. The nature and scope of the measures which may be taken by Governments to further such progress, and the timing of such measures, will require further study.[44]

Privately, however, it seemed to many on the British team that the talks had effectively killed the Collective Approach as conceived in London in the autumn of 1952.[45] Parsons cabled Cobbold on 6 March reporting 'The temperature is exceedingly cold . . . in my estimation plan in its present form is unlikely to go forward for at least another twelve months'.[46] Rowan was even less optimistic noting, 'I am sure that we cannot look for any rapid progress, and, indeed, in the long run, we may find that no satisfactory progress at all is possible under the two vital heads of finance and trade policies'.[47]

In London, Cobbold refused to accept defeat. He launched 'Operation Momentum' and wrote to Butler that

> it was inevitable that the US should feel little able to commit themselves at this stage; but you have started the ball rolling, you have got agreement on objectives, and you have established a link with US Treasury which has been missing too long. Allan Sproul [President of the Federal Reserve], I know, feels that a great step forward has been made, and that if we can keep on the up-grade and not lose impetus, we and they ought to be able to work out something sensible together.[48]

Clarke and Rowan now set about devising a way forward, before talks opened with the Organisation for European Economic Co-operation on 23 March. Government policy, they argued, should be based on four assumptions.[49] Firstly, the UK should not look for action by the United States before the end of 1953 on the two central issues – good creditor policies and support funds. Secondly, in the intervening period it was most important to keep up the momentum and the pressure on the United States, in addition to strengthening the position of the Sterling Area. Thirdly, while discussing these problems in the OEEC, and with European countries, the government must ensure that Britain remained in charge of the Collective Approach and that whatever form EPU took for 1953/54, the OEEC would be forced to consider how the EPU could be merged into a wider system. Fourthly, it was necessary to take account, in internal and external policies, of the possibility of a recession in the United States in the near future. Above all, Clarke and Rowan emphasized that in future discussions with the United States and the Europeans it was essential to 'avoid putting a "plan" which can be turned down or so modified as to represent a check to the momentum'.[50]

In his report to the Cabinet on the Washington talks, Butler accepted the fundamentals of the Clarke/Rowan memorandum.[51] The Chancellor indicated that, although the United States Government was not at present prepared to play their part in bringing into operation the proposals, they had agreed to undertake an urgent review of the means by which they could best assist in the expansion of world trade and, in particular, of the question of how their own overseas surplus was to be financed in future. The review, handled under the auspices of the National Advisory Council, would be led by Lewis Douglas, currently serving as Deputy to the Secretary of State. On the European front, Butler suggested that at the meeting of the Council of the OEEC on 23 March, he would not disclose the 'essential secret elements' of the proposals but would concentrate on the European aspects of the problem. He would impress upon the OEEC the importance of moving towards a multilateral system but in a manner which involved the minimum of risks and preserved to the maximum the gains made by co-operation in the OEEC. The Cabinet agreed that Butler and Eden propose that the EPU be extended for a further 12 months on 30 June, but that this decision be reconsidered in the event of a concerted approach to convertibility before June 1954. It was also agreed that there could be no withdrawal from the EPU except by agreement with all its members.[52]

The demise of the Collective Approach

Over the next three months it gradually became apparent to Overseas Finance and the Bank, that the Collective Approach had run its course. Otto Clarke's prediction that in a plan of this kind there was endless scope for argument and controversy, and without some pressure of external events to force the pace, discussion would become interminable, had proved correct.[53] Although the OEEC talks were hailed as a 'great success', Butler recognized that 'the Europeans, as a whole, are not with us on sterling convertibility'.[54] In general, European governments expressed great concern that the credit facilities provided by the EPU would be lost and that the UK would impose heavy restrictions against imports from Europe.[55] In private, some European representatives told Southard, representing the US Treasury, that in effect they were being given a choice: 'join the Sterling Area or operate in a kind of EPU run by the Bank of England'.[56] In addition, some European governments questioned the effects of a flexible exchange rate on their domestic economies and were fearful that a US recession might scupper the whole operation. According to Bridges,

> there was not much sign of any special pre-occupation with the effect of our proposals on European integration and federation (the Schuman Plan, EDC etc), though both the Germans and the Belgians had this aspect in mind and were clearly concerned about the weakness of France and her present inability to become an effective partner in a collective move.[57]

Visits by Rowan and Cobbold to the United States in April confirmed earlier fears that the US Administration had little real interest in the British proposals. In discussions with Rowan, Randolph Burgess 'talked of the "demise" – which he later corrected to the deferment of Plan A., – i.e. our plan – and the need for filling the resultant vacuum with an undefined Plan B'.[58] Rowan noted to Butler, 'there is no question of our ideas materialising in the next year or so'.[59] An exasperated Butler now concluded, 'we shall have to review our External Financial Policy when we have all thought things through. Our objectives are right, but how to reach them?'[60]

Burgess's 'Plan B', it transpired, was an idea to allow greater flexibility in the exchange rate without introducing convertibility. It had been suggested by Richard Bissell (Consultant to the Director for Mutual Security) at a sub-group meeting at the Washington talks and built upon an IMF paper titled 'A Wider Spread for the Spot Rate of Exchange', prepared on 6 February 1953.[61] A consensus quickly developed among British officials that a policy of floating inconvertibility be rejected for four principal reasons.[62] Firstly, with the gold/dollar link broken, there would be no longer any framework of real value for inconvertible sterling. It would be 'paper of unpredictable worth' and thus the acceptability of sterling would be greatly impaired.[63] Secondly, the rest of the Sterling Area would be opposed since their dislike of floating could not be assuaged with assurances of stability and a move to convertibility. Thirdly, all the present difficulties arising from 'cheap sterling' operations would continue except that the margin between the 'official rates' and the 'free rates' would probably widen in order to take into account the unpredictable movements in the value of 'official sterling'.[64] A degree of backdoor convertibility would thereby be introduced through the need to intervene to maintain cross-rates and keep some cohesion in the exchange rate structure. Finally, with sterling under such pressure, it was likely that floating inconvertibility would lead to a general disintegration of the pound. Floating inconvertible would therefore 'put back the prospects of the Collective Approach considerably. So far from being a move towards convertibility, it would be the reverse'.[65] Accordingly, on 15 May 1953, Bridges suggested to Butler that he could 'let the Americans know that we do not regard the proposal that we should in the near future float inconvertible as a sensible proposition, and that we have no intention of doing so'.[66]

By early June, Bolton was of the view that the Collective Approach had run into the ground.[67] The Americans, he noted, had a relatively short space of time in which to decide whether to take an active part in moulding and directing international trade and payments policy. If they failed to decide what part they should play, then 'London probably has no alternative but to seek a means of putting Commonwealth economic policies into operation through methods that may differ substantially from those included in the Collective Approach'.[68] There was now a general feeling in London that the US had 'more or less turned down our proposals ... and that the plan is dead'.[69] Robert Hall concluded, 'all this means that the ideas we formulated last December and put to the US have very few friends, in fact in my view the main friends are OF and the Bank who have been pushing convertibility and the floating rate so violently, in every conceivable form, for the past fifteen months'.[70] Butler, according to Rowan, was depressed and 'under no illusion'.[71] He was now of the view that he had 'been misinformed about the probable US reaction' and began to dissociate himself from the Clarke/Rowan faction in Overseas Finance.[72] Seizing this opportunity, Robert Hall threatened to resign from government service unless he could be found a more secure and well-paid position. He also demanded that Overseas Finance be restructured, and in particular, that Otto Clarke be removed from the division.[73] He wrote to Bridges on 10 June, that the 'relations between the Economic Section and O.F. have been very bad for more than a year, and more like those of a religious war than of reasonable men trying to make a fair presentation of a legitimate difference of opinion'.[74] Hall claimed that he 'did not want to raise this while we were in serious economic difficulties', but now that the crisis had eased, he did not think it 'fair to the country or to everyone concerned to go on as we have been doing'.[75]

On 11 June, Butler signalled his intention to retain Hall, and agreed that the Economic Section be moved into the Treasury with Hall given the title 'Economic Adviser to HMG', effective from 1 November 1953.[76] It was also agreed that Clarke be moved 'to do Social Services on the Supply side' of the Treasury,[77] and Herbert Brittain to Home Finance and Supply, also with effect from 1 November.[78] Overseas Finance, as Robert Hall clarified, had now been purged of Robot men and its structure in November would look very different from the heady days of February 1952:[79]

The Overseas Finance Division of the Treasury

February 1952		*November 1953*
Rowan	Second Secretary	Rowan
Brittain	Third Secretary	Playfair
Clarke	Under-Secretary	Copleston
Flett	Under-Secretary	Armstrong
Copleston	Under-Secretary	France

The publication in July of the Douglas Report confirmed what the government had already heard from other quarters.[80] Lewis Douglas's brief had been to follow up the Washington talks, focusing in particular on the issue of sterling convertibility. On 14 July he reported to Eisenhower that the pressures on sterling were such that 'its position may now be too sensitively balanced to submit it to the strains and stresses of free convertibility'.[81] It would be 'unfortunate' to run any risk of repeating the ill-timed and ill-fated experiment in convertibility of 1947. In the context of the increased defence burden, the reappearance of strong German and Japanese economic competition and uncertainty regarding US trade policy, 'an extension of the liberty with which sterling can be converted into other currencies would now seem to be doubtful'.[82] Thoughts that a support fund could perhaps be provided by the Federal Reserve were scotched on 29 July when Ivar Rooth reported to Hall-Patch that the Reserve would find it 'extremely difficult' to find $500 million, let alone the $1,000 million which was thought necessary.[83] Hall-Patch's assessment of the Collective Approach was that 'the momentum is not there as far as the Americans are concerned. For them this is a nebulous operation in a dim future.'[84] The next stage in the 'nebulous operation' was the creation of the Commission on Foreign Economic Policy, set up under the chairmanship of Clarence Randall (the Randall Commission), to review US economic policies and define immediate and long range objectives.[85] The Commission was not expected to report until late January 1954. In the interim, Randolph Burgess and George Humphrey at the eight annual meeting of the IMF on 16 September, made it clear that the goal of full convertibility still eluded the Fund and that there was no immediate prospect of additional funds being made available to support sterling convertibility.[86]

This chain of events was the catalyst for the development of a new approach to convertibility, sponsored by George Bolton in the Bank. In Bolton's view, the Collective Approach had become 'bogged down to trench warfare over a broad front'.[87] The government could not longer allow the pace to be dictated by the slowest but had to regain the initiative to 'establish the leadership of London'.[88] This was also the view of Otto Clarke who, in his parting shot to Overseas Finance, noted, 'we must regain control over operations on the convertibility of our own currency. This does not mean that one refrains from consulting others, but it does mean that we abandon the idea of collective decisions. Our experience with Europe seems to be quite decisive on this point, and I believe that we should get a better response from the sterling area if we gave a more definite lead of what we intended to do. I believe myself that the ropes are now being tied so closely round us that we should really have to behave like Houdinis to get rid of them'.[89] However, Clarke's solution – to go forward with an independent convertibility operation on the basis of a 10 per cent spread either side of the $2.80 parity and with whatever support fund could be obtained – lacked the imagination of Bolton's 'new look' exchange policy.

III Towards a depoliticized technical approach to convertibility

By the end of October, Bolton and Cobbold had agreed the details of a new route to convertibility.[90] In place of the 'sterile debates over words and slogans', Bolton suggested the development of a more low-key market-based solution consisting of administrative reforms in exchange control practice 'so as to get rid of the current chaotic payments situation parallel with the minimum of policy changes'.[91] The Collective Approach could be divided into two parts: a general political statement of policy and objectives, and a series of technical proposals. The statement of objectives had been useful in improving the general climate and could remain, but nothing further could be gained by pursuing in detail the technical proposals which had become 'completely bogged down' in collective high-profile discussions. Cobbold therefore suggested that whilst the Collective Approach could continue on a political level as a series of statements and policy objectives, the government should move independently on the technical side, in two stages, to simplify exchange policy.[92] It would, he noted,

> be most important to make such a move on as technical a plane as possible; to keep as far away as we could from the Convertibility issue (which arouses passions national and international, and is completely misunderstood by the public) and also from any final decision about the Fixed v. Floating Rate controversy (on which there is a genuine and profound divergence of opinion, both at home and abroad).[93]

The unification of transferable sterling

Stage One of the new route, consisted of a general simplification of exchange control practice towards non-resident sterling, other than on American accounts, with a view to allowing a regular market in a single transferable sterling to develop alongside official sterling.[94] In other words, Stage One would eliminate the '57 varieties' of non-resident sterling and create free transferability of the currency throughout the non-dollar world, for any purpose, whether current or capital. Country classifications for sterling would disappear and there would, for example, be no need for exports to Holland to be paid for in Dutch sterling or to Japan in Japanese sterling. Rather, there would simply be one kind of non-resident sterling and a single unofficial rate for transferable sterling against the dollar in free markets. In Cobbold's view, the unification of non-resident sterling would 'bring us nearer to, but would still leave to be faced, the next step of free transferability between American and other non-resident sterling'.[95] Whilst Stage One would simplify controls and thereby enhance the status of transferable sterling, it would not seek to undermine the distinction between Transferable and American accounts (although it might quicken its demise).

Stage Two, by contrast, would seek to extend the general transferability of non-resident sterling. This would be achieved by intervening in the market for transferable sterling in order to bring the official and transferable rates together alongside a policy to hold the rate at a spread of 2 per cent either side of $2.80. The multiple rate structure would have been abolished and a state of de facto convertibility would have been reached. In Stage Two, an attempt would also be made to secure parallel action from leading European countries and, although the US and the IMF would be asked to 'give their blessing', there would be no formal request for support funds or stand-by credits.[96] A variety of other moves, for example reopening the London gold market or intervening in the market for transferable sterling in order to bring the rates closer together (but not merge the rates), without widening the dealing spreads, could fit in with either stage or act as a bridge between the moves.[97]

On the difficult question of timing, Cobbold suggested that he would like some experience of Stage One before moving to Stage Two, but he emphasized to Butler that he regarded 'Stage One as committing us to Stage Two within a few months, and we should be giving some hostages to fortune in the intervening period'.[98] With the Commonwealth Finance Ministers due to meet in Sydney in January 1954, he proposed that the move to Stage One be made in November 1953, and everything readied for Stage Two immediately after Sydney. Stage One, Cobbold was at pains to stress, was to be seen as 'a technical Exchange Control step', which in his view did not require consultation with anybody outside the Commonwealth and only a brief preliminary notification to Commonwealth governments.[99]

Despite the Bank's best efforts, the Treasury refused to move to Stage One before the Sydney conference.[100] Hall and Strath urged caution, and Butler sought assurances from Cobbold that unification would not necessarily imply any change in the methods, conditions or timing of the Collective Approach.[101] By the time of the Sydney conference, the unification of sterling had been linked to the reopening of the London gold market, although the Treasury stressed that 'each proposal stands by itself and they are in no way interdependent'.[102] On 8 February 1954, Rowan reported that Stage One had been discussed with Commonwealth officials at Sydney and were 'accepted by them as a sensible and useful development'.[103] Overseas Finance and the Bank now pressed Butler for a firm decision and on 3 March 1954 he authorized the Governor to proceed with the scheme.[104] Accordingly, the Chancellor made an oral statement to the Cabinet on 17 March indicating that unification and the reopening of the gold market would take place on 22 March 1954.[105]

The press statement which accompanied the moves on 22 March was decidedly low-key and simply noted that 'these moves mark a stage in the strengthening of London as an international financial centre and of sterling as an international currency'.[106] This was certainly accurate with respect to the reopening of the gold market which, it was hoped, would help restore London as the main world centre for dealings in gold and therefore help support the worldwide value of sterling as an international currency.[107] The relaunch of the gold market was consistent with the government's intention to move towards convertibility, but could not be construed as extending new rights, since only non-residents of the Sterling Area who could pay in American or Canadian sterling (or, of course, dollars), or those receiving special licences from the Bank of England, would be allowed to purchase gold. However, with respect to the unification of sterling, the Chancellor's view that 'this is not a major move – rather a bit of administrative tidying up',[108] was rather more difficult to sustain. Bolton's depoliticized 'new look' exchange policy had, in the words of the *Economic X-Ray*, resulted in the 'maximum technical advance towards convertibility, short of the article itself'.[109] Sterling arising from current transactions would now fall into one of three categories: sterling held by residents of the Sterling Area (which remained subject to exchange control); American or Canadian account sterling (which remained fully convertible); and transferable sterling (which could be paid and received in the rest of the world and used for settlements with the Sterling Area). Not only had the number of countries in the transferable category increased from 18 to around 48, but the policing of transferable sterling had also been relaxed to the extent that the *Economic X-Ray* declared, 'this is nothing else than convertibility of all transferable sterling at a free market rate decided by the non-residents themselves'.[110] However, if Stage One had been achieved relatively painlessly, the route to Stage Two would prove considerably more difficult. Unification could, with some justification, be portrayed as part of a general 'deck-clearing' operation which also included the gradual reopening of some of London's main commodity markets (to include markets in zinc, rubber, tin, lead, copper, coffee, cocoa, raw sugar, raw fur skins, rough diamonds, wool and copra).[111] Intervention in the market for transferable sterling, with a view to encouraging coalescence of the official and transferable rates alongside the adoption of wider spreads and the virtual withering of the distinction between Transferable and American accounts, would be of an entirely different order, and could not be so easily disengaged, politically or economically, from the complexities of the Collective Approach.[112]

Intervention in transferable sterling versus the Collective Approach

Following the unification measure, non-resident sterling could now be regarded as falling into two categories – both of which were, with varying degrees of difficulty, convertible.[113] American account sterling was, of course, convertible 'officially' within the range of the 'gold points' of $2.78 to $2.82. The government's recent operation to widen the market for transferable sterling had also greatly encouraged dealing in the existing mass of convertibility operations in transferable sterling at 'unofficial' sterling/dollar rates. The markets for such transactions (still, of course, formally denied to Sterling Area residents) were widely dispersed across the globe with dealings in Bangkok, Beirut, Tangier, Milan, Rotterdam, Amsterdam and Antwerp.[114] However, the largest markets lay in Zurich and New York, where a number of the largest banks and specialized finance houses (including National City Bank, Chase, the Bank of America, Goldman Sachs, Credit Suisse, the Union Bank of Switzerland and the Swiss Bank Corporation) provided an exchange service in transferable sterling against dollars for their customers.[115] In such markets, transferable sterling was convertible at rates which fluctuated within a wide margin – with a ceiling set by the rate quoted for sterling in the official market, but with no lower limit to the range of its fluctuations. Motivations for entering the market varied. Private holders of sterling in Transferable Account countries might wish, for a number of reasons, and depending on the cost of doing so, to turn it into dollars; to buy dollar goods (in preference to those available for sterling) or to hold dollars rather than sterling; or to take a view on the rate of exchange.[116] Alternatively, private holders of dollars (not necessarily resident in the USA) in need of sterling to make payments in the Sterling Area or elsewhere, might enter the market to buy sterling as cheaply as possible. In short, sterling could be sold at a discount in order to obtain dollars, whilst, on the other hand, the market provided an opportunity of acquiring sterling at the lowest rate available. The form taken by such transactions varied enormously and included the trans-shipment of Sterling Area goods to the United States (so-called 'commodity shunting'), operations in settling invisible payments and the financing of trade between non-Sterling Area countries. In all such dealings, the extent of the convertibility of transferable sterling, at whatever rate the free market dictated, was determined by the willingness of foreign merchants to exchange dollars for sterling. Unofficial rate operations, although wide in scope, remained technically in violation of UK Exchange Control regulations and, most significantly, the cost of such operations did not fall directly on Britain's reserves.[117] This situation, however, would be radically altered if the government made a decision to intervene in the overseas markets for transferable sterling. Intervention to support the transferable rate would mean that the Exchange Equalisation Account stood, for the first time since the war, behind all non-resident sterling used in international trade. Although the formal distinction between American Account and Transferable Account sterling would remain (in other words, de jure convertibility would not have been attained), intervention in transferable markets to bring the rates closer together would finally end the government's long battle against 'cheap sterling' and result in the establishment of a form of convertibility for non-resident sterling.

On 26 April 1954, the Bank sent Overseas Finance a long memorandum outlining the case for intervention to support the transferable rate.[118] In a covering letter, Bolton noted that for some time he had felt that a move towards zero hour implying the sudden introduction of full convertibility of non-resident sterling with a flexible rate was 'not entirely realistic'.[119] The final negotiations surrounding such a move would take place in an atmosphere of considerable publicity and in the circumstances the obligation to stabilize the rate might prove an impossible task. Unification and the reopening of the gold market had been well received in exchange markets and had improved the international position of sterling with the transferable rate coming within the one per cent dealing spreads either side of the official parity.[120] By the end of April, transferable was quoted at $2.79 with the official parity standing at $2.82. The reserves had been strengthened and the tide was running in favour of sterling but, Bolton cautioned, 'it would be a serious matter if the threat of a wide discount were to re-appear'.[121] To maintain confidence, the Chancellor should therefore seize the initiative and introduce further 'technical methods' for the purpose of freeing payments. The Bank recommended three changes. Firstly, the relaxation of some exchange control procedures to allow greater freedom of transfer of blocked sterling; the free import of sterling notes; simplification of control over Securities; and improvement in travel allowances to dollar countries. Secondly, the adoption of a floating or 'moving rate' for the pound with an effective rate of $2.75 to $2.85, or 2 per cent either side of the existing par. Thirdly, intervention to support the transferable rate, 'to accelerate a market tendency for the two rates to coincide'.[122] In short, the Bank proposed bringing together the remaining rates for sterling without any formal responsibility for maintaining convertibility at a fixed rate but with an effective unofficial range of $2.75 to $2.85. In this way, Bolton clarified, the government would have 'a fairly complete experience of de facto convertibility'.[123] The step, however, would be 'irrevocable', it would be impossible to reintroduce fixed rates and if the economic position deteriorated, sterling might depreciate significantly.[124]

The technical complexity of the Bank memorandum brought a confused response from the Treasury. Bernard Gilbert, the new Deputy Secretary in Overseas Finance, interpreted Bolton as calling for 'floating inconvertibility', which of course the Bank had only recently rejected![125] However, once again, Robert Hall made a decisive intervention perceiving that the Bank's proposals were really a substitute for the Collective Approach rather than a step in the direction of what had been agreed by Cabinet.[126] In this regard he noted 'the proposal is really more like Robot (without the support fund) in that we shall have a floating rate and de facto convertibility of all non-resident sterling'.[127] Britain would have acted unilaterally without satisfying any of the conditions thought necessary when the Collective Approach was devised. By 7 May, Overseas Finance had concluded that they could not recommend to the Chancellor the adoption of the Bank's proposals.[128] A 'moving rate' would not be supported by all Commonwealth countries and several European governments had expressed doubts about a flexible rate. Moreover, the Bank's enthusiasm for 'sliding into convertibility', via intervention in the transferable rate, was at odds with convertibility as envisaged by the Commonwealth Conference and the Cabinet. Cheap sterling operations in free markets in New York already existed but this was different in scale, and kind, from 'convertibility authorised, sponsored and supported by H.M.G.'[129]

The reluctance of the Chancellor to press ahead with further 'technical changes' at this stage can also be explained, in part, by his view (shared strongly by Eden) that convertibility could not be introduced before the next General Election, lest it adversely affect the economy and thereby damage the fortunes of the Conservative Party.[130] In addition, as a result of extensive correspondence between Butler and George Humphrey (Secretary of the US Treasury), the Chancellor saw a glimmer of hope in the early months of 1954 that the Collective Approach could be revived.

IV The stand-by credit, the quid pro quo and the Humphrey–Butler talks

The Randall Report, released on 23 January 1954, had recommended that as part of a controlled and gradual approach to full convertibility, a stand-by credit should be found to strengthen Britain's reserves.[131] This could be secured through a more active utilization of the IMF's holdings of gold and currency reserves, supplemented by Federal Reserve credits. Randall had also suggested that although the EPU had achieved an impressive measure of success, it was 'a temporary mechanism with temporary objectives' and it should therefore 'not impede the attainment of a global multilateral system of trade and payments'.[132] John Williams later revealed to Rowan that he had written the section of the Report on convertibility, 'in a way which he hoped would meet our views', but as Rowan made clear, British judgement would 'depend on what action was now taken'.[133] Spurred on by the Randall Commission, the US Treasury began to push the National Advisory Council to support a stand-by credit for Britain and to accept an escape clause in the EPU renewal agreement which would enable Britain to move to convertibility during 1954, if they were prepared to do so.[134] In an attempt to out-flank the Foreign Operations Administration and the State Department, the Treasury now argued:

> We are convinced that the British position on this question is correct. Moreover, British plans for convertibility already have two years of negotiation with the Commonwealth countries behind them. If the United States should take a position on EPU which opposed the British and discouraged them from proceeding with these plans, it is unlikely that they could carry on with them or take the initiative again at least for several years to come.[135]

Accordingly on 30 March, in an address to Congress, the President reported that he had 'approved the Commission's recommendations for co-operation in strengthening the gold and dollar reserves of countries which have prepared themselves for convertibility by sound internal and external policies'.[136] The US was now committed to support the use of the resources of the IMF as a bulwark to strengthen sterling, and other currencies, involved in a move to convertibility. To cap the mood of optimism blowing across the Atlantic, Rooth reported from the IMF that the UK might look to the Fund for a stand-by credit in the region of its quota, approximately $1.3 billion.[137]

Dollar aid and Article VIII

Butler's response in London was to create the Collective Approach Committee – a small committee of officials chaired by Gilbert, to consider whether there could be 'some clearing of minds' on the Collective Approach in preparation for the Humphrey–Butler talks to be held in Washington at the end of September.[138] However, unknown to Butler, the chances of reviving the Collective Approach were suddenly to be dealt a serious blow as the Foreign Operations Administration (FOA) and the State Department initiated a move to tie stand-by credits to the liberalization of dollar imports.[139] Following FOA concerns that the Europeans might not liberalize dollar imports as rapidly as the US might wish, the State Department persuaded the National Advisory Council to accept that 'one of the tests which we shall wish to apply to any plan for sterling convertibility is the degree to which it is compatible with the maintenance and extension of European trade liberalisation'.[140]

At the informal UK–US Burgess Committee meetings opening on 2 June in Washington, it was made clear to Hall-Patch and Rickett that the US Administration would seek a quid pro quo for any financial assistance.[141] A UK stand-by agreement, Burgess clarified, would involve commitments on foreign exchange and trade policy. Countries in receipt of IMF assistance should be prepared to accept, in full, the obligations of Article VIII of the IMF Agreement and give up Article XIV which permitted restrictions on trade and payments for a transitional period (which had, in fact, become the norm).[142] In other words, Britain would be expected to end quantitative restrictions and assume non-discrimination in trade as the quid pro quo for the IMF/US stand-by credit. Although Frank Southard, of the IMF, acknowledged that quantitative restrictions were really a matter for GATT, while exchange restrictions and balance of payments matters were IMF subjects, he stressed that when countries came under Article VIII, they were generally limited in their use of discriminatory quantitative restrictions to the degree of discrimination approved by the IMF for exchange restrictions.[143] On this basis, the IMF would, 'have no trouble interpreting "restrictions" to cover trade as well as payment restrictions'.[144] Candidly, Southard admitted, this would be the price to pay for the stand-by credit. Hall-Patch reported this back to London, and at a later meeting with Burgess he indicated that the UK Government's position was that it 'could not undertake at this time a formal agreement regarding non-discrimination'.[145]

The Collective Approach Committee now recommended that the Government should not do anything which would inevitably commit Britain to carrying out the Collective Approach and convertibility in the near future or take action which might 'remove the control of events from our hands'.[146] Cobbold expressed concern that the new US stance might result in a disastrous '1945 Loan negotiation position' and this despite the progress on the European front over what might succeed EPU in the wake of convertibility.[147] At a meeting of the OEEC on 6 May, the Council had set up a Ministerial Examination Group on Convertibility, under British chairmanship, to consider the impact of convertibility on European trade and payments.[148]

On 4 June, the Council of the OEEC reported on a British proposal that when the EPU was liquidated, a new source of credit might be made available to member countries to maintain a high level of trade and further liberalization within Europe.[149] The source of credit became known as the 'European Fund', to be under the control of the Council of the OEEC, providing short-term credits to enable member countries to withstand temporary balance of payments difficulties without recourse to measures which would reduce the volume of their trade with one another and the rest of the world. It was discussed enthusiastically at a further meeting in Paris in June, and at the OEEC Ministerial Meeting on 9 July, the United States representative indicated that the US contribution to the EPU might be used as a basis for constituting the Fund. This would provide $271 million to set up the European Fund, although it was stressed that the US would 'welcome contributions by the stronger European countries of additional financial and credit facilities on a multilateral basis'.[150] It thus appeared that one of the major stumbling blocks to convertibility – what would replace the EPU and how would US interests in maintaining European co-operation be met – had finally been overcome. The future of the Collective Approach now depended on the outcome of the Humphrey–Butler discussions opening in Washington on 22 September 1954.

The Humphrey–Butler talks

In preparation for the discussions the British Treasury noted that there would be various points of difficulty on the stand-by agreement such as repurchase provisions, conditions for renewal, use of the UK's own reserves and consultation procedures.[151] However, the central issue was how Butler should handle the demand for non-discrimination in trade. On this the Treasury was unequivocal: 'the Chancellor should express the hope that Mr Humphrey will not press us to include in any stand-by agreement precise obligations about trade policies and dated obligations about moving from Article XIV to Article VIII of the Fund'.[152] Such a move would be a matter for concerted international action and agreement. It would not be at all appropriate to a specific stand-by credit agreement between the UK and the IMF. In short, the Treasury emphasized to the Chancellor that 'it is highly undesirable to make the agreement the target for attacks by critics who would say that the American price for a stand-by agreement from the IMF for the UK was the unilateral and unconditional dismantling of discrimination'.[153]

The sensitivity of this issue was also recognized by the National Advisory Council in their preparations for the meeting.[154] Andrew Overby, of the Treasury Department, indicated that the discussions concerning trade restrictions would be 'extremely difficult', in particular concerning the termination of the transition period under Article XIV of the Fund Agreement.[155] US policy, however, as Waugh of the State Department, Southard of the IMF, and Stassen of the FOA, were soon to point out, was unambiguous and could not be changed.[156]

On the second day of the meeting, Reginald Maudling opened discussions on the stand-by credit with Randolph Burgess.[157] He made it clear that the 'UK was not willing to accept any additional obligations on the trade side as part of an agreement for a stand-by credit from the Fund'.[158] In reply, Frank Southard stated that the previous discussions had made it clear that 'some sort of quid pro quo would be required in connection with the extension of a credit'.[159] Southard then suggested that countries proceeding to convertibility and requiring credits should accept higher standards of commercial policy than the rest of the world. This proposal, Maudling stated flatly, would not be acceptable to the UK and 'there would be the greatest difficulty in any attempt to put such a proposal to Parliament'.[160] Predictably, a stalemate had been reached. On the final day of the meetings, Butler indicated that the Collective Approach was deadlocked and that convertibility would not be launched in the near future. Unimpressed by Burgess's remark that it was probably no longer possible to reduce US tariff barriers, the Chancellor stated that when he went home, 'it would be thought that he had put his money on a horse that did not appear to be running too well'.[161]

Despite progress on the European Fund – now considered more important than ever by the US given the rejection by the French Assembly of the European Defence Community Treaty on 29 August – it was clear to all that Butler's last gamble on the Collective Approach had failed. The mood in the Bank, however, was less pessimistic as the door had again been opened to the pursuit of convertibility by other, less political, means. On Butler's return to London, Cobbold suggested that the next few months should be used for 'getting ahead constructively and quietly with the things we can do without anybody's permission and with support from our Commonwealth and European partners (but keeping our policy firmly in our hands and not putting it in theirs)'.[162] This, of course, meant moving ahead with Stage Two of Bolton's grand design. As the balance of payments dipped and the transferable rate fell, Cobbold prepared, once again, to push for de facto convertibility in the guise of technical market readjustment.

V 'Operation Governor' and de facto convertibility

By November 1954, the transferable rate, which had been within three cents of the official rate in May, was showing a discount of some eight cents.[163] The report of the Programmes Committee forecast a UK current account deficit of £70 million for 1955 (compared with a surplus of £165 million in 1954), while the Sterling Area as a whole, which had recorded a surplus with the rest of the world of £50 million in 1954, was forecast to move to a deficit of £75 million in 1955.[164] This would reduce the reserves by some

£35 million. The deterioration in the Sterling Area balance of payments was attributed to a rise of approximately £300 million in UK imports – less than half of which was due to price increases.[165] Although a deficit of £75 million was not large, it was, for the Programmes Committee, 'a clear indication of the trouble that may be ahead if we are not seen to be taking action to put the situation right'.[166]

The relationship between the predicted balance of payments deficit and the deterioration in the transferable rate was certainly not one of cause and effect. Government statisticians could only generalize that the discount varied because of a mixture of 'real' factors such as supply and demand for sterling, and 'confidence' based partly on experience of the Sterling Area's performance in the recent past, partly on anticipations of what its performance was likely to be, and partly on anticipation of, and rumours about, policy change.[167] However, the deterioration in the balance, alongside the weakening of the rate from the middle of 1954, provided the perfect context for the Bank to claim, once again, that internal action alone would not rectify the situation. The market in transferable sterling had, Bolton claimed, grown enormously since unification.[168] In fact, he suggested, transferable sterling was becoming 'more and more *the* sterling which foreigners know and use, and the mere extent and importance of sterling as an international currency tends to increase this'.[169] Since the collapse of the Collective Approach in September, the fall in the rate had reflected the markets' 'growing doubts about the policy of H.M.G'.[170] It was imperative, Bolton suggested, that the Government act quickly and decisively on the transferable rate to restore confidence.[171]

On 20 January 1955, Cobbold circulated two notes setting out the position of the Bank.[172] The proposals suggested by Cobbold were later referred to by the incoming Economic Secretary, Edward Boyle, as 'Operation Governor' and would dominate discussions on external economic policy for the next eight months.[173] Cobbold began by stating that although recent moves to revive the Collective Approach had failed, it would not be wise to 'sit tight', since the UK exchange system was now lagging behind both movements in trade and what was actually happening in foreign exchange markets around the world. At the root of Britain's troubles was the re-emergence of a multiple rate structure for international sterling. Once again, the strength of sterling was being sapped away, 'materially because payment to the Sterling Area is increasingly made through cheap sterling, and psychologically because of the existence of an active market in cheap sterling at a considerable discount'.[174] The loss of business to foreign competitors, the scarcity of dollars in the official London market, and the discount in what many regarded as the 'true' rate, all combined, he argued, to damage confidence, with adverse effects on sterling and the reserves. The only lasting solution would be full formal convertibility of 'non-resident' sterling to terminate the coexistence of two types of external sterling convertible at different rates. In present circumstances, however, Cobbold favoured a technical move which would fall short of formal convertibility and which was designed to eliminate the margin between the two rates, and thereby remove some of the disabilities under which UK traders now suffered. In short, he recommended action, firstly, to bring and keep official sterling and transferable sterling together without any formal act or commitment; secondly, to manage both these rates within a spread of $2.70 to $2.90 without commitments on long-term rate policy; and thirdly, to initiate a review of EPU commitments with a view to reducing obligations to provide automatic sterling credit. Alongside these measures, Cobbold suggested that the government, 'seek the blessing' of the IMF, without submitting a request for a formal stand-by agreement.[175]

Cobbold's notes caused both excitement and confusion in the Treasury. Rowan's initial assessment was that there were strong arguments, both economic and political, against the Bank plan.[176] Unsure of the technicalities, he concluded that the Governor's 'far-reaching' ideas 'could not be decided without submission to the Cabinet'.[177] By 10 February, Overseas Finance had arrived at a more balanced view which reached three principal conclusions.[178] Firstly, external action alone would not overcome the current economic difficulties. Internal measures would be required to reduce the current deficit otherwise there would continue to be pressure on sterling – and weakness in the rates. Secondly, in respect of action in the external field, Overseas Finance could not recommend the proposals contained in the Governor's notes of 20 January. In practice, Rowan noted, the Governor's proposals amounted to 'the convertibility of sterling on external account'. He clarified,

> the formal position will be maintained – i.e. we have no legal obligation to maintain the two rates near together and there is a distinction between dollar accounts and other non-sterling accounts. But these are of such a technical and narrow character that the world will assume – and that is what counts – that we are in fact convertible on external account. At any rate we shall be under such pressure that the formal distinction will soon vanish.[179]

De facto convertibility would have been reached unilaterally by a technical route, but without the support of a stand-by, favourable US trade policies or a 'settled and fair' political and economic climate. The risks associated with Operation Governor, according to Rowan, were simply too great, particularly when there was an alternative method of holding the line. Thirdly, therefore, Overseas Finance recommended a course of action which combined internal measures (an increase in the Bank Rate and deflationary measures in the Budget) and intervention in the transferable market – of a kind, however, which fell short of the Governor's proposal. In detail, Rowan suggested that the official spreads could be left where they were and the authorities could intervene in the transferable market, as they saw fit but without involving any commitment to intervene at any point or to maintain the transferable rate in any particular relationship with the official rate. The aim of this policy would be to keep the rate at a figure in relation to official sterling which it made it less profitable to deal.[180] Rowan ended by noting that intervention of this sort, without widening the official rates, 'does create some presumption in favour of fixed rates under convertibility', but he did not consider this a decisive objection.[181] On the difficult issue of timing, he concluded that internal measures should be tried at once, and, if successful, intervention might be a policy which could, with advantage, be adopted later in the process.

Intervention in the transferable market and de facto convertibility

The disagreement between the Bank and Overseas Finance, over intervention in the transferable market, was brought to a head at three critical meetings held on 21, 22 and 23 February 1955. At the first, Cobbold began by noting that ever since Robot had been turned down, he had predicted the likelihood of a currency crisis.[182] Internal action in respect of raising Bank Rate to 4.5 per cent and regaining control over hire purchase would help but 'were not enough by themselves'.[183] The market had its eyes on the exchange structure and only action to bring and keep official sterling and transferable sterling together across a wider spread would suffice. Butler's reply mirrored the objections laid out by Rowan on 10 February. The Cabinet would not approve measures which amounted to de facto convertibility – certainly not before an election – and, even if they did, he doubted whether they could be passed through Parliament. Butler, at this meeting, also rejected Rowan's form of intervention in the transferable market. He thought it 'unsound', involving 'great risks', committing the government 'definitely to take the further steps to full external convertibility'.[184] Bolton, at this point, confirmed that intervention would commit the government irrevocably to external convertibility but not to any specific form of convertibility (whether fixed or with a spread). However, lack of action on the exchange front, he claimed, might equally cost anything from $500 million to $1 billion in the next three to six months. The meeting closed deadlocked. Rowan warned that the Governor's proposals would raise major political and economic issues across Europe and the Commonwealth, and Cobbold replied that no action on the exchange structure would be misunderstood by the markets and also give rise to alarm.

The next day, Cobbold and Bolton suggested to Butler that if the Bank proposals of 20 January could not be implemented, then a modified version of Rowan's plan for intervention should be given serious consideration.[185] There was perhaps no need to widen the spread at this point or seek coalescence of the rates. Rather, the current one per cent spread could remain

and the Bank would intervene simply to reduce the discount on transferable sterling from 3 per cent to one per cent. This action, according to
Bolton, 'would not be seen as a change of policy nor as the acceptance by
the Bank of some new responsibility'.[186] The suggestion was supported by
Bernard Gilbert, who noted that the proposal, 'envisaged a quiet revolution
in the market, so that action on the exchange front would not form part of
any "packet" of severe measures'.[187] Despite opposition from Rowan, who
still preferred to hold intervention 'in suspense', Butler was attracted by
the idea and closed the meeting promising to reach a decision before they
met again at 3.15 p.m. the next day. On the morning of 23 February, Butler
met with Churchill to explain the changes which had been proposed. He
reported to the gathering at the Treasury later that afternoon that the Prime
Minister had accepted the Bank's new suggestion for intervening in the
transferable market.[188] However, he had cautioned that the matter be put to
the Cabinet, and a Cabinet meeting had therefore been arranged for 4.00
p.m. that day. Cobbold restated that the measure was 'another decisive step
in the direction of convertibility' and if the Cabinet decided against intervention, he could not 'with a clear conscience recommend to the Court an
increase in Bank Rate this week'.[189] Asked by Butler how long after intervention could the position be held without further steps in the direction of
formal convertibility, Cobbold replied, somewhat prophetically, that 'from
the technical angle it might be possible to hold the situation for quite some
time'.[190]

There was, it appears, little discussion in Cabinet about the merits of the
move to intervene in the transferable market.[191] Butler, somewhat disingenuously, indicated that the move was designed to check trafficking in transferable sterling and that intervention 'was not designed as a further step
towards convertibility of sterling'.[192] However, he clarified, intervention
would make it easier, when the time came, to take the next step towards full
convertibility. This, somewhat less than full, presentation of the facts ensured
that the Cabinet approved intervention alongside measures to increase the
Bank Rate and reintroduce controls over hire purchase facilities.

A bridge from Stage One to Stage Two had at last been constructed. A form
of external convertibility had arrived 'by the backdoor, unofficially, and
notably unacknowledged by its sponsors'.[193] The 'quiet revolution in the
market' had achieved what seemed impossible by more overt political
routes, such as the Collective Approach. This form of convertibility was not,
of course, de jure convertibility, and some doubt remained as to whether or
not it actually constituted de facto convertibility. Technically, the distinction between Transferable and American Accounts remained and there were
still two rates for sterling, albeit separated by only one per cent. The dealing
spread had not been widened, and no stand-by credit or other measures of
fortification were in sight. Nevertheless, as *The Economist* quickly pointed

out, it was wrong to dismiss intervention as 'mere technical legerdemain', as an ingenious trick intended to close the door to commodity shunting or hammer the 'wicked' foreign merchant and exchange dealer.[194] A more important and enduring issue of principle was at stake. The authorities were now reinforcing the convertibility of transferable sterling. From 24 February 1955, transferable sterling could 'confer upon its holders an undefined but nonetheless direct claim upon the Exchange Account's resources'.[195] As Cobbold was later to point out, this form of intervention meant that external sterling was 'virtually 100 per cent convertible at a 1 per cent discount in the transferable market'.[196]

In Washington, the US Treasury approved the move[197] and at the IMF, Eddie Bernstein announced that 'the United Kingdom action was the greatest single move in the history of the Fund. It meant that anybody who wanted dollars could obtain them through sterling, though at some discount, on the official rate. Official intervention had given the market a new status and a new respectability.'[198]

In Whitehall, however, the confusion, over whether a state of de facto convertibility had in fact been reached, continued well into the summer. After a month's experience of managing the two markets in sterling, Bolton began to press the Treasury to move to Stage Two by bringing the rates together and widening the spread from \$2.78–\$2.80 to \$2.70–\$2.90.[199] Once the rates were virtually identical, Bolton noted, there would be no technical advantage in retaining the distinction between Transferable and American Account Sterling. Nor, as a matter of administration, would it make much sense to demand that permission be sought for transfers from Transferable to American Account (although the separate designations could be retained for a time). At this point, Bolton clarified, 'we shall have achieved "de facto" convertibility of non-resident sterling'.[200] The question of whether to move in stages or to proceed at once to formal amalgamation of the two types of account (de jure convertibility of non-resident sterling) was, in the last instance, a political rather than a technical matter. Either step would require an approach to be made to the IMF – but only for a sympathetic response in relation to the Bank plan rather than a stand-by credit. As Cobbold was later to point out, the advantage of the technical move to Stage Two was that it would achieve convertibility without the need to abandon Article XIV of the Fund Agreement. In other words, it would be possible to move to convertibility by stealth, enabling the government to maintain certain exchange control and trade restrictions.[201] The confusion over when convertibility had in fact been reached could be used to the advantage of the government. Stage Two provided a perfect route to the prize of convertibility, at a floating rate, without encountering the interminable political and economic difficulties raised by negotiations surrounding the Collective Approach.

Overseas Finance versus the Bank

This time, however, Overseas Finance, somewhat resentful that the Bank appeared to be making the running on external policy, refused to sanction what they regarded as a policy riven with political dilemmas. Rowan noted that the distinction between the Governor's proposals and convertibility on external account was so transparent, and would be seen to be so by the world, that it would soon vanish.[202] Dennis Rickett doubted the wisdom of the Bank plan, recognizing that 'we shall be open to the charge, which has already been made with reference to the support given to transferable sterling, that we are abandoning the idea of a Collective Approach and going ahead on our own'.[203] The government would then be forced into the politically difficult position of trying to maintain that 'this was *not* convertibility'.[204] Since the difference between de facto and de jure convertibility was largely one of presentation and emphasis, why, Rickett asked, should we not make sterling convertible in name and 'take credit for doing so and not allow a step which is so important, and represents a culmination of our external economic policy over the last three years, to be taken as it were by stealth'?[205] Overseas Finance therefore recommended to the Chancellor that the Bank plan to move to Stage Two be rejected, that the present position be maintained and that the next step should be a final move to de jure convertibility.[206]

On 6 April, Winston Churchill left No. 10 and Anthony Eden assumed the office of Prime Minister in the run-up to the General Election which was held on 26 May.[207] During the Election lull, Overseas Finance prepared a position paper for the Chancellor which again argued that the distinction between the Governor's plan and de jure convertibility was so slender that 'it would be rightly regarded as a sham'.[208] The next step, Overseas Finance reiterated, should be to full formal convertibility on external account and could only be taken from a position of strength.

The return of the Conservatives to office, with a comfortable majority, provided another opportunity for Cobbold to press for the move to Stage Two. However, this was blocked once again by Rowan who argued that a unilateral decision to end the EPU would be regarded an act of 'bad faith' and that Britain would be accused of having abandoned any idea of a Collective Approach.[209] The economy, he asserted, was in an exposed position at present and convertibility could not be attempted without having established the preconditions laid out in the 1952 Commonwealth Conference communiqué. The Chancellor agreed and suggested that at the Fund/Bank meetings to be at Istanbul in September, he would adopt the line of 'stay put plus internal strengthening'.[210] This was in spite of the fact that, on 29 July, the Council of the OEEC had agreed to the renewal of the EPU and had approved the text of the new European Monetary Agreement which settled the terms of the European Fund and provided for a multilateral system to facilitate settlements between member countries should convertibility be re-established.[211] The long-running saga of the 'EPU problem' need no longer stand in the way of sterling convertibility.

At the end of three 'clarification meetings' held on 8, 9 and 10 August 1955, the Governor and the Chancellor placed on record their respective positions regarding exchange rate policy.[212] The stated positions would not change, in any fundamental sense, for the next three years. In the view of the Bank, de facto convertibility (that is, unification of the official and transferable rates) with some widening of the spread, was required to restore confidence in sterling. Doubts had arisen, particularly since the signing of the European Monetary Agreement, about whether the government was going to press ahead with convertibility. If no further action was taken, then this situation of suspicion would continue and any underlying deficit in the balance of payments would be exacerbated by general market unease. The end result might be 'a loss of confidence leading to a very dangerous situation in which drastic re-consideration of many of the government's policies might prove necessary'.[213] In such circumstances, the Governor 'could not rule out the possibility of devaluation'.[214] Furthermore, the Bank stressed that whilst a formal declaration of convertibility would almost inevitably lead to the acceptance of non-discrimination in trade, slipping into convertibility by market forces (the Bank plan) would not necessarily incur the costs of Article VIII.

In response, the Chancellor noted that the Treasury broadly agreed that it was necessary to bring the rates together, but they differed on the timing of the move. Although the Bank took the view that unification of the rates was a small step compared with those already taken, the Treasury were unable to regard it as other than the last step towards non-resident convertibility – 'it was the significant step that led over the threshold'.[215] Moreover, as regards non-discrimination, the Treasury attached far less importance than the Bank to the fact that the Bolton/Cobbold plan did not involve a formal declaration of de jure convertibility. The move would inevitably attract early notice and be considered as full convertibility, whether 'we regarded ourselves as de facto convertible or not'.[216] Consequently, the US Administration would push for Britain to accept the full obligations of Article VIII regardless of the legal position under the Fund Articles. Unknown to the British, this was indeed the direction in which the Fund was moving, although the Executive Board was split over whether the UK could remain under Article XIV for six, 12 or 18 months following convertibility.[217] Finally, the Chancellor concluded, the next move – to full de jure convertibility – was to be made when conditions were favourable, not at a time when the government was grappling with balance of payments problems.

The disagreement between the Bank and Overseas Finance over external policy was, as Fforde points out, a disappointing outcome to all they had been through together since 1951.[218] The restructuring of the Overseas

Finance Division, instigated by Robert Hall, had left Rowan isolated and, 'as he came under the influence of new people in OF', increasingly distrustful of the Bank.[219] However, despite resistance, the Bank was able to capitalize on the demise of the Collective Approach and make significant strides towards the de facto convertibility of non-resident sterling. The end of the Collective Approach signalled the end of radical attempts by the British government to remake the postwar world economy. However, it did not provide a clear path to the full restoration of currency convertibility across Europe. In the summer of 1955, it was by no means clear when, or on what terms, full convertibility would be achieved or whether the Bretton Woods institutions could be resuscitated. The next chapter documents the final moves in the convertibility saga, from Suez, through Thorneycroft's 'September measures' to the restoration of Europe-wide convertibility on Monday 29 December 1958.

8
From Suez to Operation Unicorn

From the summer of 1955 to the start of Operation Unicorn in October 1958, the Bank made numerous attempts to push to Stage Two, only to be rebutted in familiar tones by Overseas Finance and the Chancellor. The Cabinet reshuffle in December 1955, which sent Butler to the post of Lord Privy Seal and installed Harold Macmillan as Chancellor, made little difference to this stalemate.

In the early months of 1956, Cobbold sent Macmillan a personal note in which he suggested that the present arrangement was 'a three-quarter house and something of a nonsense'.[1] It was never supposed, he noted, that the existing arrangements could be a satisfactory permanent or semi-permanent technique. The fundamental issues were, firstly, whether to move to bring the two rates together; and secondly, if the rates were brought together, would it be inside the $2.78–2.82 bracket or would there be a wider spread? Cobbold was adamant that it was right to act sooner rather than later and that 'the two most important points on timing are to do it when the world sees a longish run without probable change of Government, and to do it when things have been worse and look like getting better'.[2] On the issue of wider spreads he now conceded that 'we have missed the boat for a flexible rate or wider spreads. If we had done it some years back and been content to pick up the pieces afterwards, I think we could have got away with it and derived some advantage'.[3] But, he now feared that 'after the palaver last Summer' few countries would follow a move in the direction of flexible rates and many would regard it as a first step to further devaluation. In any event, he concluded, 'the one thing we must absolutely avoid is further discussion or negotiation on the rate question. Sterling will just not stand it. We have discussed all this ad infinitum with Commonwealth, USA and Europe. We need now to decide what we want to do, and do it'.[4]

Macmillan's response was strongly influenced by Rickett and Rowan in Overseas Finance, who concluded that the state of confidence in sterling was not, at present, sufficiently strong to justify taking such a risk.[5] The move would attract a good deal of attention, act as a signal for the removal of discrimination in trade and close the door on one protective mechanism offered by the current arrangement: 'to let go of the transferable rate again and take our chance on commodity shunting', if sterling came under severe pressure.[6] By June 1956, Cobbold summed up the policy stalemate in terms familiar to those who had followed the debates since February 1952. On the vexed issue of de jure convertibility, both sides he noted, could produce 'A lot of good reasons for doing the things we ought to do and a lot of good reasons for not doing them until a lot of things happen, which never will happen'.[7]

This indecision was partly a result of disorganization in Overseas Finance, and the Treasury more broadly, in the summer of 1956. Towards the end of June, it was announced that Edward Bridges and Bernard Gilbert would retire in October, to be replaced by the long-suffering Norman Brook, and, on the economic side, by Roger Makins.[8] The appointment of Makins, who had served continuously up until this point in the Foreign Office, over Rowan, was a slap in the face for Overseas Finance. Macmillan, it seems, had wanted to 'get rid' of Rowan and send him to the War Office.[9] Rowan refused and told Macmillan that 'the appointment of Makins was the biggest blow the Civil Service had ever received'.[10] In the midst of this confusion and bitterness, news broke on 26 July that Nasser had nationalized the Suez Canal Company following the failure of negotiations, primarily with the Americans, over the financing of the High Dam on the Nile at Aswan.[11]

I The sterling crises of 1956 and 1957

The events of the Suez crisis are well documented and need not be taken up here in any detail except insofar as they have bearing on the final move to convertibility.[12] In August, as it became clear that there would be no easy settlement of the quarrel with Egypt, Cobbold and Rowan advised Macmillan that the correct course of action was to maintain firm intervention in the exchange markets.[13] There could no thought of a return to bilateralism or of letting the transferable fall, as Rickett had earlier suggested. However, in the event of war with Egypt, without American support, the strain on sterling might become so great that the existing parity could not be maintained. The Bank, in such circumstances, would favour a floating rate and recommend action be taken to bring the official and transferable rates together.[14] This course of action, however, was 'remote and undesirable', and it was therefore essential, as Bridges and Makins emphasized to Macmillan, that for the sake of the currency and the economy 'we do not go it alone, and that we have the maximum US support'.[15] In the middle of October, Cobbold reported to Macmillan the views of eight Commonwealth central bank Governors who had visited London on return from meetings in Washington. A number expressed the view that a further devaluation of sterling, which the Suez crisis might make more likely, would mean the immediate break-up of the Sterling Area and the disintegration of the currency.[16] Cobbold's reply, positively acknowledged by Macmillan, was that the government was determined to maintain the existing parity and that 'earlier ideas of wider spreads were no longer running'.[17] An obvious route to shore up the parity, already taken by France was to request a stand-by credit from the IMF. In late October, however, the Treasury accepted Cobbold's view that such an application would be taken as a sign of weakness.[18]

There seems no doubt that the Bank and most Treasury officials, including Rowan, were kept completely in the dark about the Anglo-French hostilities launched against Egypt on 31 October, until the evening of 30 October.[19] Macmillan, it seems, failed to convey the full force of the Treasury and the Bank's warnings to Eden, and, furthermore, misled the Cabinet into believing that although the Americans would issue a protest, 'they would in their hearts be glad to see the matter brought to a conclusion'.[20] Between noon on 30 October and noon on 6 November, the day the Cabinet agreed to a cease-fire, the government lost nearly $100 million in support of sterling.[21] The cease-fire, however, was only the first step towards the resolution of the crisis. By the end of the month it was clear that November had seen the reserves fall by $279 million, bringing the total down to $1,965 million, the lowest level since the end of 1952 and below the 'action level' of $2 billion.[22] In these conditions, the Treasury and the Bank discussed a number of 'crash course' programmes, including closing commodity markets and letting the transferable rate fall, and introducing unification whilst allowing sterling to float.[23] However, it was generally agreed that the right course was to maintain the stability of the currency, whilst discussing with the United States the various drastic options under consideration should US support for sterling not be forthcoming.[24] This approach was nicely emphasized in a letter from Macmillan to George Humphrey, the Secretary of the US Treasury, which noted 'The undermining of sterling would of course hurt us, but that would be far from all. It would do irreparable damage not merely to sterling but to the whole fabric of trade and payments in the Free World. This would be a major victory for the Communists'.[25]

Following the censure of Britain and France by the UN General Assembly on 24 November, Humphrey indicated that if Britain agreed to withdraw, the US would act in support of sterling.[26] On 3 December, the Foreign Secretary informed the House of Commons that British and French forces were to be withdrawn, and on 7 December the US National Advisory Council advised the US Executive Director of the IMF that it approved the UK government's request for a drawing of $561 million and a stand-by credit for one year permitting drawings up to $739 million.[27] This was followed on 21 December by National Advisory Council (NAC) approval of an Export–Import Bank line of credit of $500 million to the UK government to finance dollar requirements for US equipment, materials and services and UK dollar requirements for petroleum products.[28] Finally, NAC approved a

British request for a waiver of the December 1956 interest payments due under the terms of the Anglo-American Financial Agreement and the Canadian–United Kingdom Financial Agreement, which together totalled $104 million.[29]

The Suez crisis had revealed the precarious position of sterling and the continued dependence of the British economy on US financial assistance whenever there was a serious weakening of overseas confidence in the currency. Although concerted action had contained the drain on the reserves, it had done nothing, as Maurice Parsons (in the Bank) indicated, to change the attitude that had given rise to the underlying weakness on which the confidence crisis was built.[30] In Cobbold's view, only 'dramatic, far-reaching and convincing measures', central to which of course remained the unification of official and transferable sterling, would convince the market that sterling had recovered and that rumours of devaluation were unfounded.[31] The resignation of Anthony Eden on 9 January 1957, and the installation of Harold Macmillan as Prime Minister and Peter Thorneycroft as Chancellor, gave Cobbold some hope that convincing measures might be taken, although these were soon dashed as a new currency crisis emerged following concern about the ability of the government to contain wage inflation and the de facto devaluation of the French franc in mid-August.

Thorneycroft's brief Chancellorship is usually seen as significant because of the introduction of the infamous 'September measures' (a 2 per cent rise in Bank Rate, tightening of credit controls and assurances regarding the containment of public expenditure); because of his tussle with the Deputy Governor over a proposed ceiling on Bank advances (Thorneycroft was told that he had neither the power to direct the Bank or sack the Governor); and because of his dramatic resignation, with Birch and Powell, on 6 January 1958 over his repeated failure to convince the Cabinet of the need for tough public expenditure reductions to tackle inflation.[32] However, for our purposes the significance of the crisis of 1957 lies in the fact that it brought to the fore yet further schemes for floating rate convertibility, this time favoured by one of the arch opponents of Robot, Robert Hall.

Exchange crisis under Thorneycroft

Soon after his appointment, Thorneycroft suggested to the Cabinet that unless strong domestic measures were taken to halt wage and price increases then 'the question is not whether the pound sterling will be devalued but when'.[33] The government, he suggested, must take action to change the attitude of the country towards unrestricted collective bargaining, at least to realize that 'it cannot have this, full employment, and price stability at the same time'.[34] In the absence of such action, there was a real danger that the currency would be undermined, and the government would be faced with 'a flight from the pound through lack of confidence in policies so manifestly profligate'.[35] However, when the crisis broke, in mid-August, its cause was neither a new wave of industrial unrest nor the threat of rising costs, but the effective devaluation of the French franc which set off a wave of currency speculation in Europe.[36]

The French action, and the growing strength of the West German economy, sparked a public debate on the realignment of European exchange rates. The French, it was thought, had not gone far enough and the German mark seemed clearly undervalued. As Cobbold noted, 'this has given a new spurt to general gossip and uncertainty about currencies, which is largely concentrated on sterling and which looks likely to continue until after the Washington meetings or a change of policy by the Germans or both'.[37] In the last three weeks of August 1957, the reserves fell by $203 million, reducing total holdings to $2.14 billion.[38] Cobbold realized that nothing could be done co-operatively with the Germans until after their elections in mid-September, and so 'we should dig our toes in absolutely firmly until then (and we should encourage any other European who may come under pressure to do the same)'.[39] This effectively meant adherence to five principles. Firstly, a defence of the rate at £1 to $2.78. Secondly, a commitment to persuade the Germans to make changes in their fiscal, monetary, lending and/or exchange policy. Thirdly, material support from the IMF for any plan which might emerge from discussions. Fourthly, domestic action by the 'deficit countries' (Britain and France) to help restore confidence in their currencies and, finally, the maintenance of European co-operation to make it possible to move successfully from EPU to EMA.[40]

Thinking further ahead to the Fund/Bank meetings in Washington at the end of September, Cobbold noted that Britain could either press to maintain the existing European exchange rate pattern at all costs or move to adopt floating rates in Europe, either with or without wide top limits, but keeping the bottom rate on the dollar fixed.[41] The first course of action was fine, but, he asked, was it practicable? A move to floating was attractive, especially when combined with unification of the transferable and official rates, but the Germans would not easily allow the mark to go as far as the market wanted, and so speculation was still probable, with consequent dangers for sterling. However, a readjustment of upward margins in Europe (rather than a complete removal of top limits) to a spread of, say, $2.78–3.00, might just 'do the trick'.[42] Convincing the Germans to change current policy would still present immense difficulties, and the risks to the pound of starting an open argument on whether the German mark should be revalued against the dollar, or sterling devalued against the dollar, were all too evident. Cobbold concluded, 'it looks likely that we may get into an absolutely first-class row with Germany, in which it would be vital to have USA (and IMF) on our side and if possible having their own row with Germany'.[43]

The Treasury was somewhat sceptical of Cobbold's more radical suggestions, particularly his attempt to smuggle through unification of the rates.

Arnold France, in Overseas Finance, noted that the Treasury had to decide 'whether we can provide ourselves with big enough boots to kick the Germans into acquiescence, or whether we are prepared for some general widening of the margins both above and below the parity'.[44] The latter course, he observed, would be one of weakness unless it could be put forward as an element in a larger policy move. France repeated this advice to Rowan, with the additional observation that following a meeting with Makins and Hall, Macmillan 'raised the question of floating rates and seemed attracted; he looks on it as a sort of coping stone in the removal of controls by the Conservative Government'.[45] Makins' own recollection of the meeting was that whilst the Prime Minister was 'inclined towards "freeing the pound", he expressed the view that we should not contemplate it voluntarily except at a period when sterling was strong, e.g. in the first half of next year, and perhaps in relation to some important development, e.g. a success on the wages front'.[46] By the end of the month, Macmillan and Thorneycroft were in agreement with Cobbold, that until the Fund/Bank meetings, policy 'must be to proceed as at present, denying firmly both the need and the intention to change the parity of sterling'.[47] In the meantime, the Treasury and the Bank were instructed to continue to probe various alternative policies, including a crash programme of floating rate convertibility.[48]

The policy of defending the existing parity seemed to be paying off as there was a decline in the rate of loss of reserves in the latter part of August.[49] However, in Cabinet on 10 September, Thorneycroft announced that the mere reaffirmation of commitment to the parity at the IMF Meetings in Washington would not be sufficient to stem the drain: it had to be accompanied by the introduction of severe restrictions on expenditure, especially investment.[50] Thorneycroft had been advised by Cobbold on 22 August, before the Governor left on a three-week holiday to Sardinia, that if the situation continued to deteriorate into September, further domestic measures would have to be taken.[51] The measures would have to 'sharp and comprehensive', but, Cobbold maintained, the credit squeeze was 'played out' and no new device in that field would be worthwhile.[52] This left a rise in Bank Rate which in conjunction with a general programme might have quick effects and need not be maintained too long.[53] In Cobbold's absence, in early September Thorneycroft moved to impose a limit on bank credit together with the proposed limit on public expenditure. On 11 September, the Chancellor met with the Deputy Governor Humphrey Mynors, and the entire 11-man board of the Committee of London Clearing Bankers, and threatened to impose an advanced limit by Act of Parliament.[54] However, Mynors stood firm. He knew that a specific limit would be unacceptable to the banks, might lead to a further loss of confidence in sterling and would in any case be unworkable. He also knew, as Fforde makes clear, that the only statutory powers in existence were those contained in the Bank of England Act and that they could not be used unless the Bank considered it in the public interest; and that judging the public interest in this case was reserved by law to the Governors and their colleagues on the Court.[55] In short, neither the Chancellor nor the Treasury could order the Bank to make a particular judgement.

After much vitriol (and the return of Cobbold from Sardinia), Thorneycroft retreated to a policy of a 2 per cent increase in Bank Rate combined with a brake on public investment (which was to be kept at its nominal 1957 level for a period of two years).[56] These measures were announced on 19 September, and five days later, at the Fund/Bank meetings in Washington, he declared the government's intention to maintain sterling's existing parity. This was supported by a corresponding statement from the German authorities, who had also taken action to reduce their Bank Rate on 19 September from 4.5 to 4 per cent.[57] The UK reserves, which by the end of the month had dropped to $1,850 million (their lowest level since 1952), now began to recover and there was an underlying rise in the reserves of $120 million in October.[58] The position of sterling was strengthened further in October when the government drew $250 million of the $500 million credit arranged with the Export–Import Bank in December 1956, and, once again, claimed the waiver on the interest payments due under the American and Canadian loan agreements.[59]

The immediate crisis was over, and although Thorneycroft had a final, dramatic act to play in January 1958, the details of his demise are not the concern of this particular study. One aspect of the 1957 crisis which does, however, warrant further discussion is the apparent conversion of many Treasury officials, not least Robert Hall, to the idea of a floating rate.

Robert Hall and the floating rate

On 18 September, Macmillan asked Thorneycroft to outline a little more precisely the actual machinery that would need to be adopted if it was thought that the time had come to move to a floating rate.[60] Rickett responded three days later, indicating that in extreme circumstances, Britain could abandon the present one per cent margin on either side of the parity allowing the rate to fluctuate, and establish convertibility for non-resident sterling by bringing the transferable and official rates together.[61] An effort would be made to persuade the Germans to join in the float and if this proved possible the European Monetary Agreement would come into force, replacing the EPU. The most difficult aspect of the operation would be to decide at which point the government would give up trying to hold the parity and allow the rate to fall. In addition, there was the problem posed by upward pressure on wages and prices which would follow from the fall in the rate. This latter point was taken up in some detail by Robert Hall.[62]

In contrast to his stance throughout 1952, Hall had now come to accept the case for the floating rate.[63] It was, he noted, 'quite different when one does this because another currency is undervalued, and when one's own is weak because of one's own policies. It would be much easier to defend our action and would cast much less doubt on the position of sterling in the long run.'[64] Hall assumed that other major currencies except the dollar would float and that the German mark would appreciate against the dollar. Sterling would, of course, fall, but the extent of the fall would be cushioned by the satisfactory trading position and by the fact that 'as the rate falls, our currency gets more attractive because of what it will buy in the UK'.[65] If internal prices remained stable, a 10 per cent reduction (to a dollar rate of 2.50) would, he noted, make British goods look very cheap, particularly if the German mark floated up in terms of the dollar and the pound. Hall thus concluded that floating was an attractive option, if the balance of payments remained satisfactory and if the effect of the fall in the rate was not offset by a large and accelerating rise in domestic price levels.

Hall's assessment of the impact of floating on the internal economy provides interesting reading in the light of his specific objections to Robot in 1952. In respect of imports he now claimed that since a large proportion of Britain's imports came from Sterling Area or 'soft' currency sources, a 10 per cent depreciation would only raise the average level of import prices by 3–4 per cent. This, in turn, would raise the retail price index by little more than one per cent, since the cost of imports represented about one-third of the total cost of production of consumer goods and services. The retail price index had increased by 2 per cent between January and August 1957, and was expected to have increased by 4 per cent at the end of the first quarter of 1958. This, Hall suggested, was 'a rather surprising result; – that the retail price index after a 10 per cent devaluation may only rise very slightly more than last year'.[66] There was, after all, no reason to suppose that a strong depreciation would send prices and wages spiralling out of control.

In respect of wages, Hall suggested that the trade unions would probably regard as acceptable an increase in wage rates of between 6 and 7 per cent. This would not exceed what had been conceded in some recent years, and it was unlikely that the 6 or 7 per cent increase would be passed on fully in higher prices. In fact, through conciliation, the government could attempt to strike an early bargain with the unions. Workers, he noted, 'would have to be persuaded that everybody was making similar sacrifices to save the currency'.[67] This could be backed up by the government agreeing to a price freeze, to be reviewed after a limited period, perhaps even with subsidies for major items like bread. In short, Hall advised Macmillan that if wages and prices could be kept steady, 'the internal consequences of a floating rate do not appear to be likely to be very serious'.[68] This somewhat incredible conclusion must, of course, be read in the light of the conditions prevailing in 1957 not 1952, and of course it had no bearing on government policy in 1957 as the crisis abated. However, it does tend to put into a more realistic perspective the objections which Hall and Cherwell raised in 1952, and which were taken by many Cabinet Ministers at face value in the February Robot debates.

II Towards unification: the Treasury/Bank consensus on the move to Stage Two

By the end of January 1958, the UK's reserves had risen by $130 million, to a total of $2.4 billion, and the new Chancellor, Derick Heathcoat Amory, was soon approached by the Governor suggesting it was time to move on the exchange front.[69] Earlier, Cobbold had written to Makins that the Suez and the September 1957 crises had weakened confidence in sterling to such an extent that 'now it cannot be seen by the outside observer in which direction the next move may be'.[70] The present 'multiple rate structure' was not a 'satisfactory state for an international currency', and whilst in 'quieter waters' the time was now right to amalgamate the official and transferable account markets for sterling against the dollar.[71] Cobbold did not wish to reopen the question of wider margins, as this might 'cast doubt on our determination to hold the present sterling parity', but he still felt that there might be a technical advantage in removing the top limit at which the Exchange Equalisation Account was committed to intervene.[72] The Treasury remained unconvinced. Denis Rickett still worried about the dangers of a US recession and hankered after an assurance from the United States that they would either agree to hold sterling or increase quotas in the IMF.[73] Rowan doubted whether a unilateral move by Britain was wise and argued that 'this is not the time to divest ourselves of protective devices'.[74] Instead, he suggested a policy of continuing to remove discrimination against dollar goods and 'thereby gradually easing ourselves into formal convertibility, rather than the other way round'.[75] The situation would, however, be entirely different if, as Maurice Parsons had implied, Britain acted as part of a 'co-operative approach' with the United States and Germany.[76]

On 5 March this now-familiar debate was continued at a meeting with the Chancellor.[77] Cobbold strongly argued that failure to act would be taken as a sign that Britain's position was less strong than it appeared on the surface. The double-rate structure had a 'bad psychological effect on sterling'; even a one per cent discount had a 'discrediting effect on the official rate'; unification, which would be welcomed by the United States and the IMF, would strengthen confidence in sterling; the current structure provided no protection against bad times that might lie ahead; there could never be a time when conditions were 'perfect in every way', but market conditions were now favourable and so it was time to end this 'anomalous and unsatisfactory' system.[78] The Chancellor, having been fully briefed by Makins, concluded that he could not take an immediate decision but would 'reflect carefully on all that had been said'.[79] The policy of 'stay put but keep the situation under review' was confirmed on 10 March when Macmillan, Butler, Heathcoat Amory and Maudling agreed to defer consideration of unification at least under May, when economic conditions could be viewed with more certainty.[80] In the meantime, Macmillan, still it seems keen on moving to a floating rate, asked the Treasury and the Bank to prepare memoranda setting out the pros and cons of unification and the arguments for and against moving to a floating rate.[81]

Treasury/Bank preference for fixed rates

The joint Treasury/Bank exercise failed, of course, to produce agreement on the timing of unification. It was, however, noteworthy for the conclusions reached on the viability of a floating rate. The joint paper argued that whilst exchange adjustment might be helpful to a country seeking to avoid the need for deflation in conditions of severe world depression and falling prices, it was positively dangerous to a country pursing an inflationary policy against a background of rising or even relatively stable world prices.[82] Not only would a depreciation of the rate cause internal prices to rise, and intensify an upward wage–price spiral, but a floating rate might allow the currency to fall too quickly so that it would actually become undervalued. The unfavourable effects of the undervaluation on the terms of trade would, in that case, exceed any favourable effects on the volume of imports and exports. These dangers, it was thought, were magnified in the case of sterling where, given the large sterling balances, the effect of confidence factors were all important. Although sterling was not judged to be overvalued in terms of other currencies, the slender reserves in relation to liabilities meant that its position was extremely vulnerable. In short, the Treasury/Bank paper concluded that on balance, 'the arguments for maintaining our present policy of a sterling rate fluctuating only within narrow margins are overriding'.[83] Cobbold now apparently shared this view, noting to the Chancellor that 'neither the USA or the rest of the world would stand for our monkeying sterling about all the time against the dollar'.[84]

This was a truly remarkable conclusion in the light of the Robot debates, and as memoranda were exchanged it became clear that both the Treasury and the Bank were also now sceptical of the merits of wider spreads. Not only would raising the upper limit threaten confidence in a period of adverse pressure (it might be taken as a prelude to lowering the lower limit), but it was assumed that the rate would not work well unless it appreciated to around $2.88, and in that case the UK's competitive position would be damaged.[85] Robot, as Fforde sardonically noted, 'now belonged to another universe'.[86]

Fair weather for Unicorn?

Through the summer of 1958, Overseas Finance gradually came round to the view that the time had arrived for the unification of the transferable and official rates. The outlook for the domestic economy seemed bright and a number of developments on the international front had begun to convince even Rowan that the time was ripe to move. By the first half of 1958, the UK's reserves had increased by $803 million, bringing total holdings to $3,077 million; the UK's balance of payments on current account was in surplus to the tune of £226 million; and both wages and prices had been held steady reducing inflationary pressure.[87] Accordingly, the Bank Rate had been cut in three stages and stood at 5 per cent at the end of June. On the international level, the United States economy had begun a steady recovery and it appeared that the dollar shortage was finally coming to an end (the US reported a half-yearly fall in gold and foreign exchange reserves totalling $1,445 million).[88] A British initiative to increase the resources of the IMF (discussed in terms of increasing 'international liquidity'), and broaden the operations of the World Bank, looked to be bearing fruit as the State Department began to press for a 50 per cent increase in Fund quotas – involving a US contribution of $1.4 billion.[89] Recommending the measures to the Secretary of the US Treasury and the President, Douglas Dillon noted, 'there is no doubt in my mind that both these actions would be economically justified, would considerably strengthen the free world and would represent important counter-measures to the Soviet economic offensive'.[90] This increase in liquidity (agreed by the IMF at its September meeting held in New Delhi and operative from autumn 1959, alongside the new offshoot of the IBRD, the International Development Association) acted in many ways to resolve the long-standing issue of financial support to accompany the convertibility operation. The amount Britain could now apply for in times of difficulty had been increased automatically from $1,300 million to $2,000 million.[91] Finally, the British government had continued to make progress in respect of its dollar trade liberalization programme. Up to the beginning of 1958, controls had been removed on approximately 62 per cent of dollar imports, the relaxations covering principally raw materials and foodstuffs.[92] By the middle of the year dollar imports of industrial chemicals and allied products, including plastic-making materials, had been freed of licensing controls bringing the dollar liberalization figure up to 69 per cent. This move was capped in September by the freeing of controls on most industrial, office and agricultural machinery, along with controls on dollar salmon and newsprint, thereby increasing the dollar liberalization percentage to 75.[93] The US Treasury perceived that the liberalization lists seemed to be 'weighted in favour of products which have to be bought from the dollar area in any event or which are not competitive in the UK market because of tariffs or transportation costs',[94] but nevertheless the measures went a good way to meet Rowan's earlier observation that increased liberalization would allow the government to 'ease itself' into convertibility.

At the Commonwealth Trade and Economic Conference held in Montreal in mid-September, the Canadian Finance Minister urged that sterling convertibility for non-residents be formalized.[95] Although Heathcoat Amory replied 'in a manner which was generally interpreted as discouraging expectation of such action at this time', he was in fact simply biding his time, allowing the new dollar liberalization measures to be announced and soundings to be taken at the Fund/Bank meetings in New Delhi, before proceeding with convertibility.[96] At the Fund/Bank meetings, Per Jacobsson, who had succeeded Ivar Rooth as Managing Director of the Fund in November 1956, congratulated the Chancellor on the position of the UK economy and confirmed that a move to full convertibility now was 'absolutely right'.[97] The liberalization measures had 'impressed the Americans' and, in Jacobsson's view, 'if the UK did not act by January 1st, people would begin to think that HMG believed there was something wrong with the economy which they themselves could not detect'.[98] There were however, from Heathcoat Amory's viewpoint, two unresolved issues: firstly, the question of the renewal of the stand-by credit negotiated at the height of the Suez crisis and, secondly, the attitude of the French to convertibility. The $738.5 million which remained of the stand-by credit was due to expire on 21 December.[99] Heathcoat Amory's suggestion that the stand-by be renewed for a period of three years drew a sharp response from Jacobsson who thought it a 'great mistake' for four reasons.[100] First, such a long renewal was contrary to Fund policy and would have a 'bad effect on other countries'. Second, it would detract from UK credit. Third, it was simply unnecessary. A one-year renewal would, in his view, suffice. If events took a dive, it was 'difficult to imagine that the Fund would not respond'. Finally, some members of the Fund would 'look askance' at the proposal and would interpret it 'as a move to underwrite the possibility of a Labour Government in the UK'.[101] On the attitude of the French to convertibility, Jacobsson agreed that they appeared to lack enthusiasm but 'even in France a move to convertibility of sterling was expected', and the situation would be 'greatly eased' if British officials could speak with the French and one or two other Europeans before making a move.[102] Acting on this advice Heathcoat Amory met with the German Chancellor, Ludwig Erhard, who confirmed that as soon as the UK took action, the German government would follow suit. However, Erhard was pessimistic about the situation in France which he thought might delay the introduction of convertibility.[103]

The French exchange crisis and the European Free Trade Area negotiations

There were two aspects of the 'French problem' which exercised British officials. Firstly, in relation to Unicorn, it was recognized that the French had a number of serious, if short-term and largely administrative, anxieties surrounding the move to convertibility. The imminence of the French elections (two ballots on 23 November and 30 November followed by the Presidential election ending on 21 December) posed a problem inasmuch as an early move would force the hand of the new government on exchange rate policy and might therefore be resisted. The French policy on the rate for the franc was further complicated by rumours of devaluation and the creation of a multiple rate structure. There was also the problem of France's foreign exchange position and the repayment obligations that would be incurred if the EPU was terminated.[104] France had a debt to the EPU of $460 million in addition to a 'special credit' of $150 million, and a drawing of $393 million from the IMF.[105] In addition, it was thought that the French Government would have difficulty finding its contribution to the European Fund when the European Monetary Agreement came into force with the introduction of convertibility.

The second set of issues concerned the relation of Unicorn to French anxieties over the Free Trade Area which the Treasury noted were 'long-term and deep rooted in economic and commercial policy'.[106] Britain had developed the Free Trade Area scheme as a 'counter-initiative' to the Common Market of the Six signed on 25 March 1957 by Belgium, France, Germany, Italy, Luxembourg and the Netherlands.[107] Otto Clarke, now head of the Treasury's Home and Overseas Planning Staff, agreed that Britain could not accept the Messina/Brussels plan, but suggested that Britain develop a counter-initiative which would 'be a genuine plan, representing a significant and real tilting of our policy towards Europe'.[108] In the autumn of 1956 the Free Trade Area proposals were launched ostensibly with the purpose of merging all 17 countries of the OEEC into a single market in which there would be no barriers of tariff or quota.[109] The British Government maintained that this would prevent a division of Europe between the Six and the other 11 members of the OEEC, and tackle the problem of the reduction of tariffs and enlargement of quotas among the Six which would arise when the Market began in earnest on 1 January 1959. Each of the Six had agreed to extend these benefits to their five partners, but not to the other members of the OEEC. It was thus perceived that a situation of serious discrimination would arise in the OEEC, endangering the whole stability of the Organisation.[110] The British proposals, however, were immediately seen in Europe as an attempt to torpedo the Six.[111] When negotiations on the Free Trade Area began with the Six in autumn 1957, reports filtered through that the French thought that British proposals would 'tend to emasculate the Common Market in operation, and the French Government had come to the conclusion that the Common Market offered the most long term advantages to France from an economic and political point of view and it was going to be placed first'.[112] Moreover the US State and Treasury Departments had concluded that while the Treaty of Rome probably complicated the work of the OEEC (and the IMF and GATT), it was clear that closer economic integration among the Six would

> probably prove less harmful to US economic interests and less disruptive to world wide standards of trade and payments policy than would the development of a permanent regionalism on an OEEC-wide basis which

would probably involve the Sterling Area, Europe, and other countries maintaining or increasing discriminatory barriers against US exports.[113]

Accordingly the United States supported the Messina/Brussels proposals on both economic and political (bulwark against Communism) grounds, and made it clear that they could not support Britain in any effort to oppose or redirect these proposals through the OEEC.[114]

Despite this negative reaction, it was still thought possible in British circles that the Free Trade Area could be brought to life and introduced on 1 January 1959.[115] Discussions were due to be concluded in mid-December 1958 and it was therefore important that Unicorn did not set up pressures which might lead France to reject the Free Trade Area. In this connection, Ellis-Rees reported from Paris that Von Mangoldt, of the Bank Deutscher Länder, hoped that Britain would not unify the rates before the conclusion of the Free Trade Area discussions.[116] If the EPU crashed and France's position deteriorated as a result of the move, it would, thought Von Mangoldt, be resented by the French, co-operation would be lost and the initiative would pass to the Six. This would 'give the French a stick to beat us with', and would be seized upon as 'another example of our indifference to the impact of our policies on others'.[117] Although there was no direct linkage between Unicorn and the Free Trade Area (inasmuch as there was nothing in Unicorn which exposed the French to any more immediate pressures on the commercial policy front than they already faced), commercial policy considerations were considered important enough to figure in the timing of the move but not necessarily in the question of the validity of the move itself.

III The politics of Operation Unicorn

On 16 October 1958 the Treasury finalized a draft for Ministers recommending unification of the rates for official and transferable sterling.[118] This would make sterling convertible on external account at a single rate. There would be no change in the margins for the pound against the dollar which would continue to be $2.78–$2.82. Exchange control would be retained and trade discrimination would be eased gradually. In this regard there would be no immediate move from Article XIV (which gave 'transitional period' rights to maintain restrictions) to Article VIII (under which freedom to impose restrictions was more circumscribed). In the light of the Chancellor's discussions with Per Jacobsson, it had now been decided to request a renewal of the IMF stand-by for one year only, bearing in mind that by the end of 1959 the Fund's resources, and the UK's quota, would have been increased by 50 per cent (and the UK had in February renewed for one year the Exim Bank line of credit, making available $250 million that could be drawn at any time before 28 February 1959).[119] On unification the new European Monetary Agreement (EMA) would come into force when members of the EPU holding at least 50 per cent of the quotas in the Union notified the relevant authorities of their intention to move to the EMA. A move on the part of the UK plus Germany, and either Belgium and the Netherlands or the Scandinavians or France would be sufficient to reach 50 per cent. Under the EMA, a European Fund would be set up of $600 million with the UK initially contributing $30–40 million. The Fund would be open to all members without an accompanying gold payment. It was hoped that most European countries would follow Britain's lead in establishing convertibility and that the move would be especially welcome in Germany, Switzerland, the Netherlands, Belgium and Italy. Firm German support was thought to be important in convincing France to keep in step. In respect of the Free Trade Area negotiations, it was suggested that the move would 'reassert our leadership in Europe', and 'be a sign that we have confidence in our policies and in our position'.[120] The replacement of automatic EPU credit by the European Fund would put the UK in a position to control assistance to others, including the Six, who, it was judged, 'will therefore be disposed to take more account of our point of view'.[121] In addition, it was suggested that the forces of convertibility would be felt increasingly by the Six, who would see that discrimination and a high level of protection were not to their advantage. This in turn would help negotiate the Free Trade Area in time.[122] The Commonwealth would welcome the move and Robert Anderson, Secretary of the US Treasury, had indicated that Britain could count on the full support of the US Administration. Finally, the Treasury draft gestured in the direction of the long-standing 'preconditions' of the move to convertibility laid down in 1952, and indicated that although it was still a matter of degree of judgement as to whether the conditions had been fulfilled, in the Treasury's considered view, 'they have been fulfilled to an extent which justifies us in going forward now if this will best serve our interests'.[123]

Unicorn and the Board of Trade

The draft was sent to Heathcoat Amory on 17 October and on 23 October the Chancellor spoke to Macmillan about the proposals.[124] The Prime Minister 'agreed with the proposals in principle' but preferred that the paper be circulated to a selected group of Ministers (the so-called Unicorn Group of Ministers) rather than the full Cabinet at this stage.[125] In advance of the meeting of Ministers, Rowan discussed the proposals with senior representatives of the Foreign Office, Commonwealth Relations Office, Colonial Office and the Board of Trade.[126] It emerged from the discussion that the Board of Trade, at both Ministerial and official level, opposed the move. Somewhat surprisingly, the Board of Trade argued that the step should only be taken if the Government could negotiate with the IMF a fixed but wider spread for sterling. The flexible rate adopted by the Canadians was cited in support of this argument. Moreover, it was suggested that David Eccles, President of the Board of Trade, would regard the move as 'a financial manoeuvre dictated by the banks and as having no real appeal, and indeed in many cases no very real substance for the ordinary people'.[127] Rowan responded that the Canadian dollar was a domestic currency not held in any quantity by other countries, whereas sterling was subject to specific, and in some cases unique, pressures which ruled out a flexible rate in normal circumstances.

The following day, eight selected Ministers, plus Cobbold and Rowan, met to discuss the proposals (Macmillan, Butler, Heathcoat Amory, Lennox-Boyd, Selwyn Lloyd, Eccles, The Earl of Home and Lord Mills).[128] Cobbold opened proceedings indicating that the balance of technical advantage lay in unifying the two rates, and with sterling strong and the dollar weak, this was the most appropriate moment for the operation. The Governor was supported by the Chancellor who emphasized that the proposal was politically significant, 'inasmuch as it would represent the achievement by the Government of a purpose which they had announced in 1952'.[129] The three conditions laid down in 1952 had been broadly fulfilled and the move would command much international support. However, he added that the action 'was open to the political objection that it could be represented as a sacrifice of our freedom of manoeuvre at a time when the economic outlook was uncertain'.[130] Officials from the Trades Union Congress, he noted, had already written to him expressing their opposition to further convertibility and, internationally, France was likely to be lukewarm. On balance, however, he commended the proposals. The discussion that followed was hauntingly familiar and must have exasperated Cobbold. There was general agreement that unification was 'desirable in principle'. However, the technical advantages were to be weighed against the risk of political misrepresentation of the government's purpose. It would be easy, it was noted, to compare convertibility with

> the return to the gold standard in 1925, since both operations were based on the principle of a fixed parity; and both the Parliamentary Opposition and organised labour would undoubtedly take advantage of this fact to maintain that the Government were abandoning the protection which the economy derived from the flexibility of the present system of dual rates and were sacrificing employment and production to the interests of the international bankers.[131]

Macmillan, in summing up the discussion, noted the difficult choice facing the Government. Political embarrassment might extend also to the Free Trade Area negotiations, which, he suggested, were already in some jeopardy and might be further endangered if the French reacted unfavourably to convertibility and the establishment of the EMA. Britain would 'incur the odium of having precipitated the breakdown of the negotiations', and 'we should be confronted with the need to devise some alternative policy towards the European Common Market'.[132] Despite the propitious economic circumstances, Ministers were unable to reach a decision, and it was agreed that discussion would be resumed at a subsequent meeting once further thought had been given to the problem of France and the Free Trade Area.

When the Unicorn Group of Ministers met to continue their discussions on 5 November, it quickly became apparent that they were unable to decide whether the Free Trade Area negotiations would be helped or hindered by a move to unify the rates.[133] Unicorn could, of course, give the French an excuse to break off negotiations. Equally, Unicorn might exert pressure on France to adopt more outward-looking policies. Britain could not let decisions on sterling exchange rate policy be governed by the future of the Free Trade Area negotiations, but at the same time immediate action to unify the rates was deemed inadvisable given the present state of the negotiations and the imminence of the French elections. In summing up the discussion, Macmillan said that 'it was evidently the general view of the Meeting that no immediate steps should be taken to unify the rates, given the state of the Free Trade Area negotiations and the timing of the French elections'.[134] It might, he added, be possible to take advantage of the short interval between the French elections (30 November) and the final date for the renewal of the IMF stand-by credit (21 December) to launch the operation, but this might still cause some difficulty with the French.

Over the next two weeks, Treasury and Bank officials kept up the pressure on the Chancellor to pursue unification.[135] Rowan, in his last contribution to proceedings before resigning from the Treasury on 7 November to take up the post of Finance Director with Vickers Ltd,[136] made clear his preference for an early programme of action.[137] Cobbold relayed to Makins the gist of a conversation with Karl Blessing (President of the Deutsche Bundesbank) and Baumgartner in Basle, in which Blessing repeated his assurance that Germany would follow at once and would support the move from EPU to EMA.[138] Baumgartner stated that personally he would welcome a move by Britain soon after the French elections and that he would do his best to get De Gaulle's support.[139] On the basis of more general talk with other central bank Governors, Cobbold concluded that the Swiss, the Dutch and the Belgians would welcome an early move by Britain, and the Swedes would see no objection.[140] In addition, Roger Makins minuted the Chancellor that 'it would be a fatal step if we were to allow our exchange policy to become a pawn in our negotiations with the French about economic co-operation in Europe. They are likely to drag on for some months. In short, I do not think we can expect a more favourable conjuncture for making this move'.[141]

However, officials were further frustrated when on 17 November it was announced that the Free Trade Area negotiations were on the point of collapse.[142] De Gaulle had objected to the concept of the Area and it appeared that his objection had been accepted by the Germans.[143] The Paymaster General explained to the Cabinet that the priority now was to prevent the emergence of a discriminatory bloc, and he awaited the 'modus vivendi' proposals to be presented by the Six in early December.[144] This development threatened to delay Unicorn indefinitely.[145] On 20 November further news arrived from Paris concerning the deteriorating French economic situation.[146] Following discussions between Pinay (French Finance Minister) and Baumgartner, it had been decided that De Gaulle visit Germany to discuss an ensemble of economic questions, including the possibility of a German loan to enable France to devalue the franc and make it convertible.[147] This completely unexpected development prompted Makins to arrange an emergency meeting with the Chancellor and the Paymaster General.[148] It was decided that to get the fullest and earliest account of the De Gaulle/ Adenauer meeting, Cobbold should release John Stevens (an Executive Director of the Bank) to make enquiries through the central bank channels.[149] Until the situation could be clarified, Heathcoat Amory explained to a group of Ministers on 27 November, no action could be taken on the Unicorn front, although, as Makins subsequently noted, the sands were running out on the government, and Ministers should be readied to revert to the matter as soon as the fog had cleared.[150]

IV France, Germany and the final act

The pace quickened considerably in the first half of December. On 9 December, Cobbold, in Washington, cabled Heathcoat Amory that the United States would support the renewal of the IMF stand-by for one year and that Robert Anderson, Secretary of the US Treasury, still hoped that Unicorn could be pushed through before the end of the year.[151] The same day, Stevens saw Makins to report that Germany, Switzerland, Belgium and Holland were all anxious to move to convertibility. In France, the exchange crisis was being fuelled by rumours of an impending devaluation and De Gaulle, who was likely to be elected as President on 21 December, was expected to introduce a tough Budget alongside the devaluation of the franc which possibly might be made convertible at the same time.[152] This news produced a sharp response from Treasury officials and the Chancellor. Not only would a move by France to make the franc convertible embarrass the government (particularly on top of the Free Trade Area fiasco) but it would also threaten a new sterling crisis.[153] In the circumstances, Heathcoat Amory advised Macmillan,

> I am emphatically of the opinion that we must now decide to bring the sterling rates together so as to move as nearly as possible at the same time as the French. If we do not do this the recent weakness of sterling, which has been due mainly to the appearance of our having lost the initiative, both in regard to the Free Trade Area and unification of sterling rates, will be intensified. This would obviously be very damaging to our position.[154]

The Chancellor suggested that at the OEEC Ministerial meeting, due to open in Paris on 15 December, he should inform Pinay and Franz Etzel (German Finance Minister) that the government had decided to unify the rates and would move before the New Year.[155] Macmillan and Butler agreed.[156] It was important 'not to be forestalled by the French and the other European countries'.[157] However, it was equally important, as Stevens later confided, 'not to tell the French that the British Government would not take the convertibility step until the French considered it opportune to do so'.[158] This subtle diplomacy worked well for the British. On 14 December Erhard mentioned to Heathcoat Amory that Germany would provide up to $300 million financial assistance to France, if De Gaulle moved on convertibility.[159] It might also be advantageous, Erhard suggested, if the UK, France and Germany made the move in concert. This was also the view of Baumgartner, although on balance he favoured Anglo-French action.[160]

15 December 1958 was a momentous day for Britain and Europe. The Free Trade Area negotiations finally broke down when France refused to accept UK proposals apparently designed to ensure reciprocity and equal treatment on trade in Europe between the Six and the other eleven OEEC countries.[161] Despite a move by the German delegate, who appealed to the Americans to prevent a split in Europe, France's rejection of the 'modus vivendi' threatened the authority of the OEEC and the integrity of the principle of non-discrimination in quotas between members of the OEEC.[162] Britain was now left contemplating the value of a Uniscan Free Trade Area.[163] As these events unfolded, Heathcoat Amory, Pinay and Etzel dined together and agreed on 16 December to launch a combined convertibility operation at some point in the period between Christmas and the New Year.[164] On 17 December, Macmillan authorized the Bank of England to discuss the technicalities with the French and German central banks and to inform the Commonwealth.[165] All that remained was to agree a timetable, attend to the problem of the European Fund (which the French disliked as they would have difficulty finding their contribution) and, of course, put the matter before the Cabinet.

The Cabinet met at 10.30 a.m. on 18 December.[166] Heathcoat Amory outlined the rationale for the move in terms almost identical to those put forward in the Treasury draft of 16 October.[167] The proposal to unify the rates was agreed, although it was pointed out that the move would demand 'the maintenance of a disinflationary economic policy in the UK; and this aspect of the proposal, together with the progressive removal of dollar discrimination, would need to be presented with considerable care to public opinion in this country'.[168]

Over the next few days the French economic crisis deepened. The Bank of England reported on 19 December that the French had had their worst day on the foreign exchange markets since 1925.[169] Accordingly Baumgartner approached Cobbold to arrange a swap facility of £20 million, which the Chancellor approved.[170] Alongside this arrangement, the French agreed to the Bank's proposal on the European Fund, under which $113 million would be transferred from the EPU to the Fund but no further capital would be called for until a systematic re-examination of the provisions of the Fund had been made.[171] By 21 December it was clear that whatever the French government decided on devaluation, they would support unification and move to the EMA (with the European Fund temporarily inoperative). The severity of the crisis now meant that the French were anxious for unification and requested that the move be made on 29 December.[172] Two days later, Makins told the Chancellor that the machinery had been set in motion and at 5.50 p.m. on Saturday 27 December the Treasury announced that from 9.00 a.m. on Monday 29 December, sterling held or acquired by non-residents of the Sterling Area would be freely transferable throughout the world.[173]

The convertibility of non-resident sterling had finally been achieved at a fixed rate of exchange as part of a co-ordinated European move in which the UK was joined by all OEEC countries except Greece, Turkey and Iceland.[174] The European Payments Union was replaced by the European Monetary Agreement, and at long last the International Monetary Fund could look forward to the end of the 'transitional period' during which restrictions on payments and transfers hampered its operation. George Bolton, now Chairman of the Bank of London and South America, noted in his diary, 'EPU closes and EMA begins: Great news'.[175] Equally enthusiastic, his old sparring partner Robert Hall invoked the spirit of Robot, noting that in regard to convertibility, 'I was always against jumping out of a high window and now we have walked out of a French window'.[176]

Amid the celebrations, however, it was clear that the move to fixed rate convertibility would impose little or no new discipline on the British economy. The underlying problems, identified with clarity by Otto Clarke in 1952, remained and although convertibility had now been achieved the government had seemingly failed to enlist the support of the exchange rate in helping to grapple with the long-term position. These issues are taken up in detail in the last chapter.

9
Conclusion: Bretton Woods and British Decline

By the end of the 1950s it seemed that many of the crises that had plagued the world economy since 1945 had finally been resolved. The dollar shortage was over, trade liberalization was proceeding apace, many Western European economies were booming and the future of global multilateral trade and payments looked secure. The return to non-resident convertibility and the rebirth of the Bretton Woods twins seemed to point to a future in which the ideals espoused at New Hampshire might finally be realized.[1] But behind such predictions lay fears that new, and perhaps more fundamental, structural imbalances in the world economy were developing which would call for a radical overhaul of international economic relations. This chapter considers some of these issues and points in particular to the precarious economic position of Britain in the international system at the end of the decade.

I The crisis of the new 'Bretton Woods' system

In the early 1950s, as indicated in chapter 1, the most serious imbalance in the world economy was expressed in terms of the general dollar shortage. The dollar shortage reflected the superior competitive power of the US economy and the worldwide demand for US goods. By the end of the decade the dollar shortage was over. Total gold and dollar holdings held outside the United States increased from a level of $19.8 billion in 1951 to $36.5 billion by the end of 1958.[2] Despite recording a sizeable annual surplus on current account between 1950 and 1955, the United States recorded an overall balance of payments deficit in this period averaging $1.5 billion per year.[3] This, of course, was the result of high levels of military and economic aid, and the expansion of US private investment overseas. In 1958, however, the United States suffered a fall in exports and a rise in imports with the result that an overall deficit was recorded of $3.7 billion.[4] The current account balance of payments deteriorated still further in the first half of 1959 and by the end of the year the outflow of gold and dollars reached $4.5 billion.[5]

175

These changes reflected three important developments in the world economy.

Firstly, the changes appeared to signal the disappearance of specific commodity shortages which had provided outlets for many US products throughout much of the postwar period.[6] In this sense, it seemed that the period of reconstruction had finally come to an end. Secondly, the changes indicated that a new era of intensified competition was opening up for the United States. The quality and availability of foreign goods, especially from Europe and Japan, had improved greatly, depriving US producers of the non-price advantage they had held in the postwar years. Finally, the swollen deficits of 1958 and 1959 pointed to underlying inflationary pressure in the US economy which it was widely thought was beginning to price US goods out of world markets and weaken confidence in the value of the dollar.[7] The basic cause of the inflationary pressure was identified as excessive wage increases demanded by overpowerful labour unions, particularly in the machinery and steel sectors.[8]

The principal beneficiaries of these changes were those countries able to maintain competitive prices whilst increasing productivity in industries associated with the manufacture of export goods, particularly in the capital equipment, machinery and transport equipment sectors.[9] After 1953, the gains of Western Germany, Italy, France and Japan, in terms of increased share of world manufactures, were largely at the expense of the UK and the USA.[10] Between 1953 and 1959, the US share of the world market in manufactures fell by 4.6 per cent (and the UK by 4 per cent) whilst that of Western Germany increased by 5.8 per cent and Japan by 2.9 per cent.[11] In Germany, high levels of fixed capital investment in machinery and equipment, combined with high rates of growth of output per head, enabled industries by the mid-1950s to regain the share in world trade that they had held in 1938.[12] In the export of cars and commercial vehicles, for example, West Germany's share of the world market increased from 16.7 per cent in 1953 to 32.5 per cent by 1959, whilst the US share of the world market fell by 17.1 per cent over the same period.[13] Accordingly, throughout the 1950s West Germany's gold and dollar holdings increased at a phenomenal rate, rising from a level of $434 million in 1951 to $6,321 million at the end of 1958 (UK reserves stood at $3,069 million).[14]

This rebalancing of the world economy may have been welcome in some quarters, particularly as it now seemed unlikely that many countries would again experience dollar reserve problems. However, the continuance of a heavy United States deficit posed severe problems for both of the multilateral ideals that US authorities had struggled so long to achieve. A deepening of the deficit would fundamentally unbalance the world economy by threatening the stability of the fixed rate system (through currency speculation) and by its direct effects on world trade if US authorities responded with protectionist measures. Both of these issues are beyond the scope of the present study. It does, however, seem to be the case, as Fred Block and Susan Strange argue, that the multilateralism which was restored in 1958 was fundamentally flawed in at least two key respects.[15] Firstly, the international monetary system was now based on a version of the gold exchange standard that centred on the dollar as the 'dominant or top currency, the main component of other countries' foreign exchange reserves, their chief medium for market intervention to maintain fixed exchange rates and the pivot of other par values'.[16] US authorities had an obligation to maintain the price of gold at $35 an ounce for both private and official purchasers.[17] In the context of the continuation of large US deficits, markets became increasingly uneasy about the stability of the growing 'dollar overhang', with the predictable result that the conversion of dollars into gold began to have a major impact on US gold reserves.[18] A vicious circle had now been activated which increasingly sapped the strength and prestige of the dollar. As Block summarizes, lack of confidence in the dollar could lead to increased official gold purchases and private speculative purchases, reducing US gold reserves and further undermining confidence in the dollar.[19] Anxiety that a run on the US gold stock would prompt the United States to take unilateral action, in turn fuelled speculation about the stability of the whole international economic system: 'Each new speculative crisis was seen to have the potential of tripping the fuse of the ultimate crisis.'[20] Secondly, the extension of US military power on a global basis from 1945 provided badly needed dollars for governments in the absence of a substantial outflow of US private investment abroad.[21] However, by the late 1950s when US foreign direct investment began to increase, the worldwide US political and military apparatus could not easily be dismantled with the result that the United States continued to pump dollars abroad on capital and government account, increasing the size of the deficit.[22] Block calculates that direct US military expenditures increased from $576 million in 1950 to $3.4 billion in 1958, rising to $4.8 billion by the end of the 1960s.[23] In short, by the late 1950s the US global war on communism was beginning to threaten the basis of the international economic order – a conflict which, of course, became all too apparent with US military intervention in Vietnam.

It seems clear, then, that the system introduced in late 1958 contained a number of serious contradictions which threatened to explode once the shifts in the world economy became more pronounced and confidence in the dollar and the US economy waned. As early as 1959, Robert Triffin recognized that 'a system that kept exchange rates stable only as long as other countries were content to hold gold-convertible dollars in reserve was doomed'.[24] The volume of dollar IOUs in foreign hands would soon exceed US gold reserves, destroying confidence in the dollar, prompting currency realignment, a move to floating rates or the reimposition of inconvertibility (this time, for the dollar).[25] Despite a number of attempts to increase international liquidity, bolster the dollar and minimize dollar convertibility, by the beginning of the 1970s the dollar was in headlong retreat.[26] In mid-August 1971, the United States declared the dollar inconvertible and imposed a 10 per cent tax on dutiable imports producing what Shonfield called 'the most serious crisis in international economic relations in the Western world since the war'.[27] In the face of a mounting US payments deficit, immense speculative pressure in foreign currency markets against the dollar, and the threat of rising inflation in the United States, European governments finally moved to introduce floating rates in the early 1970s. The international economic system of the 1960s associated with Bretton Woods appeared, in some respects, to be more unstable and crisis-prone than the period associated with the move to general convertibility in the 1950s.

This conclusion does not make pleasant reading for those who advocate a return to some sort of Bretton Woods 'system'.[28] On the basis of the material presented in this study it seems self-evident that international monetary relations in the period 1944 to 1958 owed very little to the Bretton Woods Agreement. Not only was the 'transitional period' extended until 1961 (when the UK and most of Western Europe renounced the protection of Article XIV and accepted the obligations of Article VIII of the Fund Agreement)[29] but throughout the 1950s there was fundamental disagreement over the viability of the fixed rate mechanism and the Fund and Bank were marginal, at best, to the world economy. In the absence of general currency convertibility, international trade and payments were regulated less by international institutions than by national governments concerned to husband foreign currency reserves in the face of perennial balance of payments difficulties. State officials in London and Washington decided that the speed and direction of international economic relations in the 1950s partly in response to domestic political pressures, and with an eye on moving towards the agreed goals of multilateralism, but with little regard to the New Hampshire negotiations. As regards the Bretton Woods institutions, there is almost universal agreement that in the first ten years of their existence they achieved very little and were lucky to escape closure.[30] In this light, it is truly remarkable that the Bretton Woods Commission can claim that

> In the 1950s and early 1960s, the Bretton Woods par value system and the IMF worked roughly according to plan. The IMF became accepted as the referee of the system. It established its modus operandi of providing reserve credits to countries that needed them on condition that they made the necessary adjustments in their macroeconomic policies, to restore balance of payments equilibrium quickly.[31]

In fact, in the period 1947 to 1955, gross drawings on the Fund totalled no more than $1.2 billion (with the UK, France, India, Brazil and the Netherlands the principal recipients).[32] During the Jacobsson regime (1956–63), although the Fund entered a more active phase, by the end of 1959 total drawings had reached only $3.3 billion, with the UK and France again taking almost $1 billion (in 1956 the UK drew $561.5 and in 1958 France draw $393.1).[33] From 1947 to the late 1950s the very existence of the Fund was called into question by both the British and the US Treasuries, and, as Hirsch comments, when the Fund began to lend more heavily in the 1960s its activities were somewhat inconsistent with Bretton Woods intentions, in that it financed a fundamental disequilibrium 'in the hope that this would be eliminated by inflations elsewhere'.[34] A similar tale could be told of the institutions that are more peripheral to this study, the International Bank for Reconstruction and Development, and the GATT apparatus.[35] In short, the Bretton Woods system and its twins were largely irrelevant to the operation of the world economy between 1944 and 1958, and, as Cairncross points out, it was the United States not the IMF that made the 'system' work after this date, 'but only by pouring out dollars on a scale inconsistent with the stability of a reserve currency on which the whole system depended'.[36]

II The relative economic and political decline of Britain in the 1950s

The final remarks of this study focus on the position of Britain at the end of the 1950s and address what is, in many ways, the central issue under investigation: to what extent did the British government miss a golden opportunity to remake the world economy in February 1952?

By the early 1960s it was clear that the British economy suffered from three fundamental weaknesses. Firstly, the UK's share of world trade in manufactures had continued to decline throughout the 1950s with the result that receipts from exports were not sufficient to finance outgoings on current and long-term capital account.[37] It is conceivable, as Wells point out, that the UK's share in world trade could continue to decline without giving rise to serious balance of payments problems, if the volume of manufactured imports into the UK failed to grow as fast as world imports of manufactures, if there were a long-term movement of the terms of trade in favour of the UK, or if there were a curtailment of overseas investment by the UK.[38] However, throughout the 1950s the volume of imports and of capital outflow increased whilst exports failed to hold their own in competition with exports from other manufacturing countries.[39] It is noteworthy that countries whose share of world trade in manufactures increased most rapidly in this period – Japan, Italy, West Germany and France – also recorded the highest rates of productivity growth.[40] Growth rates in national product per man-year between 1954 and 1959 increased by 7.6 per cent in Japan, 3.8 per cent in Italy and 3.6 per cent in West Germany, whilst the UK recorded the lowest increase in Europe of 1.6 per cent.[41] For the decade as a whole, GDP per worker employed grew at about 2 per cent per annum in the UK, comparing favourably with 1.5 per cent in the interwar period.[42] However, growth rates on the Continent were much higher, with West Germany increasing by 5.1 per cent, and the Netherlands, Italy, Norway, France and Sweden increasing by approximately 3.5 per cent per annum.[43] By 1961 the Chancellor had concluded that unless 'national efficiency' could be improved, Britain's international competitive position would continue to weaken producing 'constant strain in the balance of payments and a threat to the maintenance of the sterling system'.[44]

The second fundamental weakness evident by the early 1960s was the instability of sterling. Susan Strange provides a powerful and persuasive account of the plight of sterling following convertibility in 1958, which deserves to be quoted in full:

> By losing its Top Currency status to the dollar, sterling was demoted into a much more vulnerable category of international currency. In place of the inherent attractions of the Top Currency – which, by definition, will be the preferred international medium – the Neutral Currency has to preserve a specially intact reputation (as does the Swiss franc) for safety and stability; it must maintain a very strong reserve position and demonstrate a patent capacity to correct any disequilibrating tendencies in its domestic economy. Unless it can do all these things – and maintain confidence that it will be able to go on doing them – it is destined to come under acute external pressure from the users.[45]

The ability of British authorities to maintain confidence in sterling, and therefore withstand the external pressure to which Strange refers, was hampered in the late 1950s and early 1960s by four main developments.[46] First, the continued outflow of British capital overseas, particularly to the Sterling Area, began to exert 'maximum demands for foreign exchange just at the time when the political dissolution of empire began to work to a climax'.[47] Second, the large sterling balances, exceeding by four times the total gold and foreign exchange reserves of the UK, were now held increasingly by private creditors and monetary authorities of countries no longer subject to British political control.[48] In 1960 UK gross liabilities stood at £4,262 million whilst UK reserves totalled £1,154 million.[49] The danger that the balances would be run down at a rate damaging to sterling was ever-present and to avert this danger the government tried all manner of policies – voluntary blocking and agreed rates of run down, floors and ceilings, generation of UK surpluses sufficient to provide for the expected run down, discouragement of increases by individual countries and international support to offset movements.[50] However, as the Treasury later admitted, 'no comprehensive long-term strategy for relieving us of this embarrassment was evolved'.[51] Third, to help avoid a situation in which the newly independent states would seek to convert their sterling balances into dollar holdings, the British government provided a number of concessions, including military aid and assistance, and economic aid in the form of loans.[52] Block calculates that the foreign exchange cost of the UK's overseas military presence doubled from 1956 to 1964, to £250 million, whilst Strange notes that the cost to the UK of 'independence loans' rose 100 per cent in the last four years of the 1950s and a further 25 per cent up to 1964 (UK Bilateral Economic Aid totalled £189.1 million in 1966).[53] Finally, the restoration of non-resident convertibility, and of London as an international financial centre, opened wide doors to volatile short-term capital movements. As Strange summarizes,

> the 'overhang' of balances over reserves and the susceptibility of sterling to large-scale shifts of capital through market operations conducted in London's Square Mile together produced a situation where, if the reserves could not be reinforced, the rate would have to be changed. Hence, quite simply, the crises of the mid-1960s.[54]

The decade began with rumours about the adoption of floating rates and ended, of course, with devaluation and the bizarre contingency measures known as Operation Brutus.[55] In summary, by the early 1960s Britain found itself at the centre of a 'decaying currency area' and having lost Master and Top Currency status, sterling was increasingly vulnerable to confidence crises at home and abroad: 'the product was a barrel of nitroglycerine which any sudden bump, any undue heat on the international scene, was liable to set off.[56]

The final set of fundamental economic problems facing the British authorities at the end of the 1950s concerned the relationship between inflation, full employment and the control of demand. By 1961 it was evident to the government that the disparity between the rate of increase of average earnings and of GDP per worker was 'the biggest single danger to healthy growth in the future'.[57] Dow calculates that between 1946 and 1960, average wages/salaries rose by 6.5 per cent a year, exceeding the rise in prices by some 2.25 per cent a year.[58] This increase in real wages and salaries was broadly in line with the average increase in output per head of about 2.25 per cent a year. But, since the average wage/salary rose by 6.5 per cent a year, and output per man increased by only 2.25 per cent, labour cost per unit of output rose 4 per cent a year on average.[59] On the basis of such calculations, Selwyn Lloyd informed the Cabinet that

> The rise in prices in the United Kingdom has been greater than in most other countries and has gradually eroded the benefits of the 1949 devaluation. If British costs go on rising at the present rate, not only will this country be unable to sell enough exports to pay for the rising volume of imports required by the potential rate of growth, but even in the home

market British goods will become less competitive, so that imports will rise still further. The deterioration of the balance of payments shows the need to prevent this continuing. Looking ahead, there can be no doubt that a continuation of past experience will carry with it a very real possibility of devaluation being forced upon this country.[60]

The essential need, the Chancellor concluded, was to find a means whereby the 'national interest' could be brought to bear on wage negotiations. In many respects these problems were a direct consequence of, what the Treasury would later call 'over-full employment'.[61] The 'politicized' style of economic management pursued since 1945,[62] when combined with over-full employment, had produced a 'climate of opinion in which moderation of claims by trade unions and a firm response to them by employers have been increasingly at a discount'.[63] As the number of industrial stoppages (and the number of days lost) increased substantially towards the end of the 1950s, the Chancellor noted pessimistically that the conception of wages and salaries as having any relationship to the increase in the national average of GDP per worker was becoming submerged in discussions of leap-frogging and pay relativities.[64] In short, the effect of maintaining demand at the levels experienced in the 1950s had greatly limited the government's room for manoeuvre and added a domestic pressure to the government's attempt to attain external solvency.[65]

In addition to these economic weaknesses, the government faced two major difficulties on the international political front. First, the collapse of the Free Trade Area negotiations had been a diplomatic disaster for the British government. In a long 'post-mortem', Frank Figgures noted that the government had 'made an error in seeking to divide the Six'; had not appreciated early enough that if the EEC had a protectionist policy it would not be possible for the Community to join the Free Trade Area without abandoning that policy; had shown an excessive woodenness in the negotiations and had persisted too long with the 17-country plan which he concluded 'really does not bear examination for five minutes'.[66] As a consequence, Western Europe was now split into two camps: the EEC and the Stockholm Group, with 'the rest' gravitating one way or the other. By early 1960, the Foreign Office had concluded that this situation was gravely damaging to the interests of the UK.[67] If political and economic integration continued, and the UK failed to reach an accommodation with the EEC, the Six would 'become a major political power which would be a strong pull on the United States away from the United Kingdom'.[68] It was conceivable that West Germany might become not only the major economy in Europe but also the 'first ally' of the United States in Europe, which would inevitably affect the UK's standing in the world.

The second area of concern was the effect of Anglo-American 'interdependence' on the long-term interests of the UK. In October 1957, in partial recognition of the growing interdependence of trade and the anti-communist military alliance, the British and US governments took the decision to promote interdependence as a policy objective.[69] The Suez crisis had indicated to the British government that against US opposition, 'we can do very little'.[70] It was therefore concluded by the Foreign Office that 'the United States is so much the most powerful nation in the Western camp that our ability to have our way in the world depends more than anything else upon our influence upon her to act in conformity with our interests'. A policy of interdependence would help achieve this aim. However, it was fraught with difficulties. First, it was recognized that in a partnership of powers of unequal strength, 'it is far more serious for the weaker than for the stronger if the partnership comes to an end'.[71] Second, the United States would exact a price for further support (for example, a resolution of the conflict between Britain and the United States over China). Finally, the danger of appearing to be an American satellite could further damage relations with Europe and paradoxically lose influence with the Americans themselves as this to some extent depended on British influence elsewhere. In short, the dwindling status of Britain as a world power since the late 1940s had produced a situation in which the UK had become increasingly dependent on the United States. This threatened to undermine the success of further British negotiations with the Six, a result which would in the long run lessen the importance of Britain to the United States. Although there was no danger of immediate decline, the Foreign Office nevertheless concluded:

> We must expect to see the United States fostering closer relations with the EEC Powers in proportion as their economic strength develops. A more intimate association will probably grow up between the United States and Western Germany, more especially if, as it's quite possible, the Germans rather than the French emerge as the natural leaders of the Six in Europe. We shall then be relatively less powerful, some of the exclusive war and post-war links will have been weakened and the United States may be less inclined than at present to take account of United Kingdom interests, more particularly if they felt that we were responsible for maintaining the split in Europe and thus weakening NATO solidarity. They will want to see us included in any new political grouping in Europe and in the closest possible relations with the Six.[72]

III Concluding remarks: Britain, Robot and the remaking of the postwar world economy

It is now possible, having sketched the depth of the economic and political difficulties facing the British government in the late 1950s, to assess the merits of the Robot scheme developed for remaking the world economy in the early months of 1952. The orthodoxy represented by Cairncross, Plowden and MacDougall is that a Robot-type scheme introduced in the early 1950s 'would have been disastrous, politically and economically'.[73] This is, of course, in the case of Plowden and MacDougall, the view of the victors (of those actively involved in defeating the plan at the time). It largely ignores the fact of Britain's declining productivity and competitiveness throughout the 1950s and skates over the political and economic problems posed for Britain by the formation of the EEC. Cairncross is somewhat more realistic, recognizing that throughout the 1950s and 1960s 'the balance of payments continued to fluctuate, the reserves remained grossly insufficient and exchange crises recurred with almost predictable regularity'.[74] Nevertheless, he joins Plowden and MacDougall in offering a broadly 'Keynesian' dismissal of Robot on the grounds that economically it was unnecessary and would have simply increased unemployment, and politically it would have endangered international relations through its effect on the EPU and the IMF.[75]

The orthodoxy has, however, been challenged by Shonfield, Brittan and Fforde.[76] Both Shonfield and Brittan argue that by delaying the introduction of convertibility, the British government ended up in the late 1950s with all the drawbacks but none of the prestige or benefits that would have flowed from full early convertibility. Given the fact of floating rate convertibility, notes Shonfield, there would have been no room for argument and hesitation from the government on a number of vital issues of policy.[77] Robot would have established a new domestic order and 'it would have been extremely difficult to go back'.[78] In short, 'if the bold stroke had been taken then, with everything risked on a single throw, it would have imparted a sharp point and a coherence to Conservative policy, instead of the havering and flabbiness that came upon it in subsequent years'.[79] Samuel Brittan goes further and places the 'dash for freedom' within the context of the comparative weakness of British economic performance after 1950.[80] His most recent conclusion is that floating rate convertibility would have freed the country 'from the throes of never-ending runs on sterling', and as such, 'the rejection by the post-war Churchill government in 1952 of Operation Robot to float sterling represented the greatest missed opportunity in British economic policy since World War II'.[81] Fforde, in more guarded fashion, concurs and adds that when fixed rate convertibility finally came to pass in late 1958, it was to prove as difficult to manage and as vulnerable to recurrent crises as the advocates of Robot had foreseen, and for the reasons they had stated.[82]

A balanced assessment of the Robot proposals must recognize two fundamental points. First, the relative economic decline of Britain in the 1950s cannot be sidestepped by advocates of the orthodoxy. The international economic system which, according to MacDougall, 'served us well during most of the period', was, in fact, unstable and prone to repeated bouts of serious crisis.[83] No solution to the problem of declining exports, falling productivity, balance of payments deficits, exchange crisis, or inflation had been found by the end of the 1950s. In this sense, the problems of the British economy, and the world economic crisis of the late 1960s, had their roots in the policies pursued a decade earlier, in the guise of 'steady as she goes'. Second, it is equally undeniable that the political decline of Britain in the international system gathered pace from the mid-1950s and could not be reversed once the Treaty of Rome had been signed and Plan G rejected. Talk of Anglo-American interdependence could not mask the fundamental changes which had occurred in the international political economy consigning Britain to awkward satellite status for the next two decades.

In this light it seems clear that Robot offered an opportunity for the British government to take a lead in restructuring the international political economy to halt economic and political decline. The real significance of the proposals lay in their impact on the politics of international economic relations. In February 1952 a pattern of events converged to produce a unique opportunity for Britain to check European integration, form a new Payments Club, and pull sterling out of its 'decaying currency area'. There is, of course, room for endless discussion about the domestic economic consequences of the plan. But what is certain is that the plan would have encouraged structural adjustment and jettisoned the politicized form of economic management, with its attendant problem of 'overload', which ensnared governments until the late 1970s. On the international level, as Otto Clarke argued, once unilateral action in the form of Robot had been rejected, Britain gradually lost control of the convertibility operation. The Collective Approach ensured that Britain moved only as fast as the slowest and least-willing country and that after years of negotiation with Europe, the Commonwealth, and the United States a so-called solution was obtainable only on other people's terms without many of the preconditions previously thought indispensable.[84] The lesson here (learnt principally in the Bank) was not that one refrained from consulting others, but that one abandoned collective decisions. In February 1952, the trapdoor was open but the squirrel took fright. Britain had lost its opportunity to remake the world economy and would spend the next thirty years presiding over decline.

Notes

1 Britain, Bretton Woods and the Crisis of the World Economy, 1945–1951

1. See for example Gilpin, 1987, pp. 131–4; Bretton Woods Commission, 1994; Balaam and Veseth, 2001, pp. 147–50; Arrighi, 1994, pp. 3, 296–9; Schild, 1995, p. 129.
2. The popular term coined by John Ruggie, 1982.
3. For accounts of the decline of the Bretton Woods 'system' see Helleiner, 1994, chapter 5; Garber, 1993, pp. 461–85; and, more generally, Soloman, 1982; and de Vries, 1985. On the move to convertibility, the best economic histories are Fforde, 1992, and Procter, 1990.
4. Keynes, 1979, pp. 256–95; also see Clarke, 1982, pp. 52–9.
5. Fforde, 1992, pp. 417–18.
6. A short dramatis personae is included at the end of this chapter providing details of the key individuals.
7. On the Bretton Woods Agreement see Van Dormael, 1978; Pressnell, 1987; Fforde, 1992; Helleiner, 1994; Schild, 1995. On the Anglo–American Loan Agreement see Gardner, 1969; Pressnell, 1987; Burnham, 1990, 1992; Fforde, 1992. On the Marshall Plan see Price, 1955; Van der Beugal, 1966; Arkes, 1972; Kindleberger, 1987; Hogan, 1987; Milward, 1984; Leffler, 1998. For literature on the European Payments Union see Triffin, 1957; Kaplan and Schleiminger, 1989; and Eichengreen, 1993, 1995.
8. PRO: T236/3071, 'The Economic Background', Memo by a group of officials, 11 July 1952.
9. HMSO, 1944, Cmd 6546; PRO: T236/3071, 'The Economic Background', Memo by a group of officials, 11 July 1952.
10. Irwin, 1995, pp. 130–2; Curzon, 1964, pp. 6–8, 34–53.
11. HMSO, 1944, Cmd 6546, p. 33; PRO: T236/3269, 'Note by the Treasury on the IMF and IBRD', 24 February 1950.
12. PRO: T236/3071, 'The Economic Background', Memo by a group of officials, 11 July 1952; PRO: T236/3269, 'Note by the Treasury on the IMF and IBRD', 24 February 1950.
13. Keynes and Morgenthau quoted in Van Dormael, 1978, pp. 2 and 222.
14. American Bankers Association report on Bretton Woods, February 1945, quoted in Van Dormael, 1978, p. 248.
15. Mikesell, 1945, pp. 563–76; Block, 1977, pp. 52–3.
16. Burnham, 1990, pp. 36–41; Williams, 1944; Mikesell, 1945, p. 569; Kolko, 1990, pp. 484–92.
17. PRO: T236/3269, 'Note by the Treasury on the IMF and IBRD', 24 February 1950; Pressnell, 1987, pp. 319–29; Fforde, 1992, pp. 62–73.
18. PRO: T236/3269, 'Note by the Treasury on the IMF and IBRD', 24 February 1950.
19. Burnham, 1990, p. 49; Fforde, 1992, pp. 72–3.
20. US National Archives: RG 56/450, 'Background Material on Dollar–Sterling Problems', December 1950; Block, 1977, pp. 57–60; Kolko, 1990, pp. 280–7.

21. Clayton to Wood (Chairman of Sears Roebuck), 26 November 1945, quoted in Gardner, 1969, p. 197.
22. PRO: T236/3071, 'The Economic Background', Memo by a group of officials, 11 July 1952.
23. Fforde, 1992, p. 160.
24. Cobbold to Eady quoted in Fforde, 1992, p. 151.
25. US National Archives: RG 59, 'Telegram: Douglas to Lovett and Snyder', 18 August 1947; Fforde, 1992, p. 153.
26. US National Archives: RG 59, 'Anglo-American Financial Discussions', 19 August 1947, and 'Discussions with the British with respect to Section 8 of the Anglo–American Financial Agreement', 11 September 1947; Fforde, 1992, p. 158.
27. PRO: T236/782, 'Dollar Crisis (European Reconstruction)', Note by Clayton, August 1947.
28. Bolton quoted in Fforde, 1992, p. 163.
29. US National Archives: RG 56/450, Box 81, 'Review of issues relating to ECU', Curtis to Willis, 9 February 1950.
30. PRO: T236/3071, 'The Economic Background', Memo by a group of officials, 11 July 1952.
31. Ibid.
32. US National Archives: RG 56/450, 'European Payments Union', Southard to Martin, 23 June 1950.
33. US National Archives: RG 59, Box 1, 'European Integration', Miriam Camp files, 6 March 1950.
34. James, 1995, p. 109.
35. US National Archives: RG 56/450, 'Memo on US Economic Foreign Policy', Frank Southard, 9 October 1952.
36. PRO: T236/3071, 'The Economic Background', Memo by a group of officials, 11 July 1952.
37. Ibid.
38. Mikesell, 1954, p. 30.
39. Ibid.
40. PRO: T236/3071, 'The Economic Background', Memo by a group of officials, 11 July 1952.
41. Ibid.
42. HMSO, 1952, Cmd 8509, p. 9, table 1.
43. HMSO, 1951, Cmd 8195, p. 3.
44. Board of Trade Journal, September 1952, 'Index Numbers of Import and Export Prices', p. 591.
45. HMSO, 1952, Cmd 8509, p. 9, table 1.
46. Dow, 1964, p. 55.
47. Ibid., p. 56, fn. 1.
48. HMSO, 1952, Cmd 8509, pp. 8–9; on de-stocking see Burnham, 1990, pp. 153–4.
49. Board of Trade Journal, 12 April 1952, 'Distribution of UK trade in 1951', p. 738.
50. Ibid.
51. HMSO, 1952, Cmd 8509, p. 16.
52. Board of Trade Journal, 12 April 1952, 'Distribution of UK trade in 1951', p. 738.
53. PRO: T273/315, 'Economic Prospects for 1952', Bridges to Butler, no date.
54. Ibid.
55. PRO: CAB 129/44, 'Economic Implications of the Defence Proposals', Memo by the Chancellor, 19 January 1951; for further details on the impact of rearmament, see Burnham, 1995.

56. HMSO, 1952, Cmd 8509, p. 15.
57. HMSO, 1952, Cmd 8509, pp. 9, 15–16.
58. HMSO, 1952, Cmd 8509, pp. 8–9.
59. PRO: T273/315, 'Economic Prospects for 1952', Bridges to Butler, no date; HMSO, 1952, Cmd 8509, p. 10.
60. HMSO, 1952, Cmd 8509, pp. 10–11.
61. Ibid., p. 10.
62. PRO: CAB 129/48, 'The Economic Position: Analysis and Remedies', Memorandum by the Chancellor, 31 October 1951.
63. HMSO, 1953, Cmd 8800, p. 7, table 1.
64. PRO: CAB 129/48, 'The Economic Position: Analysis and Remedies', Memorandum by the Chancellor, 31 October 1951.
65. PRO: PREM 11/138, 'Churchill to Eden', 21 February 1952.
66. PRO: T236/3071, 'The Economic Background', Memo by a group of officials, 11 July 1952.
67. Ibid.
68. Ibid.
69. Ibid.
70. Ibid.
71. Ibid.
72. Ibid.
73. PRO: T236/3242, 'US Dollar Shortage and UK Exports', Note by Clarke, 16 March 1952.
74. HMSO, 1952, Cmd 8509, p. 41; PRO: T236/3242, 'US Dollar Shortage and UK Exports', Note by Clarke, 16 March 1952.
75. Dow, 1964, p. 347.
76. Cairncross, 1985, pp. 40–1.
77. HMSO, 1952, Cmd 8509, pp. 23–5.
78. PRO: T273/315, 'Economic Prospects for 1952', Bridges to Butler, no date; HMSO, 1952, Cmd 8509, pp. 36–7.
79. Dow, 1964, p. 403.
80. PRO: CAB 130/78, 'Draft Synopsis of Policy Paper', Working Party on External Economic Policy, 2 July 1952.
81. US National Archives: RG 56/450, 'Summary of State Department Paper on Long-Range British Problem', 27 December 1951.
82. Ibid.
83. Ibid.
84. US National Archives: RG 56/450, 'Summary of Van Cleveland Paper on the United Kingdom', Widman to Willis, 28 December 1951.
85. PRO: CAB 130/78, 'The Problems of External Economic Policy', Memo by a Group of Officials, 22 July 1952.
86. Details have been gathered from a number of sources, including PRO and Bank files (see in particular PRO: T199/702, Treasury Organisation tables); Cairncross and Watts, 1989; Fforde, 1992; Hall, 1989 and 1991; MacDougall, 1987; Hubback, 1988; Plowden, 1989.

2 Emergency Action and the Route to Floating Rate Convertibility

1. Hall, 1989, 'Entry for 30 August 1951', pp. 165–6; Plowden, 1989, p. 133.
2. Hall, 1989, 'Entry for 30 August 1951', p. 166.

3. Hall, 1989, 'Entry for 28 August 1951', p. 164; Plowden, 1989, p. 133.
4. Hall, 1989, 'Entry for 24 October 1951', p. 174. Also see Hall, 1989, 'Entry for 25 October 1951', p. 175; Peden, 2000, pp. 432–3.
5. PRO: T273/315, 'Notes of a meeting held in Bridges' room', 11 October 1951.
6. Ibid.
7. Butler, 1971, p. 156.
8. Peden, 2000, p. 430.
9. Hall, 1989, 'Entry for 29 October 1951', p. 176.
10. Hall, 1989, 'Entry for 7 November 1951', p. 178 and 'Entry for 5 November 1951', p. 177; Fforde, 1992, pp. 440–1, fn. 26 and 27.
11. Butler Papers: RAB G24/64–67, 'Letter: Bridges to Butler', 12 August 1952.
12. Butler, 1971, p. 156.
13. PRO: T273/315, 'Economic Prospects for 1952' no date or author.
14. Butler, 1971, p. 157.
15. PRO: CAB 128/23, Cabinet conclusions, 30 October 1951.
16. BE: G1/120, Cobbold to Bridges, 22 October 1951; Fforde, 1992, p. 403.
17. PRO: CAB 129/48, 'The Economic Position: Analysis and Remedies', Memo by the Chancellor, 31 October 1951.
18. Ibid.
19. Fforde, 1992, p. 404.
20. PRO: CAB 129/48, 'The Economic Position: Analysis and Remedies', Memo by the Chancellor, 31 October 1951.
21. Hall, 1989, 'Entry for 24 October 1951', p. 174.
22. PRO: CAB 129/49, 'The Balance of Payments Situation', Memo by the Chancellor, 19 January 1952.
23. Ibid.
24. Ibid.
25. PRO: T237/315, 'Economic Situation', Bridges to Butler, 27 November 1951.
26. PRO: T237/315, 'Cuts in Government Expenditure', 29 November 1951, no author.
27. PRO: T237/315, 'Economic Situation', Bridges to Butler, 27 November 1951.
28. Hall, 1989, 'Entries for 27–29 November 1951', pp. 184–5.
29. Cairncross and Watts, 1989, p. 295; also see the papers on 'UK Post-war balance of payments' in PRO: T230/4 and T230/5.
30. PRO: T236/2311, 'Methods of Devaluation', Memo by Rowe-Dutton, 3 September 1948.
31. Ibid.; Clarke, 1982, pp. 108–9; Cairncross and Watts, 1989, p. 295.
32. PRO: T236/2311, 'Variable Rates', Memo by Bolton, 18 August 1949.
33. Ibid.
34. PRO: T230/388, 'Devaluation: the choice of the new exchange rate', Note by the Economic Section, 6 August 1949.
35. Clarke had argued with Keynes in 1945 over the sterling–dollar exchange rate, suggesting that $3.50 to the £1 rather than $4.03 would be better for the UK economy. See 'Towards a Balance of Payments', Memo by Clarke, 11 May 1945, in Clarke, 1982, pp. 96–122.
36. PRO: T236/2311, Playfair to Fleming, 10 February 1950.
37. PRO: T236/3211, Untitled memo, Fleming to Playfair, 3 March 1950.
38. PRO: T236/2311, Playfair to Clarke and Flett, 4 March 1950.
39. PRO: T236/3211, Untitled memo, Fleming to Playfair, 3 March 1950.
40. Ibid.
41. Ibid.

42. PRO: CAB 129/40, 'Economic Report', Note by the Chancellor, 12 June 1950.
43. PRO: T236/2311, Hall's handwritten comments on Fleming's memo, 3 March 1950.
44. PRO: T236/2311, Playfair to Clarke and Flett, 4 March 1950.
45. PRO: T236/2311, Flett and Brittain's untitled handwritten comments, 16–18 March 1950.
46. PRO: T236/2311, Clarke's handwritten comments on Playfair to Clarke and Flett, 7 March 1950.
47. Ibid.
48. Ibid.
49. Ibid.
50. BE: G1/97, 'Extracts from the Governor's Diary', 22 March 1951.
51. MRC: MSS. 292/560.1/7, 'TUC Economic Committee Minutes', 11 October 1950; MSS. 292/567/12/6, 'Economic Planning Board Minutes', 2 November 1950; PRO: T236/2944, Memo to Henry Wilson Smith, 2 January 1951; Fforde, 1992, p. 309.
52. BE: G1/97, 'Extracts from the Governor's Diary', 22 March 1951.
53. PRO: T236/2944, Wilson Smith to Brittain, 3 January 1951.
54. PRO: T236/2944, Herbert Brittain to Wilson Smith, 10 January 1951.
55. PRO: T236/2944, 'Revaluation of Sterling', Note by Brittain and Clarke, 10 January 1951.
56. Ibid.
57. Ibid.
58. PRO: T236/2944, 'A note on revaluation', Nita Watts, 12 March 1951; PRO: T236/2944, Clarke to Brittain, 21 March 1951.
59. PRO: T236/2944, Gaitskell to Brittain, 5 June 1951; BE: G1/97, 'Governor's Note', 6 June 1951.
60. PRO: T236/2944, 'A note on revaluation', Nita Watts, 12 March 1951.
61. BE: G1/97, 'Floating Sterling', Memo by Fisher to the Governor, 14 March 1951; Fforde, 1992, p. 309.
62. BE: G1/97, 'Floating Sterling', Memo by Fisher to the Governor, 14 March 1951.
63. Ibid.
64. BE: G1/97, 'Floating Sterling', Memo by Bolton, 22 March 1951 (also in PRO: T236/2944).
65. PRO: T236/2944, 'Exchange Rates', Brittain to Bridges, 20 April 1951.
66. BE: G1/97, 'Floating Sterling', Memo by Bolton, 22 March 1951; Fforde, 1992, p. 309.
67. BE: G1/97, 'Floating Sterling', Memo by Bolton, 22 March 1951.
68. Ibid.
69. BE: G1/97, 'Extracts from the Governor's Diary', 22 March 1951.
70. BE: G1/97, 'Floating Sterling', Comments by Thompson-McCausland, 9 April 1951.
71. Ibid.
72. Ibid.
73. BE: G1/97, 'Note to the Governor', Thompson-McCausland, 4 May 1951.
74. Ibid.
75. Ibid.
76. Ibid.
77. Ibid.
78. Ibid.
79. Fforde, 1992, p. 310.

80. BE: G1/97, 'Lucius Thompson-McCausland's memo on Floating Sterling and controlling the rate of exchange', Memo by Fisher to the Governor, 17 May 1951.
81. BE: G1/97, 'Lucius Thompson-McCausland's memo on Floating Sterling and controlling the rate of exchange', Memo by Fisher to the Governor, 17 May 1951.
82. BE: G1/97, 'Fluctuating Exchange Rate', Memo by William Allen, 17 May 1951.
83. Ibid.
84. Fforde, 1992, p. 311.
85. Ibid.
86. PRO: T236/2944, 'Implications of US Inflation', Clarke to Hall, 21 March 1951.
87. Ibid.
88. PRO: T236/2944, 'Exchange Rates', Memo by Bridges, 26 April 1951; PRO: T236/2944, Memo by Plowden, 27 April 1951.
89. PRO: T236/3067 contains minutes of the Finance Ministers' meetings held between 15 and 21 January. This was preceded by meetings of officials which began on 8 January.
90. PRO: T236/3969, 'The Market in Transferable Sterling', Memo by the Bank of England, 31 January 1955.
91. Ibid.
92. Ibid.
93. PRO: T236/3937, 'Cheap sterling and the unification plan', Memo by Symons to Copleston, 26 January 1954.
94. Fforde, 1992, pp. 221–49; Interview with John Fforde, 22 November 1999.
95. 'Backdoor Convertibility', *The Economist*, 5 March 1955, p. 828.
96. Fforde, 1992, p. 222.
97. PRO: T230/388, 'Cheap Sterling', Note by the Economic Section, 19 December 1949; PRO: T325/38, 'Cheap Sterling', Note by the Bank of England, 8 April 1952; Fforde, 1992, p. 225.
98. Siepmann quoted in Fforde, 1992, p. 241.
99. Ibid. p. 222.
100. PRO: T236/3969, 'The Market in Transferable Sterling', Memo by the Bank of England, 31 January 1955.
101. Fforde, 1992, p. 222.
102. PRO: T325/38, 'Cheap Sterling', Note by the Bank of England, 8 April 1952.
103. Ibid.
104. Ibid.
105. Ibid.
106. BE: G1/120, Untitled Memo, Thompson-McCausland to the Governor, 31 October 1951.
107. Ibid.
108. Ibid.
109. BE: G1/120, 'Some Consequences of Convertibility', Thompson-McCausland to Cobbold (also shown to Rowan), 26 November 1951.
110. BE: G1/120, Untitled Memo, Thompson-McCausland to the Governor, 31 October 1951.
111. Fforde, 1992, p. 421.
112. BE: G1/120, 'Notes on "Convertibility"', Bolton to Cobbold, 25 January 1952.
113. Ibid.
114. Ibid. Fforde, 1992, p. 426; BE: G1/121, 'Untitled and unsigned note', 6 February 1952; 'Memo by Flett' to Rowan, 6 February 1952; BE: ADM 14/30, 'Plan for "Overseas Sterling"', Bolton to Thompson-McCausland, first draft, 9 February 1952.

115. BE: ADM 14/30, 'Note by Cobbold', 28 November 1951.
116. BE: G1/120, 'Extract from Governor's Note, 21 November 1951', 21 November 1951.
117. For details see Burnham, 1990, chapters 2 and 3.
118. US National Archives: RG 56/450, Box 78, 'Memo on US Economic Foreign Policy', Southard, 9 October 1952.
119. US National Archives: RG 56/450, Box 78, 'Memo on US Economic Foreign Policy', Southard, 9 October 1952; RG 56/450, Box 78, 'Background material on dollar–sterling problems', December 1950.
120. US National Archives: RG 56/450, Box 77, 'The Question of Aid to Britain', Polk to Willis, 28 July 1951.
121. US National Archives: RG 56/450, Box 81, 'Review of issues relating to ECU', Curtis to Willis, 9 February 1950.
122. US National Archives: RG 56/450, Box 81, 'Review of issues relating to ECU', Curtis to Willis, 9 February 1950.
123. US National Archives: RG 56/450, Box 81, 'Review of issues relating to ECU', Curtis to Willis, 9 February 1950.
124. PRO: T236/3245, 'Emergency Action', Memo by Rowan, 8 February 1952.
125. PRO: T236/5329, 'Postwar Anglo-American Discussions on International Trade and Payments', Memo by J. Mark, 28 October 1953.
126. PRO: CAB 130/73, 'Economic Aid – Historical Background', GEN. 396/37, 21 December 1951.
127. Ibid.
128. Procter, 1993, p. 32; also see Leigh-Phippard, 1995, especially chapter 5.
129. PRO: CAB 130/73, 'Economic Aid – Historical Background', GEN. 396/37, 21 December 1951.
130. PRO: T236/2989, 'Record of conversation', Memo to Brittain, Flett, Copleston and Clarke, 26 November 1951.
131. PRO: CAB 130/73, 'Economic Aid – Historical Background', GEN. 396/37, 21 December 1951.
132. Ibid.; Procter, 1993, p. 34.
133. Procter, 1993, p. 34.
134. This was based on Otto Clarke's draft 'Emergency Action', 31 January 1952, see PRO: T235/37; Procter, 1993, pp. 33–4.
135. US National Archives: RG 56/450, Box 78, 'The Dollar Area and the Sterling Area', US Treasury, International Affairs, December 1952.
136. PRO: T236/3240, 'Convertibility', Memo by Clarke, 25 January 1952.
137. Ibid.
138. US National Archives: RG 56/450, 'Plan for British Solvency', Memo by Polk to Willis, 5 January 1952.
139. Ibid.
140. Ibid.
141. Fforde, 1992, p. 426.
142. BE: ADM 14/30, 'Sterling in the Future', Memo by John Fisher, 24 January 1952; Fforde, 1992, p. 427.
143. PRO: T236/3069, 'Commonwealth Finance Ministers', Note by Strath to Brittain, 2 January 1952.
144. Ibid.
145. PRO: T236/3069, 'Commonwealth Finance Ministers', Note by Strath to Brittain, 2 January 1952.

146. PRO: T236/3069, 'Commonwealth Finance Ministers', Butler's handwritten comments on Strath's note, 2 January 1952.
147. PRO: CAB 128/44, Cabinet Conclusions, 10 January 1952.
148. Ibid.
149. Fforde, 1992, p. 427, fn. 17; Macmillan Papers: MS. Macmillan, Dep. c. 14/1, 'Diary for 1952', Entry for 29 February.
150. PRO: T236/3067, 'Minutes of the Meeting of the Commonwealth Finance Ministers', 15 January 1952.
151. Ibid.
152. PRO: T236/3067, 'Minutes of the Meeting of the Commonwealth Finance Ministers', 18 January 1952.
153. PRO: T236/3067, 'Minutes of the Meeting of the Commonwealth Finance Ministers', 15 January 1952.
154. Ibid.
155. Ibid.
156. PRO: T236/3067, 'Minutes of the Meeting of the Commonwealth Finance Ministers', 18 January 1952.
157. Ibid.
158. Ibid.
159. PRO: T236/3069, 'Tactics to be followed by the UK: Note of a meeting held in Sir H. Brittain's room', 22 January 1952.
160. BE: ADM 14/30, 'Note by Cobbold', Cobbold's handwritten comments, 28 November 1951.
161. PRO: T236/3069, 'Tactics to be followed by the UK: Note of a meeting held in Sir H. Brittain's room', 22 January 1952.
162. PRO: T236/3069, 'Working Party on Convertibility', Note by Herbert Brittain to Mr Mitchell, 25 January 1952.
163. PRO: CAB 128/24, 'Balance of Payments Conclusion', 25 January 1952.
164. PRO: CAB 129/49, 'The Balance of Payments Situation', Memo by the Chancellor, 19 January 1952.
165. Ibid.
166. PRO: T171/408, 'Budget 1952: Chronology of Events'; Hansard, 'Financial and Economic Situation', pp. 40–62, 29 January 1952.
167. PRO: T236/3240, 'Convertibility', Memo by Clarke, 25 January 1952.

3 Operation Robot: Restructuring the Domestic and the World Economy

1. PRO: T236/3242, 'Economic Situation: Balance of Payments', C.C. (52) 23rd, 24th and 25th Conclusions: Cabinet Conclusions 28th and 29th February 1952 (also in PRO: CAB 128/40); Plowden, 1989, p. 144.
2. Cairncross, 1985, p. 244; MacDougall, 1987, p. 86.
3. Dell, 1996, p. 166; Plowden, 1989, p. 143.
4. PRO: T236/3240, 'Convertibility', Memo by Clarke to Rowan, 25 January 1952.
5. BE: G1/120, 'Untitled memo', Thompson-McCausland to Cobbold, 31 October 1951; BE: G1/120, 'Notes on Convertibility', Memo by Bolton, 25 January 1952.
6. BE: G1/120, 'Notes on Convertibility', Memo by Bolton, 25 January 1952.
7. PRO: T236/3240, 'Convertibility', Memo by Clarke to Rowan, 25 January 1952.
8. Ibid.

9. Ibid.
10. Ibid.
11. Ibid.
12. Ibid.
13. Ibid.
14. Ibid.
15. Ibid.
16. Ibid.
17. BE: ADM 14/30, 'Causes of Inconvertibility', Thompson-McCausland to Cobbold, 28 January 1952; BE: G1/120, 'Notes on Convertibility', Bolton to Cobbold, 25 January 1952.
18. BE: ADM 14/30, 'Causes of Inconvertibility', Thompson-McCausland to Cobbold, 28 January 1952.
19. BE: G1/120, 'Notes on Convertibility', Bolton to Cobbold, 25 January 1952; PRO: T325/38, 'Sir George Bolton on "Convertibility"', Clarke to Brittain, 29 January 1952.
20. PRO: T325/38, 'Sir George Bolton on "Convertibility"', Clarke to Brittain, 29 January 1952.
21. PRO: T325/37, Memo by Clarke to Rowan, 29 January 1952.
22. Ibid.
23. Ibid.
24. PRO: T325/37, 'Emergency Action', Memo by Clarke to Rowan, First Draft, 31 January 1952.
25. Cairncross, 1985, p. 241, fn. 20, and Procter, 1993, p. 35, both seem to be unaware that Clarke's first draft of 'Emergency Action' was very different to the finished document which had been worked on by Hall and others, and which can be found in PRO: T236/3245 dated 8 February 1952.
26. PRO: T325/37, 'Emergency Action', Memo by Clarke to Rowan, First Draft, 31 January 1952.
27. Ibid.
28. Ibid.
29. Ibid.
30. Ibid.
31. Ibid.
32. Ibid.
33. Hall, 1989, p. 201, 'Entry for 8 February'; PRO: T236/3245, 'Note for Record', by Robert Hall, 4 March 1952.
34. PRO: T236/3245, 'Emergency Action', Final Draft, 8 February 1952.
35. BE: C160/24, 'Sir George Bolton's Diary 1952', 5 and 6 February 1952; BE: G3/5, 'Governor's Diary', 6 February 1952.
36. BE: G1/121, 'Untitled and unsigned note', 6 February 1952; Fforde, 1992, p. 431 fn. 18 suggests that the author was Fisher writing under instructions from Bolton.
37. BE: G1/121, 'Untitled and unsigned note', 6 February 1952; Fforde, 1992, p. 431.
38. BE: G3/5, 'Governor's Diary', 7 February 1952.
39. BE: G3/107, 'Note for Record', Cameron Cobbold, 18 March 1952.
40. Ibid.
41. BE: C160/24, 'Sir George Bolton's Diary 1952', 8 February 1952.
42. BE: C160/24, 'Sir George Bolton's Diary 1952', 8 and 9 February 1952; BE: ADM 14/30, 'Plan for "Overseas Sterling"', First Draft, 9 February 1952; BE: C160/144, 'Plan for "Overseas Sterling"', Memo by Bolton, 16 February 1952; BE: G3/107,

'Note for Record', by Cameron Cobbold, 18 February 1952; BE: G1/121, Cobbold to Butler, 13 January 1952.

43. BE: C160/24, 'Sir George Bolton's Diary 1952', 8 and 9 February 1952.
44. BE: G1/121, 'Governor's notes for meeting with Cabinet', 28 February 1952.
45. BE: C160/144, 'Plan for "Overseas Sterling"', Memo by Bolton, 16 February 1952.
46. Ibid.
47. BE: G1/121, Cobbold to Butler, 13 January 1952; Fforde, 1992, p. 433.
48. BE: G1/121, 'Cobbold's remarks on External Action', 22 February 1952.
49. PRO: T236/3240, 'Septuagesima Plus', Memo by Clarke, 12 February 1952.
50. Ibid.
51. Ibid.
52. PRO: T325/38, 'Plan for "Overseas Sterling"', Memo by Clarke, 19 February 1952.
53. Ibid.
54. BE: C160/24, 'Sir George Bolton's Diary 1952', 18 and 19 February 1952; Cairncross, 1985, p. 248; Fforde, 1992, p. 433.
55. BE: C160/24, 'Sir George Bolton's Diary 1952', 18 and 19 February 1952; Hall, 1989, pp. 204–5, 'Entries for 19 and 20 February 1952'.
56. BE: G3/107, 'Note for Record' by Cameron Cobbold, 18 March 1952; PRO: T236/3245, 'Note for Record', by Robert Hall, 4 March 1952.
57. BE: G3/107, 'Note for Record' by Cameron Cobbold, 18 March 1952.
58. Ibid.
59. PRO: T236/3245, 'Note for Record', by Robert Hall, 4 March 1952.
60. Ibid.
61. PRO: T236/3245, 'Note for Record', by Robert Hall, 4 March 1952; Hall, 1989, p. 205, 'Entry for 22 February 1952'. Crookshank announced to the House on 25 February that the Budget would now fall on 11 March. The *Times* recorded that the postponement was due to 'technical difficulties involved in introducing a Budget before the end of the preceding financial year' exacerbated by the 'unhappy event of the King's death. This and the consequent ceremonies interrupted both the Chancellor's own work and his consultations with some of his principal official advisers'. *The Times*, Tuesday 26 February 1952.
62. BE: C160/24, 'Sir George Bolton's Diary 1952', 20 and 21 February 1952.
63. BE: ADM 14/30, 'External Sterling Plan', Report from Overseas Finance to the Chancellor, 4 April 1952.
64. PRO: T236/3244, 'External Sterling Plan: First draft of Chancellor's Paper', Clarke, 26 June 1952; also see Clarke's comments in PRO: T236/3241, 'E.S.P.: Causes and Consequences', Minute by Clarke, 26 February 1952, where he notes, 'this is not a plan to put the balance of payments right. It is a dismal necessity which results from our failure to put the balance of payments right.'
65. Butler Papers: RAB G24/64, 'Letter: Bridges to Butler', 12 August 1952.
66. PRO: T236/3241, 'Robot Walks Again', Clarke to Rowan, 11 March 1952.
67. PRO: CAB 130/73, 'German Industrial Recovery and Competition', Brief by the Board of Trade, 20 December 1951.
68. Ibid.
69. Ibid.
70. Ibid.
71. BE: ADM 14/30, 'External Sterling Plan', Report from Overseas Finance to the Chancellor, 4 April 1952; also see PRO: T236/3240, 'Septuagesima Plus', Memo by Clarke, 12 February 1952, in which Clarke notes, 'We stand on our competitive power, with exchange rate as a safety valve.'
72. PRO: T236/3245, 'External Action', Clarke to Rowan, 22 February 1952.

73. BE: ADM 14/30, 'External Sterling Plan', Report from Overseas Finance to the Chancellor, 4 April 1952.
74. Ibid.
75. Ibid.
76. PRO: T236/3242, 'Economic Situation: Balance of Payments', C.C. (52) 23rd, 24th and 25th Conclusions: Cabinet Conclusions 28th and 29th February 1952 (also in PRO: CAB 128/40).
77. BE: ADM 14/30, 'External Sterling Plan', Report from Overseas Finance to the Chancellor, 4 April 1952.
78. PRO: T236/3241, 'External Action', Clarke to Butler, 26 February 1952.
79. PRO: T236/3241, 'ESP: Causes and Consequences', Minute by Clarke, 26 February 1952.
80. BE: ADM 14/30, 'External Sterling Plan', Report from Overseas Finance to the Chancellor, 4 April 1952.
81. PRO: T236/3242, 'Setting the Pound Free', Cherwell to Churchill, 18 March 1952.
82. Ibid.
83. BE: G1/121, 'Letter: Peacock to Governor', 29 February 1952.
84. PRO: T236/3241, 'ESP: Causes and Consequences', Minute by Clarke, 26 February 1952.
85. PRO: T236/3245, External Action', Clarke to Rowan, 26 February 1952; also see Butler's comments in PRO: T236/3242, 'Economic Situation: Balance of Payments', C.C. (52) 23rd, 24th and 25th Conclusions: Cabinet Conclusions 28th and 29th February 1952 (also in PRO: CAB 128/40).
86. PRO: T236/3241, 'Operation Robot: Proposed timetable and draft telegrams', 26 February 1952 and 27 February 1952.
87. PRO: T236/3241, 'The Plan and Europe', Memo by Bolton, 27 February 1952.
88. PRO: T236/3241, 'External Action', Memo by Butler, 26 February 1952.
89. PRO: T236/3241, 'Telegram number 3: Substance and Commentary', Memo by Overseas Finance to Butler, 26 February 1952.
90. For a wider discussion of the significance of the Sterling Area see Schenk, 1994.
91. PRO: T236/3241, 'External Action', Memo by Butler, 26 February 1952.
92. PRO: T236/3241, 'Funding of Sterling Area Balances', Note by the Bank of England, 27 February 1952.
93. PRO: T236/3241, 'External Action', Memo by Butler, 26 February 1952.
94. PRO: T236/3241, 'Draft telegrams', 26 February 1952.
95. PRO: T236/3241, 'Draft telegrams', 26 February 1952; PRO: T236/3241,'External Action' Memo by Butler, 26 February 1952.
96. PRO: T236/3243, 'External Sterling Plan', Memo by Overseas Finance to Butler, 4 April 1952.
97. PRO: T276/29, 'Sterling Balances Since the War', Treasury Historical Memorandum 16, January 1972. The fifth Agreement, outlined on 8 February 1952, provided for the release of £310 million and for annual releases of £35 million between 1952 and 1957.
98. PRO: T276/29, 'Sterling Balances Since the War', Treasury Historical Memorandum 16, January 1972.
99. For a breakdown of the size of the balances see Schenk, 1994, pp. 20–6.
100. BE: G3/107, 'Governor's Note', 4 June 1952; BE: C160/24, 'Sir George Bolton's Diary', 16 June 1952; PRO: T276/29, 'Sterling Balances Since the War', Treasury Historical Memorandum 16, January 1972; Fforde, 1992, p. 463.
101. BE: G3/107, 'Governor's Note', 16 June 1952; BE: C160/24, 'Sir George Bolton's Diary', 16 June 1952; Fforde, 1992, p. 463.

102. PRO: T236/3241, 'External Action', Memo by Butler, 26 February 1952.
103. PRO: T236/3241, 'The Plan – the Colonies', Butler to Rowan, 25 February 1952; PRO: T236/3241, 'Financial Situation', Memo by Lyttelton, 26 February 1952.
104. In any case the Treasury decided that 'on economic grounds we have no major interest in keeping Pakistan in the Sterling Area', PRO: T236/3243, 'External Sterling Plan', Memo by Overseas Finance to Butler, 4 April 1952.
105. PRO: T236/3241, 'External Action', Memo by Butler, 26 February 1952; PRO: T236/3243, 'External Sterling Plan', Memo by Overseas Finance to Butler, 4 April 1952.
106. PRO: T236/3241, 'External Action', Memo by Butler, 26 February 1952.
107. PRO: T236/3241, 'Robot Walks Again', Clarke to Rowan, 11 March 1952.
108. Ibid.
109. For general discussions on the workings of EPU see Kaplan and Schleiminger, 1989; Eichengreen, 1995, pp. 169–98; and Burnham, 1990, pp. 137–49.
110. PRO: T236/3241, 'ESP: Causes and Consequences', Memo by Clarke, 26 February 1952.
111. PRO: T236/3241, 'The Plan and Europe', Memo by Bolton, 27 February 1952.
112. Ibid.
113. Ibid.
114. Ibid.
115. Ibid.
116. BE: G1/121, 'Europe', Beale to the Governor, 28 February 1952.
117. Ibid.
118. Ibid.
119. BE: OV 44/20, 'EPU: Plan of Action', Bridge to Bolton, 22 February 1952.
120. PRO: T236/3241, 'The Plan and Europe', Memo by Bolton, 27 February 1952; BE: OV 44/20, 'EPU: Plan of Action', Bridge to Bolton, 22 February 1952; Fforde, 1992, pp. 453–54.
121. BE: OV 44/20, 'EPU: Plan of Action', Bridge to Bolton, 22 February 1952.
122. Ibid.
123. PRO: T236/3241, 'Europe – Payments', Note by the Bank, 29 February 1952.
124. Ibid.
125. BE: OV 44/20, 'Probable Reactions of EPU Countries', 22 February 1952; PRO: T236/3241, 'Europe – Payments', Note by the Bank, 29 February 1952.
126. PRO: T236/3241, 'Europe – Payments', Note by the Bank, 29 February 1952.
127. PRO: T236/3243, 'External Sterling Plan', Report from Overseas Finance to Butler, 4 April 1952.
128. Ibid.
129. Fforde, 1992, p. 457.
130. PRO: FO371/96057, 'The Proposed Anglo-French Talks', Strang to Morrison, September 1951.
131. PRO: FO371/96057, Memo by Strang, 4 September 1951.
132. Fforde, 1992, p. 461.
133. Ibid., p. 457.
134. Ibid., p. 457, fn. 43.
135. PRO: T237/174, 'New French Import Control Measures', Paris to Foreign Office, 8 February 1952.
136. PRO: T237/175, 'French Trade and Payments Situation' and *Financial Times* extract, 17 March 1952.

137. PRO: T237/174, Memo: Berthoud to Harvey, 4/2/52; and PRO: T237/175, 'Suspension of French Measures of Liberalisation', French Delegation to OEEC, 2 March 1952.
138. US National Archives: RG 59, Box 2, 'Letter: Labouisse to Cleveland', 17 March 1952.
139. PRO: T236/3243, 'External Sterling Plan', Report from Overseas Finance to Butler, 4 April 1952.
140. PRO: CAB 128/16, Cabinet Conclusions, CM(49)41, August 1949.
141. Fforde, 1992, p. 461.
142. PRO: T236/3243, 'External Sterling Plan', Report from Overseas Finance to Butler, 4 April 1952.
143. Fforde, 1992, p. 459.
144. PRO: T325/38, 'Plan for "Overseas Sterling"', Note by Clarke, 19 February 1952.
145. US National Archives: RG 56/450, Box 30, 'Summary of State Department paper on Long-Range British Problem', 27 December 1951.
146. Ibid.
147. PRO: T273/377, 'Gold Questions', Memo by Rowan, 21/10/52; PRO: T236/3695, 'Note of a meeting held at the US Treasury', 28 January 1954.
148. PRO: T273/377, 'Gold Questions', Memo by Rowan, 21 October 1952.
149. Ibid.
150. PRO: T236/3695, 'Note of a meeting held at the US Treasury', 28 January 1954. W. Randolph Burgess, a former US banker, was now Under-Secretary for Monetary Affairs at the US Treasury – see Fforde, 1992, p. 489.
151. PRO: T236/3937, 'London Gold Market', Butler to Churchill, 15 March 1954; PRO: T236/4048, 'Note of a Meeting held at the US Treasury on 23 September 1954', 23 September 1954.
152. PRO: T325/38, 'Plan for "Overseas Sterling"', Note by Clarke, 19 February 1952; PRO: T236/3243, 'External Sterling Plan', Report from Overseas Finance to Butler, 4 April 1952.
153. US National Archives: RG 56/450, 'Notes on the European Exchange Rate Situation', Memo by Eddie Bernstein, 2 January 1952.
154. Ibid.
155. Ibid.
156. Ibid.
157. US National Archives: RG 56/450, 'Bernstein Memorandum on Exchange Rate Policy', Abramson to Willis, 7 February 1952.
158. Ibid.
159. US National Archives: RG 56/450, 'Memo on US Economic Foreign Policy', Frank Southard, 9 October 1952.
160. Ibid.
161. US National Archives: RG 59, Box 106, 'Concepts and Principles of a Long-Term US Foreign Policy', 16 October 1956; Box 55, 'Probable Developments in the World Situation Through Mid-1953', CIA memo, 24 September 1951.
162. PRO: T236/5329, 'UK Trade and Financial Policies', December 1950.
163. PRO: T236/5329, 'Drawing of sterling from the Fund', Bolton to Gutt, 29 October 1950.
164. PRO: T236/5712, 'The Future of the IMF', Treasury Report, 26 August 1952.
165. PRO: T236/3241, 'External Action', Memo by Butler, 26 February 1952.
166. US National Archives: RG 56/450, 'Bernstein Memorandum on Exchange Rate Policy', Abramson to Willis, 7 February 1952.

167. For a wider discussion of the Anglo-American mutual security relationship in the early 1950s see, Leigh-Phippard, 1995, pp. 152–8; and Dobson, 1988, chapters 4 and 5.
168. US National Archives: RG 56/450, 'United States Policy in EPU', Treasury Department to the National Advisory Council Staff Committee, 13 February 1952.
169. Ibid.
170. Ibid.
171. Ibid.
172. Ibid.
173. US National Archives: RG 56/450, 'EPU: An Evaluation in the light of US Policy', Mutual Security Agency to National Advisory Council Staff Committee, 21 February 1952.
174. Ibid.
175. Ibid.
176. US National Archives: RG 56/450, 'NAC: Minutes, Meeting 190', 13 March 1952.
177. Ibid.
178. Ibid.
179. Ibid.
180. Ibid.
181. PRO: T236/3244, 'Robot', Salter to Butler, 24 January 1952.
182. Butler Papers: RAB G24/60, 'Unfinished Symphony', Butler to Churchill, August 1952.
183. Macmillan Papers: MS. Macmillan, Dep. c. 14/1, 'Diary for 1952', Entry for 29 February 1952; also see MacDougall, 1987, p. 87, who notes that for Cherwell this was 'one of the most exciting periods in his life', and Cairncross, 1985, pp. 245 and 270, who refers to the controversy as producing the 'fullest' and 'most sophisticated' debate on exchange rate policy, as well as being 'the most bitter of the postwar years in Whitehall'.

4 The Battle for Robot

1. PRO: T236/3245, 'Note for Record', Robert Hall, 4 March 1952.
2. Hall, 1989, 'Entry for Wednesday 20 February', p. 205.
3. Hall, 1989, 'Entry for Tuesday 4 March and Wednesday 5 March', p. 207.
4. BE: C160/24, 'Sir George Bolton's Diary 1952', 21 and 22 February 1952; PRO: T236/3245, 'Note for Record', Robert Hall, 4 March 1952.
5. PRO: T236/3245, 'Note for Record', Robert Hall, 4 March 1952; Hall, 1989, 'Entry for Saturday 23 February', p. 206.
6. Hall, 1989, 'Entry for Saturday 23 February', p. 206; Plowden, 1989, pp. 145–7.
7. Peden, 2000, p. 438.
8. Hall, 1989, 'Entry for Saturday 23 February', p. 205.
9. Cairncross and Watts, 1989, p. 304.
10. Ibid., p. xi; Peden, 2000, pp. 372–5 and 437–1.
11. PRO: T236/3242, 'Economic Situation: Balance of Payments', C.C. (52) 23rd, 24th and 25th Conclusions: Cabinet Conclusions 28th and 29th February 1952 (also in PRO: CAB 128/40).
12. PRO: T230/388, 'What happens when the reserves run out?', Watts to Hall, 19 February 1952.
13. Ibid.

14. PRO: T230/388, 'Notes on the current controversy', Butt to Downie, no date; PRO: T230/388, 'Freeing the Exchange Rate', Note to Downie, 21 February 1952.
15. PRO: T230/388, 'Freeing the Exchange Rate' Note to Downie, 21 February 1952.
16. PRO: T230/389, 'What we should do', Jukes to Watts and Neild, 27 February 1952.
17. PRO: T230/389, 'External Policy', Downie to Hall, 27 February 1952; PRO: T230/389, 'A Course of Action', Downie to Watts, no date.
18. PRO: T230/389, 'External Policy', Downie to Hall, 27 February 1952.
19. PRO: T230/389, 'Jukes's Folly and Downie's Desperation', Butt to Watts, 29 February 1952.
20. PRO: T230/389, Memo by Neild to Downie, 28 February 1952.
21. Ibid.
22. PRO: T236/3242, 'The Future of Sterling', Memo by Robert Hall, 25 March 1952.
23. PRO: T230/389, 'Alternative Exchange Policies', Memo by Watts, 25 February 1952; 'Alternative Exchange Policies if the Reserves Run Out', Butt to Watts, no date; 'The Mechanics of Sterling Union', memo by Neild, no date; 'Sterling Union: An Alternative to Robot', Butt to Hall, 20 March 1952.
24. PRO: T230/389, 'Alternative Exchange Policies if the Reserves Run Out', Butt to Watts, no date.
25. PRO: T230/389, 'The Future of Sterling: Summary of Opposing Views', no author indicated, 29 March 1952.
26. MacDougall, 1987, p. 100; also see Plowden, 1989, p. 154.
27. PRO: T230/389, Hall to Butt, 21 March 1952.
28. Birkenhead, 1961, p. 278; MacDougall, 1987, p. 82.
29. Birkenhead, 1961, p. 280.
30. MacDougall, 1987, p. 89; Plowden, 1989, p. 148.
31. Fforde, 1992, pp. 440–1.
32. MacDougall, 1987, pp. 92–4.
33. PRO: T236/3240, 'The Balance of Payments: Memo by the Paymaster General', Cherwell to Butler and Churchill, no date.
34. Ibid.
35. Ibid.
36. Ibid.
37. Ibid.
38. Cherwell Papers: J122/315, Cherwell to Churchill, 26 February 1952.
39. Cherwell Papers: J122/311, Cherwell to Churchill, 26 February 1952.
40. Fforde, 1992, pp. 441–2, fn. 28.
41. BE: G3/107, 'Note for Record', by Cameron Cobbold, 18 March 1952; Fforde, 1992, p. 441, fn. 28; p. 446, fn. 33.
42. Peden, 2000, p. 430.
43. BE: G1/121,'Letter: Peacock to Cobbold', 29 February 1952; also see Fforde, 1992, p. 446.
44. MacDougall, 1987, p. 94.
45. Plowden, 1989, p. 145; Fforde, 1992, p. 439.
46. PRO: T235/72, 'Note on UK Relationship with European Supranational Institutions and particularly the EDC', Crawford to Arnold France, 16 February 1953; Fforde, 1992, p. 439.
47. PRO: PREM 11/138, Churchill to Eden, 21 February 1952; PRO: T236/3245, 'Note for Record', Robert Hall, 4 March 1952; Plowden, 1989, p. 147.
48. PRO: T236/3245, 'Note for Record', Robert Hall, 4 March 1952; Plowden, 1989, p. 147.

49. Plowden, 1989, p. 147; Peden, 2000, p. 461.
50. Plowden, 1989, p. 147.
51. PRO: PREM 11/138, Churchill to Eden, 21 February 1952.
52. Avon Papers: AP20/16/29, Butler to Eden, 22 February 1952.
53. MacDougall, 1987, p. 97.
54. Shuckburgh, 1986, pp. 37–8.
55. Avon Papers: AP20/16/37, 'Note to Eden by Shuckburgh', diary extract, 31 December 1952.
56. Avon Papers: AP20/16/34c, 'Operation Robot', Berthoud to Shuckburgh, 19 February 1953.
57. Avon Papers: AP20/1/28, Eden's Diaries, Diary for 1952: entry for 14 February 1952 (it was obviously written after this date).
58. Avon Papers: AP20/16/34c, 'Operation Robot', Berthoud to Shuckburgh, 19 February 1953.
59. PRO: PREM 11/138, Eden to Churchill, 23 February 1952.
60. MacDougall, 1989, p. 94.
61. PRO: T236/3243, 'Passage from Edwin Plowden', no date; BE: ADM 14/32, 'The Plan: Note of a meeting of Permanent Secretaries with Sir Leslie Rowan', 24 March 1952; Plowden, 1989, pp. 148–9.
62. PRO: T236/3241, 'Notes of a talk with Professor Robbins', 27 February 1952; PRO: T236/3244, 'Supplementary Notes', Memo by L. Robbins, no date.
63. PRO: T236/3244, 'Supplementary Notes', Memo by L. Robbins, no date.
64. PRO: T236/3244, 'Supplementary Notes', Memo by L. Robbins, no date.
65. MacDougall, 1987, p. 94.
66. Butler, 1971, p. 159.
67. PRO: T236/3241, 'Notes of a Meeting of Ministers held at No. 10 Downing Street', 27 February 1952.
68. Ibid.
69. Ibid.
70. Ibid.
71. BE: G3/107, 'Note for Record', C. Cobbold, 18 March 1952.
72. BE: G1/121, Cobbold's handwritten remarks on Butler's draft 'External Action', 22 February 1952.
73. BE: G1/121, 'Governor's Notes for Meeting with Cabinet', 28 February 1952.
74. PRO: T236/3241, Bridges to Butler, 26 February 1952.
75. PRO: T236/3241, Memo by the Chancellor, 28 February 1952.
76. PRO: T236/3241, Butler's handwritten comments on 'Plowden to Butler', 27 February 1952.
77. PRO: T236/3241, Bridges to Chancellor, 26 February 1952.
78. MacDougall, 1987, p. 97.
79. Avon Papers: AP20/16/29, 'Letter', Cherwell to Eden, 27 February 1952.
80. Avon Papers: AP20/1/28, Eden's Diary: Entry for 14 February 1952 (obviously written after this date).
81. PRO: PREM 11/138, Brook to Churchill, 27 February 1952.
82. Ibid.
83. Ismay had been in Lisbon with Eden and was present for part of the discussion of the proposals with Berthoud. Berthoud records that Ismay 'seemed prepared to accept them'. Avon Papers: AP20/16/34c, 'Operation Robot', Note to Shuckburgh from Berthoud, 19 February 1953.
84. PRO: PREM 11/138, Brook to Churchill, 28 February 1952.
85. BE: G3/107, 'Note for Record', C. Cobbold, 18 March 1952: Avon Papers:

AP20/1/28, Eden's Diary: Entry for 14 February 1952 (obviously written after this date).

86. BE: G1/121, 'Governor's notes for meeting with Cabinet', 28 February 1952.
87. Ibid.
88. Ibid.
89. Ibid.
90. Ibid.
91. Avon Papers: AP20/1/28, Eden's Diary: Entry for 14 February 1952 (obviously written after this date).
92. BE: G3/107, 'Note for Record', C. Cobbold, 18 March 1952.
93. MacDougall, 1987, p. 98.
94. Hall, 1989, 'Entry for Friday 29 February', p. 206; MacDougall, 1987, p. 98.
95. Macmillan Papers: MS. Macmillan, Dep. c. 14/1, 'Diary for 1952', Entry for 29 February 1952.
96. Ibid.
97. PRO: T236/3241, 'External Action', Memo by the Chancellor, 26 February 1952; PRO: T236/3240, 'The Balance of Payments', Memo by the Paymaster General, no date.
98. Macmillan Papers: MS. Macmillan, Dep. c. 14/1, 'Diary for 1952', Entry for 29 February 1952.
99. PRO: T236/3242, 'Economic Situation: Balance of Payments', C.C. (52) 23rd, 24th and 25th Conclusions: Cabinet Conclusions 28th and 29th February 1952 (also in PRO: CAB 128/40).
100. PRO: T236/3241, 'External Action', Memo by the Chancellor, 26 February 1952.
101. Ibid.
102. Macmillan Papers: MS. Macmillan, Dep. c. 14/1, 'Diary for 1952', Entry for 29 February 1952.
103. PRO: T236/3241, 'External Action', Memo by the Chancellor, 26 February 1952.
104. PRO: T236/3242, 'Economic Situation: Balance of Payments', C.C. (52) 23rd, 24th and 25th Conclusions: Cabinet Conclusions 28th and 29th February 1952 (also in PRO: CAB 128/40).
105. Ibid.
106. Ibid.
107. Ibid. Plowden, 1989, p. 151.
108. PRO: T236/3242, 'Economic Situation: Balance of Payments', C.C. (52) 23rd, 24th and 25th Conclusions: Cabinet Conclusions 28th and 29th February 1952 (also in PRO: CAB 128/40).
109. Macmillan Papers: MS. Macmillan, Dep. c. 14/1, 'Diary for 1952', Entry for 29 February 1952.
110. Macmillan Papers: MS. Macmillan, Dep. c. 14/1, 'Diary for 1952', Entry for 29 February 1952; PRO: T236/3241, 'Financial Situation', Memo by Lyttelton, 26 February 1952.
111. Crookshank Papers: Diary of Viscount Crookshank, M.S. Eng. Hist. d. 361, 'Entry for 29 February'.
112. Woolton Papers: MS. Woolton 25, 'Letter: Woolton to Churchill', 21 July 1952.
113. PRO: T236/3242, 'Economic Situation: Balance of Payments', C.C. (52) 23rd, 24th and 25th Conclusions: Cabinet Conclusions 28th and 29th February 1952 (also in PRO: CAB 128/40).
114. Ibid.
115. MacDougall, 1987, p. 98; Butler, 1971, p. 159.

116. Macmillan Papers: MS. Macmillan, Dep. c. 14/1, 'Diary for 1952', Entry for 29 February 1952.
117. Macmillan Papers: MS. Macmillan, Dep. c. 14/1, 'Diary for 1952', Entry for 29 February 1952.
118. MacDougall, 1987, p. 98; Macmillan Papers: MS. Macmillan, Dep. c. 14/1, 'Diary for 1952', Entry for 29 February 1952; BE: C160/24, 'Sir George Bolton's Diary 1952', 28 February 1952.
119. BE: C160/24, 'Sir George Bolton's Diary 1952', 29 February 1952.
120. PRO: CAB 128/24, 24th Cabinet Conclusions (52), 'Meeting held 29 February 1952 at 1100am'.
121. Macmillan Papers: MS. Macmillan, Dep. c. 14/1, 'Diary for 1952', Entry for 29 February 1952.
122. Ibid.
123. Ibid.
124. Ibid.
125. Avon Papers: AP20/16/31, 'The Plan: Notes for Cabinet', no date.
126. Ibid.
127. Ibid.
128. Ibid. On Plowden and the floating rate see BE: ADM 14/32, 'The Plan: Note of a meeting of Permanent Secretaries with Sir Leslie Rowan, 24 March 1952'.
129. Avon Papers: AP20/16/34c, 'Operation Robot', Note to Shuckburgh from Berthoud, 19 February 1953; Macmillan Papers: MS. Macmillan, Dep. c. 14/1, 'Diary for 1952', Entry for 29 February 1952.
130. Macmillan Papers: MS. Macmillan, Dep. c. 14/1, 'Diary for 1952', Entry for 29 February 1952.
131. PRO: T236/3242, 'Economic Situation: Balance of Payments', C.C. (52) 23rd, 24th and 25th Conclusions: Cabinet Conclusions 28th and 29th February 1952 (also in PRO: CAB 128/40).
132. Macmillan Papers: MS. Macmillan, Dep. c. 14/1, 'Diary for 1952', Entry for 29 February 1952.
133. Ibid.
134. Avon Papers: AP20/1/28, Eden's Diary for 1952: Entry for 14 February 1952 (obviously written after this date).
135. PRO: CAB 128/24, (52) 25th Conclusions, 'Meeting 29th February at 3.00 p.m.'.
136. PRO: T236/3241, 'Memo by the Chancellor', 28 February 1952.
137. Macmillan Papers: MS. Macmillan, Dep. c. 14/1, 'Diary for 1952', Entry for 29 February 1952.
138. PRO: T236/3242, 'Economic Situation: Balance of Payments', C.C. (52) 23rd, 24th and 25th Conclusions: Cabinet Conclusions 28th and 29th February 1952; PRO: CAB 128/24, (52) 25th Conclusions, 'Meeting 29th February at 3.00pm'.
139. Ibid.
140. Hall, 1989, 'Entry for Tuesday 4 March', p. 206.
141. BE: C160/24, 'Sir George Bolton's Diary 1952', 29 February 1952; BE: G3/107, 'Note for Record', C. Cobbold, 18 March 1952; Fforde, 1992, p. 440, fn. 25.
142. BE: G3/107, 'Note for Record', C. Cobbold, 18 March 1952.
143. BE: G1/121, Cobbold to Butler, 3 March 1952.
144. Hall, 1989, p. 211, 'Entry for Wednesday, 19 March'.
145. BE: G1/121, Cobbold to Churchill, 3 March 1952.
146. BE: G3/107, 'Note for Record', C. Cobbold, 18 March 1952.
147. Avon Papers: AP20/16/30, 'Letter: Butler to Eden', 1 March 1952.

148. Macmillan Papers: MS. Macmillan, Dep. c. 14/1, 'Diary for 1952', Entry for 29 February 1952.
149. Ibid.
150. Hall, 1989, 'Entry for Tuesday 4 March', p. 207.
151. Butler Papers: RAB G24/64, 'Letter: Bridges to Butler', 12 August 1952.
152. BE: C160/24, 'Sir George Bolton's Diary 1952', 29 February 1952.
153. Avon Papers: AP20/16/34c, 'Operation Robot', Note to Shuckburgh from Berthoud, 19 February 1953.
154. Avon Papers: AP20/1/28, Eden's Diary for 1952: Entry for 14 February 1952 (obviously written after this date); Macmillan Papers: MS. Macmillan, Dep. c. 14/1, 'Diary for 1952', Entry for 29 February 1952.
155. Macmillan Papers: MS. Macmillan, Dep. c. 14/1, 'Diary for 1952', Entry for 29 February 1952.
156. Fforde, 1992, pp. 448–9.
157. BE: C160/24, 'Sir George Bolton's Diary 1952', 29 February 1952.

5 Robot Walks Again

1. Hall, 1989, p. 210.
2. *The Financial Times*, 8 March 1952; Dow, 1964, p. 81; Cairncross, 1985, pp. 255–6.
3. PRO: T171/408 Budget Committee Minutes 1952.
4. BE: G1/72, Niemeyer to Cobbold, 5 January 1952; Fforde, 1992, p. 447.
5. Butler, 1971, p. 158.
6. PRO: T171/408, 'The General Budgetary Problem: note by Hall', 5 March 1952.
7. PRO: T171/408, 'Budget 1952: Meeting 29 February 1952'.
8. PRO: T171/408, 'The Budget 1952'; Cairncross, 1985, p. 256.
9. BE: G1/72, 'Reaction to the Budget', 12 March 1952.
10. US National Archives: RG 56/450, 'Some Political Aspects of the Budget', London to US State Department, 1 April 1952.
11. Butler, 1971, p. 158.
12. MacDougall, 1987, p. 101; Fforde, 1992, p. 448.
13. US National Archives: RG 56/450, 'British Budget', 12 March 1952.
14. BE: G1/97 Extracts from the Governor's Diaries: 2 April and 4 July 1952.
15. Hall, 1989, p. 211.
16. PRO: T230/389, 'Sterling Union: An Alternative to Robot', 20 March 1952.
17. PRO: T230/389, 'The Mechanics of Sterling Union', Memo by R. Neild, no date.
18. PRO: T230/389, 'Proposals for a Sterling Union', 21 March 1952.
19. Hall, 1989, p. 213.
20. PRO: T236/3242, 'The Future of Sterling', Hall to Armstrong, 25 March 1952; Hall, 1989, p. 213; Cairncross and Watts, 1989, p. 306.
21. PRO: T236/3242, 'The Future of Sterling', Hall to Armstrong, 25 March 1952.
22. MacDougall, 1987, p. 100; Plowden, 1989, p. 154.
23. BE: ADM 14/30, 'Notes on memorandum: The Future of Sterling', WMA to Bolton, 27 March 1952.
24. PRO: T236/3242, 'Alternative Approach', Bridges to Hall, 27 March 1952.
25. PRO: T236/3242, 'US Dollar Shortage and UK Exports', memo by Clarke, 26 March 1952.
26. Ibid.
27. Ibid.

28. Ibid.
29. PRO: SUPP 14/332, 'The Market for British Cars in the USA', 8 September 1950.
30. PRO: T236/3242, 'US Dollar Shortage and UK Exports.,' memo by Clarke, 26 March 1952.
31. Ibid.
32. Hall, 1989, p. 214.
33. Hall, 1989, p. 214; Plowden, 1989, p. 154.
34. BE: C160/24, 'Sir George Bolton's Diary 1952', 13 and 14 March 1952.
35. BE: ADM 14/30, Thompson-McCausland to Governor, 12 March 1952.
36. BE: G1/121, Cobbold's remarks on External Action, 22 February 1952.
37. PRO: T236/3241, 'Robot walks again', Clarke to Rowan, 11 March 1952.
38. PRO: T236/3241, 'The Plan, 4th Revision', Bolton to Clarke, 14 March 1952.
39. BE: G1/123, 'Range', memo to Bolton, 25 June 1952.
40. PRO: T236/3241, 'Robot walks again', Clarke to Rowan, 11 March 1952.
41. Ibid.
42. Ibid.
43. Ibid.
44. Fforde, 1992, p. 462.
45. Fforde, 1992, p. 462; BE: C160/24, 'Sir George Bolton's Diary 1952', 13 March 1952. Bolton noted that Cobbold was interested in softening the Sterling Area balance proposal and would 'endeavour fudge plan for EPU'.
46. PRO: T236/3244, 'The Sterling Balances', Flett to Rowan, 26 June 1952.
47. Ibid.
48. PRO: T236/3244, 'External Financial Policy', memo by Butler, 28 June 1952.
49. Fforde, 1992, p. 463.
50. BE: G1/97, 'Extract from Governor's Diaries', 29 May 1952.
51. BE: G3/107, Governor's Note, 4 June 1952.
52. BE: G3/107, Governor's Note, 16 June 1952.
53. BE: C160/24, 'Sir George Bolton's Diary 1952', 16 June 1952.
54. PRO: T236/3244, 'External Sterling Plan', memo by Butler, first draft 26 June 1952; BE: C160/24, 'Sir George Bolton's Diary 1952', 26 March 1952.
55. PRO: T236/3241, 'Robot walks again', Clarke to Rowan, 11 March 1952.
56. Fforde, 1992, p. 454.
57. PRO: T236/3241, 'Robot walks again', Clarke to Rowan, 11 March 1952.
58. BE: OV44/20, 'EPU: Plan of Action', Bridge to Bolton, 22 February 1952.
59. Ibid.
60. BE: C160/24, 'Sir George Bolton's Diary 1952', 27 March 1952; Fforde, 1992, p. 455.
61. Fforde, 1992, pp. 455–6.
62. Roy Bridge quoted in Fforde, 1992, p. 456.
63. BE: G1/123, 'The Plan: Programme and Timetable', Bolton to Cobbold, 27 June 1952.
64. Ibid.
65. Ibid.
66. PRO: T236/3244, 'External Financial Policy' memo by Butler, 28 June 1952.
67. Fforde, 1992, pp. 457–9.
68. BE: G1/72, 'Secret Letter', Cobbold to Baumgartner, 6 March 1952.
69. Ibid.
70. BE: G1/97, 'Extracts from Governor's Diaries', 14 March 1952.
71. PRO: T237/175, 'Suspension of French Measures of Liberalisation', 5 March 1952; *Financial Times*, 17 March 1952.

72. PRO: T237/175, 'Suspension of French Measures of Liberalisation', 5 March 1952.
73. PRO: T237/175, 'French Deficit in EPU', Hall-Patch to Foreign Office, 16 March 1952.
74. PRO: T236/3244, 'Record of an informal discussion after lunch with the Governor of the Bank of France', dated 6 May 1952 but other Treasury and Bank files confirm that this should read 6 June 1952; also see Fforde, 1992, p. 458.
75. PRO: T236/3244, 'Record of an informal discussion after lunch with the Governor of the Bank of France', 6 June 1952.
76. PRO: T236/3244, 'Record of an informal discussion after lunch with the Governor of the Bank of France', 6 June 1952.
77. PRO: T236/3244, 'Record of an informal discussion after lunch with the Governor of the Bank of France', 6 June 1952.
78. Baumgartner's discussions with Bolton recorded in Fforde, 1992, p. 458.
79. PRO: T236/3244, 'Record of an informal discussion after lunch with the Governor of the Bank of France', 6 June 1952.
80. PRO: T236/3244, 'Note by Rowan', 12 June 1952.
81. Bolton quoted in Fforde, 1992, p. 458.
82. PRO: T325/38, Note, 20 June 1952.
83. PRO: T236/3244, 'Europe and Convertibility', paper by the Bank of England, 17 June 1952.
84. BE: G1/123, 'The Plan: Programme and Timetable', Bolton to Cobbold, 27 June 1952.
85. BE: G1/123, 'The Plan: Programme and Timetable', Bolton to Cobbold, 27 June 1952.
86. BE: G1/97 Extracts from the Governor's Diaries, 27 June 1952.
87. BE: G3/107, Cobbold to Butler, 30 June 1952.
88. Ibid.
89. BE: G3/108, Cobbold to Butler, 2 July 1952.
90. Ibid.
91. Macmillan Papers: MS. Macmillan, Dep. c. 14/1, 'Diary for 1952', Entry for 30 June 1952.
92. PRO: T236/3244, 'External Financial Policy', 28 June 1952. The memorandum was circulated on 27 June but erroneously dated 28 June, see MacDougall, 1987, p. 102.
93. PRO: T236/3244, 'External Financial Policy', 28 June 1952.
94. Ibid.
95. Ibid.
96. Macmillan Papers: MS. Macmillan, Dep. c. 14/1, 'Diary for 1952', Entry for 30 June 1952.
97. PRO: CAB 129/53, 'External Financial Policy', memo by Lord Cherwell, 30 June 1952; also see MacDougall, 1987, pp. 102–3.
98. PRO: CAB 129/53, 'External Financial Policy', memo by Lord Cherwell, 30 June 1952.
99. Ibid.
100. Ibid.
101. PRO: T236/3244, 'Note for Record', by Rowan, 30 June, 1952.
102. PRO: T236/3244, 'Supplementary Notes', by Robbins, 1 July 1952.
103. Ibid.
104. Ibid.
105. PRO: CAB 129/53, 'External Financial Policy', memo by Lord Cherwell, 30 June 1952.

106. Ibid.
107. Ibid.
108. PRO: T236/3244, 'Robot', memo by Salter, 24 June 1952.
109. PRO: T236/3244, Plowden to Butler, 24 June 1952.
110. PRO: T236/3241, 'Robot', Rowan to Bridges, 13 March 1952.
111. Ibid.
112. Ibid.
113. BE: G1/121, Peacock to the Governor, 29 February 1952.
114. Macmillan Papers: MS. Macmillan, Dep. c. 14/1, 'Diary for 1952', Entry for 30 June to 4 July, 1952.
115. Ibid.
116. Ibid.
117. Ibid.
118. BE: C160/24, 'Sir George Bolton's Diary 1952', 1 July 1952.
119. Macmillan Papers: MS. Macmillan, Dep. c. 14/1, 'Diary for 1952', Entry for 30 June to 4 July, 1952.
120. BE: C160/24, 'Sir George Bolton's Diary 1952', 1 July 1952.
121. Ibid.
122. BE: C160/24, 'Sir George Bolton's Diary 1952', 5 July 1952.
123. BE: G1/97, Extracts from the Governor's Diaries, 4 July 1952.
124. Ibid.
125. BE: G3/108, Note by Cobbold, 25 July 1952.
126. BE: G3/108, Cobbold to Butler, 30 July 1952.

6 The Collective Approach to Freer Trade and Currencies

1. BE: G3/107, 'Exchange Policy', Cobbold to Butler, 6 May 1952.
2. BE: G3/107, 'Exchange Policy', Cobbold to Butler, 6 May 1952.
3. PRO: PREM 11/22, Cabinet Conclusions, CC. (52) 60, Minute 7, 17 June 1952.
4. Ibid.
5. Hall, 1989, p. 232.
6. PRO: T236/3071, 'External Economic Policy: Memorandum by the President of the Board of Trade', 28 July 1952.
7. Ibid.
8. PRO: T236/3248, 'Record of meeting held in Secretary's room, Board of Trade', 29 April 1952. The Committee had been set up on the instruction of the Economic Policy Committee on 26 March 1952. For further details see PRO: T236/3248, 'Review of Future External Commercial Policy', Note by Chairman, 23 May 1952.
9. PRO: T236/3248, Clarke to Rowan, 12 May 1952.
10. PRO: T236/3248, 'Commercial Policy', Clarke to Rowan and Mitchell, 23 May 1952.
11. Hall, 1989, p. 232.
12. Hall, 1989, p. 232; pp. 234–5; p. 293 fn. 2; and PRO: T236/3071.
13. PRO: CAB 130/78, 'Working Party on External Economic Policy: Minutes', 1 July 1952.
14. Ibid.
15. PRO: T236/3089, 'Convertibility, Multilateralism, Etc', Clarke to Rowan, 17 July 1952.
16. Ibid.

17. Ibid.
18. MacDougall, 1987, p. 104.
19. PRO: CAB 21/3068, Clarke to Morland, 1 July 1952.
20. PRO: CAB 130/78, 'The Problems of External Economic Policy', Memo by a Group of Officials, 22 July 1952.
21. PRO: T236/3089, 'Convertibility, Multilateralism, Etc', Clarke to Rowan, 17 July 1952.
22. PRO: T236/3071, 'The Economic Background', Memo by a Group of Officials, 11 July 1952.
23. PRO: CAB 130/78, 'The Problems of External Economic Policy', Memo by a Group of Officials, 22 July 1952.
24. Ibid.
25. PRO: T236/3089, 'Convertibility, Multilateralism, Etc', Clarke to Rowan, 17 July 1952.
26. Ibid.
27. Ibid.
28. Ibid.
29. PRO: T236/3071, 'PEC (52) 1', Cabinet Committee Minutes, 30 July 1952; PRO: CAB 130/78, 'Preparations for Commonwealth Economic Conference', Note by Morland, 30 July 1952.
30. PRO: T236/3071, 'PEC (52) 1', Cabinet Committee Minutes, 30 July 1952.
31. Hall, 1989, p. 244; Fforde, 1992, p. 470.
32. PRO: T236/3368, 'Steps Towards Convertibility', Memo by a Group of Officials, 30 August 1952.
33. PRO: T236/3071, 'External Economic Policy', Memo by the Paymaster General, 1 August 1952.
34. MacDougall, 1987, p. 106.
35. Ibid.
36. PRO: T236/3071, 'External Economic Policy', Memo by the Paymaster General, 1 August 1952.
37. PRO: T236/3076, 'Atlantic Payments Union', first draft of Working Party on Sterling Convertibility Report, 29 August 1952.
38. Fforde, 1992, p. 472.
39. PRO: T236/3076, 'Atlantic Payments Union', first draft of Working Party on Sterling Convertibility Report, 29 August 1952.
40. Ibid.
41. Hall, 1989, p. 243.
42. PRO: T236/3076, 'The Cherwell/MacDougall Plan', Clarke to Figgures, 1 August 1952.
43. PRO: T236/3071, 'Atlantic Payments Union', Figgures to Brittain, 5 August 1952.
44. Ibid.
45. Ibid.
46. PRO: T236/3076, 'Paymaster General's Memorandum: PEC (52) 7', Lucius Thompson-McCausland to Figgures, 5 August 1952.
47. Ibid.
48. Ibid.
49. PRO: T236/3076, 'Atlantic Payments Union', WPSC (52) 7, 29 August 1952. The final report was circulated to Ministers on 2 September.
50. PRO: T236/3076, 'Atlantic Payments Union', Figgures to Brittain, 2 September 1952.

51. PRO: T236/3076, 'Atlantic Payments Union', Brittain's handwritten comments, 2 September.
52. Hall, 1989, p. 244; Fforde, 1992, p. 470.
53. BE: OV44/51, 'Preparation for the Commonwealth Economic Conference on External Policy – the state of the game', Rootham to Cobbold, 26 August 1952; 'Convertibility Working Party', Rootham to Bolton, 27 August 1952.
54. Ibid.
55. Hall, 1989, p. 245.
56. Ibid.
57. BE: OV44/51, 'Preparation for the Commonwealth Economic Conference on External Policy – the state of the game', Rootham to Cobbold, 26 August 1952; 'Convertibility Working Party', Rootham to Bolton, 27 August 1952.
58. PRO: T236/3368, 'Steps Towards Convertibility', Memo by a Group of Officials, 30 August 1952.
59. PRO: T236/3368, 'Steps Towards Convertibility', Memo by a Group of Officials, 30 August 1952.
60. PRO: T236/3368, 'Report of Convertibility Working Party', Brittain to Armstrong, 1 September 1952.
61. PRO: T236/3368, 'The Objectives Paper', Clarke to Brittain, 1 September 1952; and Brittain's handwritten comments on that memorandum, 1 September 1952.
62. PRO: T236/3368, 'Steps Towards Convertibility', Memo by a Group of Officials, 30 August 1952.
63. Ibid.
64. Ibid.
65. PRO: T236/3368, Cobbold to Butler, 29 August 1952.
66. Ibid.
67. PRO: T236/3368, 'Steps Towards Convertibility', Memo by a Group of Officials, 30 August 1952.
68. PRO: T236/3368, 'The Objectives Paper', Clarke to Brittain, 1 September 1952.
69. PRO: T236/3368, Cobbold to Butler, 29 August 1952.
70. PRO: T236/3072, Minutes of Cabinet (PEC) Committee (52) 4, 4 September 1952.
71. PRO: T236/3368, 'The Collective Approach to Convertibility', Memo by a Group of Officials, 8 September 1952; PRO: T236/3072, ' The Collective Approach to Convertibility', Memo by a Group of Officials, 10 September 1952; PRO: T236/3368, 'Collective Approach to Convertibility' Memo by the Paymaster-General, 10 September 1952.
72. PRO: T236/3072, Minutes of a meeting of the Committee, PEC (52) 8, 12 September 1952.
73. Cherwell Papers: J122/115, 'Letter: Cherwell to Churchill', 18 September 1952.
74. PRO: T236/3072, Minutes of a meeting of the Committee, PEC (52) 8, 12 September 1952.
75. Ibid.
76. Cherwell Papers, J122/121, 'Letter: Cherwell to Churchill', 18 September 1952.
77. PRO: T236/3072, 'Preparatory Meeting of Officials – General Report', 15 October 1952.
78. PRO: T236/3368, Cobbold to Rowan, 19 September 1952.
79. PRO: T236/3368, 'Convertibility: Notes for Statement', Rowan to Butler, 16 September 1952.
80. Bolton's remarks are recorded in Fforde, 1992, p. 478.
81. PRO: T236/3072, 'The Next Stage', memo by Eden to Cabinet PEC Committee, 17 October 1952.

82. Ibid.
83. Ibid.
84. PRO: T236/3089, 'Collective Approach – Mark II', memo by Clarke to Rowan, 6 October 1952; PRO: T236/3089, 'The new scheme compared with the old', Clarke to Rowan, 23 October 1952.
85. PRO: T236/3089, 'The new scheme compared with the old', Clarke to Rowan, 23 October 1952.
86. Ibid.
87. PRO: T236/3073, 'The Economic Conference of Prime Ministers', memo by Butler and Thorneycroft, no date.
88. Ibid.
89. PRO: T236/3073, 'Minutes of a meeting of the PEC Committee, PEC (52) 10', 30 October 1952.
90. PRO: T236/3073, 'The Collective Approach and all that', Bridges to Butler, 24 October 1952.
91. BE: C160/24, 'Sir George Bolton's Diary 1952', 16 and 27 October 1952. Bolton noted that Cherwell was 'still intriguing' but appeared now to have 'overplayed his hand'.
92. PRO: CAB 128/25, 'Cabinet Conclusions, CC (52) 92', 3 November 1952.
93. Ibid.
94. MacDougall, 1987, p. 107.
95. PRO: DO 35/6504, 'Commonwealth Economic Conference: telegrams W186 and W187', 4 November 1952.
96. PRO: PREM 11/22, 'Commonwealth Conference: Collective Approach', memo by Eden to the Cabinet, 6 December 1952.
97. PRO: CAB 128/25, 'Cabinet Conclusions, CC (52) 103', 8 December 1952.
98. PRO: T236/3369, 'Draft by Cobbold: after personal discussion with Sir C. Deshmukh', 5 December 1952; Fforde, 1992, p. 484.
99. PRO: CAB 128/25, 'Cabinet Conclusions, CC (52) 103', 8 December 1952.
100. PRO: PREM 11/22, 'Communiqué', 11 December 1952.
101. PRO: T273/377, 'Procedure for further consultations on the Collective Approach', Brook to Eden, 24 November 1952.
102. PRO: DO 35/6504, 'Commonwealth Economic Conference', 13 December 1952.
103. PRO: T236/3521, 'Collective Approach', Washington to Foreign Office, 28 January 1953.
104. PRO: CAB 128/25, 'Cabinet Conclusions, CC (52) 105', 16 December 1952.
105. PRO: FO 371/99075, 'Record of Butler's conversation with Mr Pella during his visit to Paris', 15 December 1952; PRO: FO 371/99075, 'Record of Butler's conversation with Monsieur Pinay during his visit to Paris', 15 December 1952.
106. PRO: T236/3369, 'The Commonwealth Conference and OEEC', memo by Hugh Ellis-Rees, 25 November 1952.
107. PRO: T236/3089, 'Alternatives if things go badly', memo by Clarke, 26 November 1952.
108. Ibid.
109. Ibid.
110. Ibid.
111. PRO: T236/3089, 'What the UK policy should be if things go badly', Plowden to Bridges, 3 December 1952.
112. PRO: T236/3089, 'Alternatives if things go badly', memo by Clarke, 26 November 1952.

7 Anglo-American Negotiations and a New Bank Route to Convertibility

1. PRO: T236/3813, 'Commonwealth Conference', Foreign Office to Washington, 10 December 1952; US National Archives: RG 56/450, 'Official text of the Commonwealth Economic Conference Communique', National Advisory Council, document 1734, 13 December 1952.
2. US National Archives: RG 56/450, 'Official text of the Commonwealth Economic Conference Communique', National Advisory Council, document 1734, 13 December 1952.
3. BE: G1/98, Governor's Files, 'Letter: Cobbold to Bolton', 12 January 1953.
4. PRO: T236/4035, 'The Approach to USA', Clarke to Rowan, 19 December 1952.
5. Ibid.
6. Ibid.
7. PRO: T273/378, 'Note of an informal Meeting between Monsieur Marjolin, Secretary-General of the OEEC and UK Officials held in Mr Strath's Room on Friday 16 January 1953'.
8. PRO: T273/378, 'OEEC and the Collective Approach to Convertibility', 13 January 1953.
9. BE: G1/98, Governor's Files, 'Letter: Cobbold to Bolton', 12 January 1953.
10. BE: G3/6 Governor's Diaries, Entry for 17 February 1953.
11. PRO: CAB 128/26, Cabinet Conclusions, CC (53) 6, 3 February 1953.
12. PRO: T273/378, 'Note: Rowan to Bridges', 14 January 1953.
13. PRO: T236/4037, 'A Collective Approach to Freer Trade and Currencies', Memo submitted to the US Administration by HM Government in the UK, 10 February 1953.
14. Ibid.
15. Ibid.
16. PRO: T236/3813, 'Note for Mr Rooth: Collective Approach', Stevenson to Rowan, 23 January 1953.
17. PRO: T236/3527, Ellis Rees to Foreign Office, 29 January 1953.
18. BE: OV44/60, 'Letter: Brittain to Cobbold', 2 March 1953.
19. Hall, 1989, 'Entry for 24 February 1953', p. 265.
20. PRO: T273/378, 'A Collective Approach to Freer Trade and Currencies: Memorandum to certain European Governments from the UK Government', Rowan to Bridges, 26 February 1953.
21. Ibid.
22. US National Archives: RG 59, 'Telegram: Gifford to Acheson', No: 2252 and 2253, 16 October 1952.
23. US National Archives: RG 56/450, 'American Economic Foreign Policy', Memorandum by George Willis, 7 October 1952.
24. US National Archives: RG 56/450, 'Proposed Staff Review of American Economic Foreign Policy', Memorandum by Leddy, 25 October 1952.
25. Ibid.
26. US National Archives: RG 56/450, 'American Economic Foreign Policy', Memorandum by George Willis, 7 October 1952.
27. US National Archives: RG 56/450, 'The Dollar Area and the Sterling Area', Treasury Department Briefing Book, December 1952.
28. Ibid.
29. Ibid.

30. Ibid.
31. Ibid.
32. Ibid.
33. Ibid.
34. Ibid.
35. Ibid.
36. US National Archives: RG 59, Box 55, 'Probable Developments in the World Situation Through Mid-1953', Central Intelligence Agency, 24 September 1951; US National Archives: RG 59, Box 77, 'Substance of Discussions of State-DMS-JCS Meeting', Pentagon, 28 January 1953.
37. US National Archives: RG 56/450, 'The Dollar Area and the Sterling Area', Treasury Department Briefing Book, December 1952.
38. BE: G1/98, 'Letter: Rowan to Bridges and Cobbold', 8 March 1953; Shuckburgh, 1986, p. 79.
39. BE: G1/98, 'Letter: Rowan to Bridges and Cobbold', 8 March 1953.
40. BE: OV44/60, 'Discussions on the Collective Approach to Freer Trade and Currencies', Meeting held at the State Department, 3 p.m., 5 March 1953.
41. PRO: T273/378, 'Discussions of the Collective Approach to Freer Trade and Currencies', Meeting held at the US Treasury, 10 a.m., 6 March 1953.
42. Ibid.
43. Ibid.
44. PRO: T273/378, 'Discussions of the Collective Approach to Freer Trade and Currencies, Annex A: Joint Communique', Meeting held in State Department, 5 p.m., 6 March 1953.
45. Fforde, 1992, p. 491.
46. BE: G1/98, 'Telegram: Parsons to Cobbold', 6 March 1953.
47. BE: G1/98, 'Letter: Rowan to Bridges and Cobbold', 8 March 1953.
48. PRO: T273/378, 'Letter: Cobbold to Butler', 13 March 1953.
49. PRO: T273/378, 'The Collective Approach – Discussions with the US and Canada', Rowan to Bridges, 12 March 1953.
50. Ibid.
51. PRO: CAB 128/26, Cabinet Conclusions, CC (53) 20, 17 March 1953.
52. PRO: CAB 128/26, Cabinet Conclusions, CC (53) 21, 20 March 1953.
53. PRO: T236/4035, 'The Approach to the US', Clarke to Rowan, 19 December 1952.
54. BE: G1/98, 'Memorandum: Bolton to Brittain', 25 March 1953.
55. US National Archives: RG 56, Box 55, 'Report on Paris Meetings, March 23–27, 1953', Southard to Burgess, 30 March 1953.
56. Ibid.
57. PRO: T236/3527, 'The Collective Approach and Europe', Bridges to Rowan, 9 June 1953.
58. PRO: T236/5725, 'Visit to Washington, Sunday 19–21 April 1953', Rowan to Butler, 21 April 1953.
59. PRO: T236/5725, 'Visit to Washington, Sunday 19–21 April 1953', Rowan to Butler, 21 April 1953.
60. PRO: T236/5725, Butler's handwritten comments, dated 26 April 1953, on Rowan's memorandum 'Visit to Washington, Sunday 19–21 April 1953', 21 April 1953.
61. PRO: T273/378, 'Discussion on Collective Approach to Freer Trade and Currencies', Meeting of sub-Group held in US Treasury, 2.15 p.m., 6 March 1953; PRO: T236/5725, 'A Wider Spread for the Spot Rate of Exchange', IMF Paper prepared by I. G. Patel, 6 February 1953.

62. PRO: T236/5725, 'Floating Semi-Convertible', Clarke to Rowan, 23 April 1953; PRO: T236/5725, 'Minute: Rowan to Butler', 30 April 1953; BE: OV44/60, 'Note: Hamilton to Parsons', 27 March 1953.
63. PRO: T236/5725, 'Minute: Rowan to Butler', 30 April 1953.
64. PRO: T236/5725, 'Minute: Bolton to Rowan', 8 April 1953.
65. PRO: T236/5725, 'On Floating Inconvertible', Brittain to Rowan, 4 May 1953.
66. PRO: T236/5725, 'Floating Inconvertible', Bridges to Butler, 15 May 1953.
67. BE: OV44/60, 'Commonwealth Economic Policy – Next Stage', Bolton to Cobbold, 6 June 1953.
68. Ibid.
69. Hall, 1989, 'Entry for 25 June 1953', p. 274.
70. Ibid., p. 274.
71. BE: OV44/60, 'Letter: Rowan to Hall-Patch', 25 July 1953.
72. Hall, 1989, 'Entry for 25 June, 1953', p. 275.
73. Hall, 1989, 'Entry for 25 June, 1953', p. 276; Cairncross and Watts, 1989, p. 154; PRO: T236/138, 'Letter: Butler to Bridges', 11 June 1953.
74. PRO: T236/138, 'Letter: Hall to Bridges', 10 June 1953.
75. Ibid.
76. PRO: T236/138, 'Letter: Butler to Bridges', 11 June 1953; PRO: T199/257, 'Economic Section', Note by Brook, 27 July 1953.
77. Hall, 1989, p. 278.
78. Ibid., p. 273.
79. The table detailing the changes to Overseas Finance is taken from ibid., p. 278.
80. BE: OV44/60, 'Letter: Rowan to Hall-Patch', 25 July 1953.
81. US National Archives: RG 56/450, 'Letter from Lewis Douglas to President Eisenhower', 14 July 1953.
82. Ibid.
83. BE: OV44/60, 'Letter: Hall-Patch to Bolton', 29 July 1953.
84. Ibid.
85. US National Archives: RG 56/450, 'Letter: Neidlinger to National Committees of ICC', 18 August 1953.
86. US National Archives: RG 56/450, 'Statement by Burgess on the annual report of the IMF at the eight annual meeting', 16 September 1953; Fforde, 1992, p. 497.
87. BE: OV44/61, 'Extract from letter: Bolton to Cobbold', 15 September 1953.
88. BE: OV44/61, 'An Outline of Foreign Exchange Policy', Bolton to Parsons, 17 October 1953.
89. PRO: T235/41, 'Questions about 1954 – and perhaps earlier', Clarke to Rowan, 23 October 1953.
90. BE: G1/98, 'Note: Cobbold to Butler', 30 October 1953.
91. BE: OV44/61, 'An Outline of Foreign Exchange Policy', Bolton to Parsons, 17 October 1953.
92. BE: G1/98, 'Note: Cobbold to Butler', 30 October 1953; Fforde, 1992, pp. 499–500.
93. BE: G1/98, 'Note: Cobbold to Butler', 30 October 1953.
94. BE: G1/98, 'Letter: Cobbold to Butler', 4 November 1953.
95. Ibid.
96. BE: G1/98, 'Note: Cobbold to Butler', 30 October 1953.
97. Fforde, 1992, pp. 499–501.
98. BE: G1/98, 'Note: Cobbold to Butler', 30 October 1953.
99. Ibid.

100. PRO: T236/3937, 'Note: BWS to Bridges', 23 November 1953.
101. PRO: T236/3937, Cobbold to Butler, 24 November 1953; PRO: T236/3937,'Unification of Non-Resident Sterling', Hall to Gilbert, 9 February 1954;
102. PRO: T236/3937, 'Unification of Non-Resident Sterling', Treasury 2nd draft, 19 November 1953.
103. PRO: T236/3937, 'Unification of Non-Resident Sterling', Rowan to Gilbert, 8 February 1954.
104. PRO: T236/3937, 'Handwritten note: Butler to Rowan', 3 March 1954.
105. PRO: T236/3937, 'London Gold market: Unification of Sterling', Butler to Churchill, 15 March 1954.
106. PRO: T236/3938, 'Press Announcement', 22 March 1954.
107. PRO: T236/3939, 'Commonwealth Liaison Committee Minutes', 19 March 1954.
108. PRO: T236/3938, 'Extract from Chancellor's letter of 10 March 1954', 10 March 1954.
109. PRO: T236/3939, 'Economic X-Ray: No 963', 22 March 1954.
110. Ibid.
111. US National Archives: RG 56/450, 'Free Commodity Markets and Progress toward Sterling Convertibility', Memo by William Dale, 10 February 1953.
112. Fforde, 1992, pp. 505 and 528.
113. PRO: T273/379, 'Uses of Transferable Sterling', Memo by the Bank, 10 February 1955; 'Backdoor Convertibility', *The Economist*, 5 March 1955.
114. PRO: T236/3969, 'The Market in Transferable Sterling', Bolton to Rowan, 31 January 1955.
115. Ibid.
116. PRO: T273/379, 'Uses of Transferable Sterling', Memo by the Bank, 10 February 1955.
117. PRO: T236/3937, 'Cheap sterling and the unification plan', Symons to Copleston, 26 January 1954; 'Backdoor Convertibility', *The Economist*, 5 March 1955.
118. PRO: T236/5725, 'Sterling Exchange in the Transitional Stage', Bolton to Rowan, 26 April 1954.
119. PRO: T236/5725, 'Letter: Bolton to Rowan', 26 April 1954.
120. PRO: T236/3999, 'Transferable Sterling: Underlying balance of payments factors', no author, 8 February 1955; Fforde, 1992, p. 506.
121. PRO: T236/5725, 'Letter: Bolton to Rowan', 26 April 1954.
122. Ibid.; PRO: T236/5725, 'Sterling Exchange in the Transitional Stage', Bolton to Rowan, 26 April 1954.
123. PRO: T236/5725, 'Sterling Exchange in the Transitional Stage', Bolton to Rowan, 26 April 1954.
124. Ibid.
125. PRO: T236/5725, 'Memorandum on Bank Proposals', Stevenson to Rowan, 29 April 1954.
126. PRO: T236/5725, 'Proposals from the Bank', Hall to Gilbert, 5 May 1954.
127. Ibid.
128. PRO: T236/5725, 'Sterling Exchange in the Transitional Period', Gilbert to Petch, 7 May 1954.
129. Ibid.
130. Hall, 1991, 'Entry for 12 August 1954', p. 10.
131. US National Archives: RG 56/450, 'Report to the President and the Congress by the Commission on Foreign Economic Policy', Advance copy, 21 January 1954.
132. Ibid.

133. PRO: T236/3695, 'Record of discussions in New York, 2 February 1954', Note by Rowan, no date.
134. US National Archives: RG 56/450, 'Treasury views on the Report of the Commission on Foreign Economic Policy', 12 February 1954.
135. Ibid.
136. US National Archives: RG 56/450, 'Excerpt from President's message to Congress on 30 March 1954, on report of the Foreign Economic Policy Commission', 30 March 1954.
137. PRO: T236/3695, 'Note of a meeting at the IMF, 28 January 1954', no author, 28 January 1954.
138. PRO: T236/4044, 'The Collective Approach', Letter from Bridges to Lee, 27 April 1954.
139. US National Archives: RG 56/450, 'National Advisory Council on International Monetary and Financial Problems: Minutes no. 210', 15 April 1954.
140. US National Archives: RG 56/450, 'Department of State Comment on Treasury Memorandum entitled US Approach at the OEEC Meeting', 15 April 1954.
141. US National Archives: RG 56/450, 'Draft minutes of Burgess Committee meetings', 2 June 1954.
142. Ibid.
143. Ibid.
144. Ibid. June 1954.
145. Ibid.
146. PRO: T236/4045, 'The Collective Approach: Where We Stand', Collective Approach Committee, 15 June 1954.
147. Cobbold quoted in Fforde, 1992, p. 509.
148. US National Archives: RG 56/450, 'OEEC Ministerial Examination Group on Convertibility', NAC document 1734, Report from Paris, 22 December 1954.
149. US National Archives: RG 56/450, 'OEEC Report on Convertibility', 4 June 1954.
150. US National Archives: RG 56/450, 'US Position for Ministerial Meeting on Problems of Convertibility', NAC document 1734, Paper 19, 9 July 1954; 'Survey of Convertibility Problems', NAC Meeting 212, 2 July 1954; PRO: T236/4046, 'European Exchange Arrangements after the termination of EPU', 10 July 1954.
151. PRO: T236/5726, 'Discussions on draft stand-by credit arrangement', W.B.C.A. (54), Treasury, 13 September 1954.
152. Ibid.
153. Ibid.
154. US National Archives: RG 56/450, 'Agenda for Fund and Bank Meetings (including Discussions of Convertibility)', NAC Minutes 213, 17 September 1954.
155. US National Archives: RG 56/450, 'Agenda for Fund and Bank Meetings (including Discussions of Convertibility)', NAC Minutes 213, 17 September 1954.
156. Ibid.
157. PRO: T236/4048, 'Note of a Meeting held at the US Treasury on 23 September 1954', 23 September 1954; US National Archives: RG 56/450, 'Excerpts from Minutes of Humphrey–Butler Conversations, 23 September 1954'.
158. PRO: T236/4048, 'Note of a Meeting held at the US Treasury on 23 September 1954', 23 September 1954.
159. US National Archives: RG 56/450, 'Excerpts from Minutes of Humphrey–Butler Conversations, 23 September 1954'.
160. PRO: T236/4048, 'Note of a Meeting held at the US Treasury on 23 September 1954', 23 September 1954; US National Archives: RG 56/450, 'Excerpts from Minutes of Humphrey–Butler Conversations, 23 September 1954'.

161. US National Archives: RG 56/450, 'Excerpts from Minutes of Humphrey–Butler Conversations, 29 September 1954'.
162. Cobbold quoted in Fforde, 1992, p. 514.
163. PRO: T236/3999, 'Transferable Sterling – Underlying Balance of Payments Factors', Memo by Kahn, 8 February 1955.
164. PRO: T236/3969, 'Programmes Committee Report', 11 February 1955.
165. Ibid.
166. Ibid.
167. PRO: T236/3999, 'Rates and movements of Sterling liabilities', Mitchell to Kahn, 2 February 1955.
168. PRO: T236/5416, 'Letter: Playfair to Rowan', 2 December 1954; 'Letter: Bolton to Playfair', 2 December 1954.
169. PRO: T236/5416, 'Letter: Playfair to Rowan', 2 December 1954.
170. PRO: T236/5416, 'Letter: Bolton to Playfair', 2 December 1954.
171. Ibid.
172. PRO: T236/5416, 'Exchange Policy', Cobbold to Bridges, 20 January 1955; 'The Outlook for Transferable Sterling', Note by Cobbold, 20 January 1955.
173. PRO: T273/379, 'Letter: Boyle to the Chancellor', 9 August 1955.
174. PRO: T236/5416, 'Exchange Policy', Cobbold to Bridges, 20 January 1955.
175. Ibid.; 'The Outlook for Transferable Sterling', Note by Cobbold, 20 January 1955.
176. PRO: T236/5416, 'Annex A', Note by Rowan, 27 January 1955.
177. PRO: T236/5416, 'Exchange Policy', Rowan to Gilbert, 24 January 1955.
178. PRO: T236/5416, 'Exchange Policy', Memo by Rowan, 10 February 1955.
179. Ibid.
180. Ibid.
181. Ibid.
182. PRO: T273/379, 'Record of a Discussion at the Treasury on Exchange Rate Policy and the General Economic Situation, Monday 21 February 1955'.
183. Ibid.
184. Ibid.
185. PRO: T236/379, 'Economic Situation and Exchange Rate Policy: Record of discussion at the Treasury, Tuesday 22 February 1955'.
186. Ibid.
187. Ibid.
188. PRO: T236/379, 'Economic Situation and Exchange Rate Policy: Record of Discussion at the Treasury, Wednesday 23 February 1955'.
189. Ibid.
190. Ibid.
191. PRO: CAB 128/28, 'Conclusions of a meeting held in the Prime Minister's Room, 23 February 1955', C.C. (55) 17th Conclusions.
192. Ibid.
193. Fforde, 1992, p. 527.
194. 'Backdoor Convertibility', *The Economist*, 5 March 1955, p. 827.
195. Ibid.
196. PRO: T273/379, 'Note of a meeting in Sir Edward Bridges' Room, 8 August 1955'.
197. PRO: T236/3969, 'Telegram: Harcourt to Rowan, 15 March 1955', 16 March 1955.
198. PRO: T236/3969, 'Telegram: Makins to Foreign Office, 17 March 1955', 19 March 1955.
199. PRO: T236/4361, 'Exchange Policy: Technical Procedures', Memo by Bolton, 30 March 1955.
200. Ibid.

201. PRO: T273/379, 'Note of a meeting in Sir Edward Bridges' Room', 8 August 1955'.
202. PRO: T273/379, 'The Future of Exchange Policy', Rowan to Gilbert, 25 March 1955.
203. PRO: T236/4361, 'Convertibility: The Next Step', Rickett to Rowan, 22 April 1955.
204. PRO: T273/379, 'The Future of Exchange Policy', Rowan to Gilbert, 25 March 1955.
205. PRO: T236/4361, 'Convertibility: The Next Step', Rickett to Rowan, 22 April 1955.
206. Ibid.
207. Moran, 1966, p. 649; Hall, 1991, p. 28.
208. PRO: T236/3941, 'External Economic Policy', Memo prepared by Overseas Finance, Bridges to the Chancellor, 27 May 1955.
209. PRO: T273/379, 'Exchange Rate Policy', Memo by Rowan, 28 June 1955.
210. PRO: 273/379, 'Note: Butler to Bridges', 8 August 1955.
211. PRO: T236/4362, 'The Renewal of the EPU and a European Monetary Agreement: Report by the Managing Board of the EPU', 16 July 1955; Fforde, 1992, pp. 537–8.
212. PRO: T273/379, 'Note of a meeting held in the Chancellor's Room, 10 August 1955', 11 August 1955.
213. PRO: T273/379, 'Note of a meeting held in the Chancellor's Room, 10 August 1955', 11 August 1955.
214. Ibid.
215. PRO: T273/379, 'Note of a meeting held in Edward Bridges' Room, 8 August 1955', 8 August 1955.
216. PRO: T273/379, 'Note of a meeting held in the Chancellor's Room, 10 August 1955', 11 August 1955.
217. US National Archives: RG 56/450, 'Fund Policy Respecting Articles VIII and XIV', Southard to Glendinning, 10 June 1955.
218. Fforde, 1992, p. 541.
219. Hall, 1991, 'Entry for Wednesday 30 July 1958', p. 166.

8 From Suez to Operation Unicorn

1. PRO: T236/5403, 'Extract from Private and Personal Note From the Governor to Chancellor', 12 April 1956.
2. Ibid.
3. Ibid.
4. Ibid.
5. PRO: T236/5403, 'Exchange Rate Policy: Note of a meeting held in the Chancellor's room, 24 April 1956', 24 April 1956; PRO: T236/5403, Memo: Rickett to Rowan, 29 May 1956, and Rowan's handwritten response, 10 June 1956.
6. PRO: T236/5403, Memo: Rickett to Rowan, 29 May 1956.
7. Cobbold quoted in Fforde, 1992, p. 529.
8. Hall, 1991, p. 71.
9. Ibid.
10. Ibid.
11. Peden, 2000, p. 446; Fforde, 1992, p. 550; Procter, 1990, p. 434.
12. For details of the economics of the crisis, see Kunz, 1991; Johnman, 1989; Fforde, 1992, pp. 549–63; Procter, 1990, pp. 434–48.
13. Fforde, 1992, p. 553.

14. Procter, 1990, p. 435.
15. Fforde, 1992, p. 553; Peden, 2000, p. 446.
16. Fforde, 1992, p. 554.
17. Fforde, 1992, p. 554; Procter, 1990, p. 435.
18. Procter, 1990, p. 436.
19. Fforde, 1992, p. 549; Peden, 2000, p. 447. Dell, 1996, p. 218, notes that Makins was told on 28 October.
20. Peden, 2000, p. 446; Dell, 1996, p. 217; Johnman, 1989, p. 179.
21. Fforde, 1992, p. 555.
22. Procter, 1990, p. 443.
23. Procter, 1990, p. 443; Fforde, 1992, p. 558; Dell, 1996, p. 219.
24. PRO: T236/5403, 'Note of a meeting at the Treasury, Monday 19 November 1956', 19 November 1956.
25. Fforde, 1992, p. 560.
26. Ibid.
27. US National Archives: RG 56/450, 'National Advisory Council Minutes, Meeting 253', 7 December 1956.
28. US National Archives: RG 56/450, 'National Advisory Council Minutes, Meeting 254', 21 December 1956.
29. US National Archives: RG 56/450, 'National Advisory Council Minutes, Meeting 255', December 1956.
30. Fforde, 1992, p. 562.
31. Ibid.
32. For an overview, see Green, 2000, pp. 409–30; Dell, 1996, pp. 223–41; Peden, 2000, pp. 486–93; Dow, 1964, pp. 95–103; Fforde, 1992, pp. 669–93.
33. PRO: CAB 129/087, 'Wages, Prices and the Pound Sterling', Memo by the Chancellor, C. (57) 103, 27 April 1957.
34. Ibid.
35. Ibid.
36. Dow, 1964, p. 97. French exports received a 20 per cent subsidy, and French imports other than essential raw materials a 20 per cent tax. The Bank treated this as devaluation. See Dow, 1964, p. 97, fn. 1.
37. PRO: T236/5403, Untitled memo by the Governor, 22 August 1957.
38. Fforde, 1992, p. 569.
39. PRO: T236/5403, Untitled memo by the Governor, 22 August 1957.
40. Ibid.
41. Ibid.
42. Ibid.
43. Ibid.
44. PRO: T236/5403, Untitled memo, France to Makins, 23 August 1957.
45. PRO: T236/5403, Untitled memo, France to Rowan, 23 August 1957.
46. PRO: T236/5403, Untitled note, Makins to Thorneycroft, 23 August 1957.
47. PRO: T236/5403, 'Untitled note, Collier to Makins, 26 August 1957.
48. PRO: T236/5403, 'Sterling', Wilson to Rowan, 28 August 1957.
49. Procter, 1990, p. 451.
50. Ibid., p. 452.
51. Fforde, 1992, p. 677.
52. Ibid.
53. Cobbold quoted in Fforde, 1992, p. 677.
54. Ibid., p. 680.
55. Ibid., p. 681.

56. Procter, 1990, p. 452.
57. Ibid., p. 453; Fforde 1992, p. 572.
58. Fforde, 1992, p. 572, fn. 7; US National Archives: RG 56/450, 'United Kingdom Report, NAC Document 59-2, Supplement 4', National Advisory Council, 23 April 1959.
59. Procter, 1990, p. 453; Fforde, 1992, p. 572, fn. 7.
60. PRO: T236/5403, Minute: Macmillan to Thorneycroft, 18 September 1957.
61. PRO: T236/5403, 'Exchange Policy', Memo by Rickett, 21 September 1957.
62. PRO: T236/5403, 'Internal Effects of a Floating Exchange Rate', Hall to Rickett, 23 September 1957.
63. Hall, 1991, p. 122, 'Entry for 19 August 1957'.
64. Ibid.
65. PRO: T236/5403, 'Internal Effects of a Floating Exchange Rate', Hall to Rickett, 23 September 1957.
66. Ibid.
67. Ibid.
68. Ibid.
69. PRO: T236/5403, 'Letter: Cobbold to Heathcoat Amory', 3 March February 1958; PRO: T236/5403, 'Exchange Rates', Makins to Heathcoat Amory, 19 February 1958; Fforde, 1992, p. 586.
70. PRO: T236/5403, 'Letter: Cobbold to Makins', 4 February 1958.
71. Ibid.
72. Ibid.
73. PRO: T236/5403, 'Bringing the Rates Together', Rickett to Rowan, 6 February 1958.
74. PRO: T236/5403, 'Exchange Policy', Rowan to Makins, 7 February 1958.
75. Ibid.
76. Ibid.
77. PRO: T236/5403, 'Exchange Rate Policy: Note of a meeting held in the Chancellor's Room at 4.30pm on 5 March 1958', 6 March 1958.
78. Ibid.
79. Ibid.
80. Procter, 1990, p. 457.
81. Fforde, 1992, pp. 587, 589.
82. PRO: T236/5403, 'Advantages and Disadvantages of Flexible Exchange Rates', 26 March 1958.
83. Ibid.
84. Fforde, 1992, p. 590.
85. Ibid, p. 588.
86. Ibid, p. 589.
87. HMSO, 1960, Cmnd 976, tables 24, 25, 31 and 32.
88. PRO: T236/5315, 'World Gold and Foreign Exchange Report: 13th Report', W.E.P. (59) 2, January 1959.
89. US National Archives: RG 56/450, 'Prime Minister Macmillan's Letter to the President on Economic Interdependence', Memo by Douglas Dillon to The Secretary, 4 June 1958.
90. Ibid.
91. PRO: T236/4818, 'Operation Unicorn', Treasury Memo for Ministers, M.S. (58) 11 (Revise), 16 October 1958.
92. US National Archives: RG 56/450, 'United Kingdom Report, NAC Document 59-2, Supplement 4', National Advisory Council, 23 April 1959.

93. Ibid.
94. Ibid.
95. US National Archives: RG 56/450, 'Sterling Convertibility', Telegram from Robert Bean to the State Department, 17 September 1958.
96. US National Archives: RG 56/450, 'Sterling Convertibility', Telegram from Robert Bean to the State Department, 17 September 1958; Fforde, 1992, p. 592.
97. PRO: T236/4818, 'Operation Unicorn: Discussions at New Delhi', Makins to Rowan, 16 October 1958.
98. Ibid.
99. PRO: T236/4818, 'Operation Unicorn', Treasury Memo for Ministers, M.S. (58) 11 (Revise), 16 October 1958.
100. PRO: T236/4818, 'Operation Unicorn: Discussions at New Delhi', Makins to Rowan, 16 October 1958.
101. Ibid.
102. Ibid.
103. PRO: T236/4818, 'Note of a talk between the Chancellor and Dr Erhard', 7 October 1958.
104. PRO: T236/4819, 'Unicorn', Treasury note, no date.
105. Fforde, 1992, p. 595, fn. 20.
106. PRO: T236/4819, 'Unicorn', Treasury note, no date.
107. PRO: T234/100, 'European Integration', Note by Treasury, 21 February 1956; Ellison, 1996, pp. 1–34; Schaad, 1998, pp. 39–60; Peden, 2000, pp. 448–52.
108. PRO: T234/100, 'European Integration', Note by Treasury, 21 February 1956; Peden, 2000, p. 451.
109. PRO: T234/357, 'Free Trade Area Negotiations: Current Position', Treasury Memo, 17 December 1958.
110. Ibid.
111. US National Archives: RG 56/450, 'Developments in the UK Regarding a Partial Free Trade Area', US Embassy, London to the Department of State, 7 November 1956; PRO: T234/720, 'Free Trade Area Negotiations: Post Mortem', Figgures to Clarke, 17 July 1959.
112. US National Archives: RG 56/450, 'French Position on the Free Trade Area', US Embassy in Paris to the Department of State, 23 September 1957.
113. US National Archives: RG 56/450, 'European Integration', Overby to Humphrey, 19 January 1956.
114. Ibid.
115. PRO: T234/357, 'Free Trade Area Negotiations: Current Position', Treasury Memo, 17 December 1958.
116. PRO: T236/4819, 'Letter: Ellis-Rees to Rickett', 31 October 1958.
117. Ibid.
118. PRO: T236/4818, 'Operation Unicorn', Treasury Memo for Ministers, M.S. (58) 11 (Revise), 16 October 1958.
119. PRO: T236/4819, 'Unicorn: Export/Import Bank Line of Credit', 30 October 1958.
120. PRO: T236/4818, 'Operation Unicorn', Treasury Memo for Ministers, M.S. (58) 11 (Revise), 16 October 1958.
121. Ibid.
122. PRO: T236/4819, 'Unicorn: Free Trade Area', Arnold France to Rowan, 30 October 1958.
123. PRO: T236/4818, 'Operation Unicorn', Treasury Memo for Ministers, M.S. (58) 11 (Revise), 16 October 1958.

124. Procter, 1990, p. 461; PRO: T236/4818, Bell to Rowan, 23 October 1958.
125. PRO: T236/4818, Note to Rowan, 23 October 1958.
126. PRO: T236/4819, 'Unicorn', Rowan to Heathcoat Amory, 27 October 1958.
127. Ibid.
128. PRO: T236/4819, 'Exchange Rate Policy: Note of a meeting held at No. 10, Downing Street on 28 October 1958', 28 October 1958.
129. Ibid.
130. Ibid.
131. Ibid.
132. Ibid.
133. PRO: T236/4819, 'Exchange Rate Policy: Note of a meeting held at No. 10, Downing Street on 5 November 1958', 6 November 1958.
134. Ibid.
135. Procter, 1990, p. 465.
136. Hall, 1991, pp. 165, 180; Fforde, 1992, p. 595.
137. PRO: T236/4820, Rowan's handwritten comments on 'Unicorn', Ricketts to Rowan, 6 November 1958.
138. PRO: T236/4820, 'Note of Conversation', Cobbold to Makins, 11 November 1958.
139. Ibid.
140. Ibid.
141. PRO: T236/4820, 'Unicorn', Makins to the Chancellor, 13 November 1958.
142. Fforde, 1992, p. 597.
143. PRO: T236/4820, 'Unicorn', Makins to the Chancellor, 28 November 1958.
144. Procter, 1990, pp. 466, 499 fn. 245; PRO: T236/4820, 'Unicorn', Makins to the Chancellor, 28 November 1958.
145. Hall, 1991, p. 181 notes that 'Makins told me it was put off sine die'.
146. PRO: T236/4820, 'Telegram: Paris to Foreign Office', 20 November 1958.
147. Ibid.
148. PRO: T236/4820, 'Untitled note', Makins to Bell (with handwritten comments by Rickett), 21 November 1958.
149. PRO: T236/4820, Rickett to Makins, 25 November 1958.
150. PRO: T236/4820, 'Exchange Rate Policy: Note of a meeting held at No. 10 Downing Street on 27 November 1958', 27 November 1958; PRO: T236/4820, 'Unicorn', Makins to the Chancellor, 28 November 1958.
151. PRO: T236/4821, 'Telegram: Cobbold to the Chancellor', 9 December 1958.
152. PRO: T236/4821, 'Basle Meeting: 6–8 December 1958', Note by John Stevens, 9 December 1958.
153. PRO: T236/4821, 'Unicorn', Heathcoat Amory to the Prime Minister, 10 December 1958.
154. Ibid.
155. Ibid.
156. PRO: T236/4821, 'Unicorn', Phelps to Bell, 11 December 1958.
157. Ibid.
158. US National Archives: RG 59, 'Anglo-French Convertibility Negotiations', Bean to State Department, 5 January 1959.
159. PRO: T236/4821, 'Record of Conversation: Unicorn', 14 December 1958.
160. PRO: T236/4821, 'Record of Conversation: Unicorn', Note by Stevens, 14 December 1958.
161. PRO: T234/357, 'Free Trade Area Negotiations: Current Position', 17 December 1958.

162. PRO: T234/357, 'United States and European Economic Co-operation', 16 December 1958.
163. PRO: T236/357, Untitled memo to Rickett, 16 December 1958.
164. US National Archives: RG 59, 'Anglo-French Convertibility Negotiations', Bean to State Department, 5 January 1959; Fforde, 1992, p. 599.
165. PRO: T236/4822, Note to Bell, 17 December 1958.
166. PRO: CAB 128/32, Cabinet Conclusions, CC (58) 86, 18 December 1958.
167. PRO: T236/4818, 'Operation Unicorn', Treasury Memo for Ministers, M.S. (58) 11 (Revise), 16 October 1958.
168. PRO: CAB 128/32, Cabinet Conclusions, CC (58) 86, 18 December 1958.
169. PRO: T236/4822, 'Unicorn', Rickett to Makins, 19 December 1958.
170. Ibid. Fforde, 1992, P. 600.
171. Fforde, 1992, p. 600; PRO: T236/4823, 'Unicorn: Possible Press Queries', 23 December 1958.
172. PRO: T236/4822, 'Telegram: Stevens to Cobbold and Rickett', 21 December 1958.
173. PRO: T236/4823, 'Draft Press Announcement', no date; Procter, 1990, p. 470; Fforde, 1992, p. 602.
174. Procter, 1990, p. 470.
175. BE: C160/30, 'Sir George Bolton's Diary: 1958', 29 December 1958.
176. Hall, 1991, p. 181, 'Entry for Tuesday 30 December 1958'.

9 Conclusion: Bretton Woods and British Decline

1. Strange, 1976, pp. 33–4.
2. PRO: T236/5313, 'The World Gold and Dollar Position', 1957; PRO: T277/2368, 'Working Party on World Economic Problems: World Trade and Economic Conditions, 16th Report', W.E.P. (59) 32 (Final), July 1959.
3. PRO: T236/5313, 'Working Party on World Economic Problems: World Trade and Economic Conditions, 10th Report', W.E.P. (57) 18 (Final), 2 July 1957; Lary, 1963, p. 43.
4. Lary, 1963, p. 30.
5. PRO: T277/2368, 'Working Party on World Economic Problems: World Trade and Economic Conditions, 16th Report', W.E.P. (59) 32 (Final), July 1959; Lary, 1963, p. 30.
6. Lary, 1963, p. 30.
7. PRO: T236/5315, 'Current Economic Problems of the United States', Note by the Treasury, 13 May 1959.
8. Lary, 1963, pp. 56–68.
9. Wells, 1964, p. 4.
10. Ibid., p. 3.
11. Ibid., p. 15, table 1.1.
12. Ibid., p. 3.
13. Ibid., p. 137, table 9.1.
14. PRO: T236/5313, 'The World Gold and Dollar Position', 1957; PRO: T277/2368, 'Working Party on World Economic Problems: World Trade and Economic Conditions, 16th Report', W.E.P. (59) 32 (Final), July 1959.
15. Block, 1977, p. 134; Strange, 1976, chapter 11.
16. Strange, 1976, p. 320.
17. Block, 1977, p. 165.
18. Strange, 1976, p. 320; Block, 1977, 135.

19. Block, 1977, p. 165.
20. Ibid., p. 166.
21. Ibid., p. 135.
22. Ibid., p. 136.
23. Ibid., p. 141, table 1.
24. Strange, 1994, p. 105.
25. Ibid., pp. 105, 107
26. Shonfield, 1976, p. 1.
27. Ibid., p. 72.
28. Bretton Woods Commission, 1994; Bordo and Eichengreen (eds), 1993.
29. Rees, 1963, p. 262, fn. 1.
30. Hirsch, 1969, p. 370; Cairncross, 1994, p. 22; Cooper, 1968, p. 36.
31. Bretton Woods Commission, 1994, p. B-8.
32. Hirsch, 1969, p. 372; Cooper, 1968, p. 211, table 8.1; PRO: T312/929, 'The Liquidity Position of the IMF', IMF Paper by A.F.W.P., 6 May 1964.
33. Cooper, 1968, p. 211; PRO: T312/929, 'The Liquidity Position of the IMF', IMF Paper by A.F.W.P., 6 May 1964.
34. Hirsch, 1969, p. 372.
35. See, for instance, Oliver, 1975; Curzon, 1965; Shonfield, 1976; Curzon and Curzon, 1976.
36. Cairncross, 1994, p. 22.
37. Wells, 1964, p. xix.
38. Ibid.
39. Ibid., p. xx; Black, 1962. pp. 114–32.
40. Wells, 1964, p. 69; Brittan, 1964, p. 280; also see Crafts, 1995, p. 249.
41. Wells, 1964, p. 72, table 5.4.
42. PRO: CAB 129/105, 'Economic Growth and National Efficiency', Memo by the Chancellor of the Exchequer, C. (61) 94, 10 July 1961.
43. Ibid.
44. Ibid.
45. Strange, 1971, p. 299.
46. Ibid., p. 129; Block, 1977, p. 186.
47. Strange, 1971, p. 129.
48. Ibid., p. 120.
49. PRO: T267/29, 'Sterling Balances Since the War', Treasury Historical Memorandum No. 16, January 1972; HMSO, 1961, Cmnd 1334, p. 68, table 31.
50. PRO: T267/29, 'Sterling Balances Since the War', Treasury Historical Memorandum No. 16, January 1972.
51. Ibid.
52. Strange, 1971, p. 191; Block, 1977, pp. 186–7.
53. Block, 1977, p. 187; Strange, 1971, p. 195, table 6.VIII.
54. Strange, 1976, pp. 120–1; Strange, 1971, pp. 129–30.
55. PRO: T312/1485, 'Floating Rates', Memorandum by the Bank of England, 13 January 1961; Operation Brutus can be traced in files PRO: T295/489–492 and T295/604. For an overview of the 1960s, see Cairncross, 1996.
56. Strange, 1971, pp. 74, 300–1.
57. PRO: CAB 129/105, 'Economic Growth and National Efficiency', Memo by the Chancellor of the Exchequer, C. (61) 94, 10 July 1961.
58. Dow, 1964, p. 345.
59. Ibid., p. 347.

60. PRO: CAB 129/105, 'Economic Growth and National Efficiency', Memo by the Chancellor of the Exchequer, C. (61) 94, 10 July 1961.
61. PRO: T267/28, 'Special Study of Incomes Policy', Treasury Historical Memorandum No. 29, February 1976.
62. Burnham, 1999, 2001.
63. PRO: CAB 129/105, 'Economic Growth and National Efficiency', Memo by the Chancellor of the Exchequer, C. (61) 94, 10 July 1961.
64. PRO: CAB 129/105, 'Industrial Relations', Memorandum by the Minister of Labour, C. (61) 64, 16 May 1961; PRO: CAB 129/105, 'Economic Growth and National Efficiency', Memo by the Chancellor of the Exchequer, C. (61) 94, 10 July 1961.
65. This supports Nick Crafts' assertion that 'the "social contract" impeded growth', see Crafts, 1995, p. 247.
66. PRO: T234/720, 'Free Trade Area Negotiations: Post Mortem', Note by Frank Figgures, 17 July 1959.
67. PRO: T236/5329, 'The Future of Anglo-American Relations', Note by the Planning Section of the Foreign Office, 5 January 1960.
68. Ibid.
69. PRO: T236/5329, 'The effects of Anglo-American interdependence on the long-term interests of the UK', Paper by the Foreign Office Steering Committee, SC (58) 8 3rd Revise, 2 April 1958.
70. Ibid.
71. Ibid.
72. PRO: T236/5329, 'The Future of Anglo-American Relations', Note by the Planning Section of the Foreign Office, 5 January 1960.
73. Cairncross, 1985, p. 270. Also see Plowden, 1989, p. 157; MacDougall, 1987, p. 108.
74. Cairncross, 1985, p. 265.
75. Ibid., pp. 265–71.
76. Shonfield, 1958, pp. 217–23; Brittan, 1964, pp. 173–5; Brittan, 2002 and 2003; Fforde, 1992, pp. 449–51, 469, 545.
77. Shonfield, 1958, p. 219.
78. Ibid., p. 218.
79. Ibid., pp. 218–219.
80. Brittan, 1964, p. 177.
81. Brittan, 2002, 'Black or White Wednesday: UK ERM membership in retrospect', Samuel Brittan talk at the Institute of Economic Affairs, 16 September 2002, downloaded from *http://www.samuelbrittan.co.uk/spee23_p.html* accessed on 2 December 2002; Brittan, 2003, 'The changing economic role of government', Samuel Brittan: Contribution to 50th Anniversary Vol. Soc. of Bus. Economists 2003 downloaded from *http://www.samuelbrittan.co.uk/text131_p.html* accessed on 2 December 2002.
82. Fforde, 1992, p. 469.
83. MacDougall, 1987, p. 108.
84. PRO: T325/41, 'Questions about 1954 – and perhaps earlier', Clarke to Rowan, 23 October 1953; Fforde, 1992, p. 469.

Bibliography

Manuscript collections

UK public records
Public Record Office (Kew)

Cabinet
CAB 128 – Cabinet: Minutes (CM and CC Series) 1945–1974
CAB 129 – Cabinet: Memoranda (CP and C Series) 1945–1972
CAB 130 – Cabinet: Miscellaneous Committees: Minutes and Papers (GEN, MISC and REF Series) 1945–1970
CAB 21 – Cabinet Office and predecessors: Registered Files (1916 to 1965) 1916–1973

Dominions and Commonwealth Relations Office
DO 35 – Dominions Office and Commonwealth Relations Office: Original Correspondence 1915–1971

Foreign Office
FO 371 – Foreign Office: Political Departments: General Correspondence 1906–1966

Prime Minister's Office
PREM 11 – Prime Minister's Office: Correspondence and Papers 1951–1964

Ministry of Supply
SUPP 14 – Ministry of Supply Files 1917–1958

Treasury
T171 – Chancellor of the Exchequer's Office: Budget and Finance Bill Papers 1859–1979
T230 – Cabinet Office, Economic Section, and Treasury, Economic Advisory Section: Registered Files (EAS and 2EAS Series) 1939–1971
T234 – Treasury: Home and Overseas Planning Staff Division and successors: Registered Files (HOP Series) 1939–1961
T235 – Treasury: Mutual Aid Division: Registered Files (MA Series) 1948–1956
T236 – Treasury: Overseas Finance Division: Registered Files (OF and 2OF Series) 1920–1964
T237 – Treasury: Overseas Finance (Marshall Aid) Division: Registered Files (OFM Series) 1948–1960
T267 – Treasury: Historical Memoranda 1957–1976
T273 – Treasury: Papers of Lord Bridges 1920–1956
T276 – Treasury: Accounts Branch: Registered Files (A/CS C Series) 1952–1969
T277 – Treasury: Committee Section: Minutes and Papers 1948–1971
T312 – Treasury: Finance Overseas and Co-ordination Division: Registered Files (2F Series) 1954–1972

T325 – Treasury and other departments: Sir R. W. B. (Otto) Clarke Papers 1941–1977

Bank of England Archive (Threadneedle Street, London)
BE: ADM 14 – L.P. Thompson-McCausland's Papers 1941–1965
BE: C160 – Sir George Bolton's Papers
BE: G1 – Governor's Files 1913–1981
BE: G3 – Governor's Diaries 1916–1979
BE: OV44 – Sterling and Sterling Area Policy 1929–1975

United States public records

National Archives and Records Administration (College Park, Maryland)
RG 56 – General Records of the Department of the Treasury
RG 59 – General Records of the Department of State

Private papers and interviews

Avon Papers: Special Collections Department, University Library, University of Birmingham.
Butler Papers: Trinity College Library, Cambridge University.
Cherwell Papers: Nuffield College Library, Oxford University.
Clarke Papers: Churchill Archive Centre, Churchill College, Cambridge University.
Crookshank Papers and Diaries: Department of Western Manuscripts, Bodleian Library, Oxford University.
MacDougall Papers, Churchill Archive Centre, Churchill College, Cambridge University.
Macmillan Papers and Diaries: Department of Western Manuscripts, Bodleian Library, Oxford University.
Woolton Papers: Department of Western Manuscripts, Bodleian Library, Oxford University.
TUC Economic Committee Minutes: Modern Records Centre, University of Warwick.
Interview with John Fforde, 22 November 1999.
Interview with Fred Atkinson, 30 November 1999.
Interview with Donald MacDougall, 3 March 2003.

Official records

United Kingdom (HMSO)

HMSO, 1944, *United Nations Monetary and Financial Conference: Bretton Woods, New Hampshire, USA., July 1 to July 22, 1944* (Cmd 6546).
HMSO, 1952, *Economic Survey for 1952* (Cmd 8509).
HMSO, 1953, *Economic Survey for 1953* (Cmd 8800).
HMSO, 1960, *Economic Survey for 1960* (Cmnd 976).
HMSO, 1961, *Economic Survey for 1961* (Cmnd 1334).
House of Commons, *Parliamentary Debates* (Hansard)
House of Lords, *Parliamentary Debates* (Hansard)

International

Bank for International Settlements, *Annual Reports*
United Nations, *Economic Survey of Europe 1963* (E/ECE/542; Geneva, 1964).

Newspapers and periodicals

The Banker
Board of Trade Journal
The Economist
Financial Times
The Guardian
The Times

Unpublished works

Procter, S. (1990), 'Towards Convertibility: the Sterling Policy of the Conservative Governments 1951–1958', PhD thesis, University of Bristol.

Published works

Arkes, H. (1972), *Bureaucracy, the Marshall Plan and the National Interest* (Princeton, Princeton University Press).
Arrighi, G. (1994), *The Long Twentieth Century* (London, Verso).
Balaam, D. and Veseth, M. (2001), *Introduction to International Political Economy*, second edition (New Jersey, Prentice-Hall).
Birkenhead, F. (1961), *The Prof in Two Worlds* (London, Collins).
Black, J. (1962), 'The Volume and Prices of British Exports', in G. Worswick and P. Ady (eds), *The British Economy in the Nineteen-Fifties* (Oxford, Clarendon Press).
Block, F. (1977), *The Origins of International Economic Disorder: a Study of United States International Monetary Policy from World War II to the Present* (London, University of California Press).
Bordo, M. and Eichengreen, B. (1993), *A Retrospective on the Bretton Woods System* (London, University of Chicago Press).
Bretton Woods Commission, (1994), *Bretton Woods: Looking to the Future* (Washington, Bretton Woods Commission).
Brittan, S. (1964), *The Treasury under the Tories 1951–1964* (Harmondsworth, Penguin).
Brittan, S. (2002), 'Black or White Wednesday: UK ERM membership in retrospect', talk at the Institute of Economic Affairs, 16 September 2002 downloaded from *http://www.samuelbrittan.co.uk/spee23_p.html* accessed on 2 December 2002.
Brittan, S. (2003), 'The changing economic role of government', Samuel Brittan: Contribution to 50th Anniversary Vol. Soc. of Bus. Economists 2003 downloaded from *http://www.samuelbrittan.co.uk/text131_p.html* accessed on 2 December 2002.
Bulpitt, J. and Burnham, P. (1999), 'Operation Robot and the British Political Economy in the Early-1950s: the Politics of Market Strategies', *Contemporary British History*, 13, 1, 1–31.
Burnham, P. (1990), *The Political Economy of Postwar Reconstruction* (London, Macmillan).
Burnham, P. (1992), 'Re-evaluating the Washington Loan Agreement: a Revisionist View of the Limits of Postwar American Power', *Review of International Studies*, 18, 3, 241–259.
Burnham, P. (1995), 'Rearming for the Korean War: the Impact of Government Policy on Leyland Motors and the British Car Industry', *Contemporary Record*, 9, 2, 343–67.
Burnham, P. (1999), 'The Politics of Economic Management in the 1990s', *New Political Economy*, 4, 1, 37–54.

Burnham, P. (2001), 'New Labour and the Politics of Depoliticisation', *The British Journal of Politics and International Relations*, 3, 2, 127–49.

Butler, R. (1971), *The Art of the Possible* (London, Hamish Hamilton).

Cairncross, A. (1985), *Years of Recovery: British Economic Policy 1945–51* (London, Methuen).

Cairncross, A. (1994), 'Forget Bretton Woods – Recovery was Born in the USA', in *Guardian Studies, IMF and the World Bank: the Next 50 years* (London, Guardian Newspapers), 22–4.

Cairncross, A. (1996), *Managing the British Economy in the 1960s* (London, Macmillan).

Cairncross, A. and Watts, N. (1989), *The Economic Section 1939–1961: a Study in Economic Advising* (London, Routledge).

Clarke, R. (1982), *Anglo-American Economic Collaboration in War and Peace 1942–1949* (Oxford, Oxford University Press).

Coates, D. (1994), *The Question of UK Decline* (Hemel Hempstead, Harvester Wheatsheaf).

Cooper, R. (1968), *The Economics of Inter-Dependence: Economic Policy in the Atlantic Community* (London, McGraw-Hill).

Crafts, N. (1995), ' "You've Never Had It So Good?": British Economic Policy and Performance, 1945–1960', in B. Eichengreen (ed.), *Europe's Post-War Recovery* (Cambridge, Cambridge University Press), 246–70.

Curzon, G. (1965), *Multilateral Commercial Diplomacy: the General Agreement on Tariffs and Trade and its Impact on National Commercial Policies and Techniques* (London, Michael Joseph).

Curzon, G. and Curzon, V. (1976), 'The Management of Trade Relations in the GATT', in A. Shonfield (ed.), *International Economic Relations of the Western World 1959–1971, Volume 1: Politics and Trade* (London, Oxford University Press), 143–286.

De Vries, M. (1985), *The International Monetary Fund, 1972–1978*, three volumes (Washington DC, IMF).

Dell, E. (1996), *The Chancellors* (London, HarperCollins).

Dobson, A. (1988), *The Politics of the Anglo-American Economic Special Relationship 1940–1987* (Brighton, Wheatsheaf).

Dow, C. (1964), *The Management of the British Economy 1945–60* (London, Cambridge University Press).

Eichengreen, B. (1995), 'The European Payments Union: an Efficient Mechanism for Rebuilding Europe's Trade?', in B. Eichengreen (ed.), *Europe's Post-War Recovery* (Cambridge, Cambridge University Press), 169–98.

Ellison, J. (1996), 'Perfidious Albion? Britain, Plan G and European Integration, 1955–56', *Contemporary British History*, 10, 3, 1–34.

Fforde, J. (1992), *The Bank of England and Public Policy, 1941–1958* (Cambridge, Cambridge University Press).

Garber, P. (1993), 'The Collapse of the Bretton Woods Fixed Exchange Rate System', in M. Bordo and B. Eichengreen (eds), *A Retrospective on the Bretton Woods System* (London, University of Chicago Press), 461–85.

Gardner, R. (1969), *Sterling–Dollar Diplomacy* (Oxford, Oxford University Press).

Gilpin, R. (1987), *The Political Economy of International Relations* (Guildford, Princeton University Press).

Grant, W. (2002), *Economic Policy in Britain* (London, Palgrave).

Green, E. H. (2000), 'The Treasury Resignations of 1958: a Reconsideration', *Twentieth Century British History*, 11, 4, 409–30.

Hall, R. (1989), *The Robert Hall Diaries 1947–1953*, edited by A. Cairncross (London, Unwin Hyman).

Hall, R. (1991), *The Robert Hall Diaries 1954–1961*, edited by A. Cairncross (London, Unwin Hyman).

Helleiner, E. (1994), *States and the Reemergence of Global Finance* (Ithaca, Cornell University Press).

Hirsch, F. (1969), *Money International* (Harmondsworth, Pelican).

Hogan, M. (1987), *The Marshall Plan: America, Britain and the Reconstruction of Western Europe, 1947–1952* (Cambridge, Cambridge University Press).

Hubback, D. (1988), 'Sir Richard Clarke – 1910–1975: a Most Unusual Civil Servant', *Public Policy and Administration*, 3, 1, 19–34.

Irwin, D. (1995), 'The GATT's Contribution to Economic Recovery in Post-war Western Europe', in B. Eichengreen (ed.), *Europe's Post-War Recovery* (Cambridge, Cambridge University Press), 127–50.

James, H. (1995), 'The IMF and the Creation of the Bretton Woods System, 1944–58', in B. Eichengreen (ed.), *Europe's Post-War Recovery* (Cambridge, Cambridge University Press), 93–126.

Johnman, L. (1989), 'Defending the Pound: the Economics of the Suez Crisis', in A. Gorst, L. Johnman and W. Lucas (eds), *Postwar Britain, 1945–64: Themes and Perspectives* (London, Pinter), 166–81.

Kaplan, J. and Schleiminger, G. (1989), *The European Payments Union: Financial Diplomacy in the 1950s* (Oxford, Oxford University Press).

Keynes, J. M. (1979), 'Overseas Financial Policy in Stage III', in *Collected Writings of John Maynard Keynes, Volume XXIV* (London, Macmillan), 256–95.

Kindleberger, C. (1987), *Marshall Plan Days* (Boston, Allen and Unwin).

Kolko, G. (1990), *The Politics of War*, revised edition (New York, Pantheon Books).

Kunz, D. (1991), *The Economic Diplomacy of the Suez Crisis* (Chapel Hill, University of North Carolina Press).

Kynaston, D. (2001), *The City of London, Volume IV: a Club No More, 1945–2000* (London, Chatto & Windus).

Lary, H. (1963), *Problems of the United States as World Trader and Banker* (New York, National Bureau of Economic Research).

Leffler, M. (1998), 'The United States and the Strategic Dimensions of the Marshall Plan', *Diplomatic History*, 12, 807–25.

Leigh-Phippard, H. (1995), *Congress and US Military Aid to Britain* (London, Macmillan).

MacDougall, D. (1987), *Don and Mandarin: Memoirs of an Economist* (London, John Murray).

Mikesell, R. (1945), 'The Key Currency Proposal', *Quarterly Journal of Economics*, 59, 563–76.

Mikesell, R. (1954), *Foreign Exchange in the Postwar World* (New York, Twentieth Century Fund).

Milward, A. (1984), *The Reconstruction of Western Europe, 1945–1951* (London, Methuen).

Moran, Lord, (1966), *Winston Churchill: the Struggle for Survival 1940–1965* (London, Constable).

Oliver, R. (1975), *International Economic Co-operation and the World Bank* (London, Macmillan).

Peden, G. C. (2000), *The Treasury and British Public Policy 1906–1959* (Oxford, Oxford University Press).

Plowden, E. (1989), *An Industrialist in the Treasury: the Postwar Years* (London, Andre Deutsch).

Pressnell, L. S. (1987), *External Economic Policy Since the War: Volume 1 The Postwar Financial Settlement* (London, HMSO).

Price, H. (1955), *The Marshall Plan and its Meaning* (Ithaca, Cornell University Press).

Procter, S. (1993), 'Floating Convertibility: the Emergence of the Robot Plan, 1951–1952', *Contemporary Record*, 7, 1, 24–43.

Rees, G. (1963), *Britain and the Postwar European Payments Systems* (Cardiff, University of Wales Press).

Ruggie, J. (1982), 'International Regimes, Transactions, and Change: Embedded Liberalism in the Postwar Economic Order', *International Organization*, 36, 379–415.

Schaad, M. (1998), 'Plan G: A "Counterblast"? British Policy Towards the Messina Countries, 1956', *Contemporary European History*, 7, 39–60.

Schenk, C. (1994), *Britain and the Sterling Area: From Devaluation to Convertibility in the 1950s* (London, Routledge).

Schild, G. (1995), *Bretton Woods and Dumbarton Oaks* (London, Macmillan, 1995).

Seldon, A. (1981), *Churchill's Indian Summer: the Conservative Government 1951–55* (London, Hodder & Stoughton).

Shonfield, A. (1958), *British Economic Policy Since the War* (Harmondsworth, Penguin).

Shonfield, A. (1976), 'International Economic Relations of the Western World: an Overall View', in A. Shonfield (ed.), *International Economic Relations of the Western World 1959–1971, Volume 1: Politics and Trade* (London, Oxford University Press), 1–142.

Shuckburgh, E. (1986), *Descent to Suez: Diaries 1951–56* (London, Weidenfeld & Nicolson).

Soloman, R. (1982), *The International Monetary System, 1945–1981* (New York, Harper & Row).

Strange, S. (1971), *Sterling and British Policy: a Political Study of an International Currency in Decline* (London, Oxford University Press).

Strange, S. (1976), 'International Monetary Relations', in A. Shonfield (ed.), *International Economic Relations of the Western World 1959–1971, Volume 2: International Monetary Relations* (London, Oxford University Press), 18–359.

Strange, S. (1994), *States and Markets*, second edition (London, Pinter).

Tomlinson, J. (1997), *Democratic Socialism and Economic Policy: the Attlee Years 1945–1951* (Cambridge, Cambridge University Press).

Triffin, R. (1957), *Europe and the Money Muddle* (New Haven, Yale University Press).

Van der Beugal, E. (1966), *From Marshall Aid to Atlantic Partnership* (London, Elsevier).

Van Dormael, A. (1978), *Bretton Woods: Birth of a Monetary System* (London, Macmillan).

Wells, S. J. (1964), *British Export Performance: a Comparative Study* (London, Cambridge University Press).

Williams, J. (1944), 'International Monetary Plans: After Bretton Woods', *Foreign Affairs*, 23, 1, 38–56.

Index